The Other Side of God

The Other Side of God

A Polarity in World Religions

Edited by Peter L. Berger

ANCHOR PRESS/DOUBLEDAY
GARDEN CITY, NEW YORK
1981

The Other Side of God: A Polarity in World Religions is published simultaneously in hardcover and paperback editions.

Library of Congress Cataloging in Publication Data
Main entry under title:
The Other Side of God.

1. Religion—Addresses, essays, lectures. 2. Religions—Addresses, essays, lectures. I. Title: Polarity in world religions. II. Berger, Peter L.
BL48.O78   291   AACR2
ISBN (hardcover): 0-385-17424-1
ISBN (paperback): 0-385-17423-3
Library of Congress Catalog Card Number 80-2844

Contents

Preface

The papers assembled in this volume emerged from a seminar that met, in New York and Boston, from 1978 to 1980. The seminar, under the title "Monotheism and the World Religions," was sponsored by the Radius Institute of New York, which is concerned with the implications of contemporary social and cultural trends for Jewish life and values. Funding was raised by the Radius Institute from the Emet Foundation of Los Angeles and several private contributors. The seminar was chaired by Peter Berger.

The basic presupposition of the seminar was simple—namely, that the contemporary situation, in which the monotheistic traditions of the West find themselves in an increasingly massive encounter with the great religions of southern and eastern Asia, calls for a rethinking of certain fundamental aspects of monotheism. The agenda of the seminar, though it ranged over a vast territory of highly complex religious data, was also essentially simple. At the outset it was proposed by the chairman that two distinct types of religious experience may be found in history, respectively designated "confrontation" and "interiority." In the first type, the divine is experienced as a reality external to, often acutely threatening to, the subjective consciousness of the individual; in the second type, the divine, or more broadly the object of the religious experience, is sought or believed to be discovered within the depths of consciousness itself. Both types, it was proposed, are to be found in all the major religious traditions, but the first type was always normative in the great revelation traditions originating in western Asia, notably Judaism, Christianity, and Islam. Still, the understanding of the other type of religious experience and interpretation has always been important for the self-definition of the monotheistic traditions. The seminar was designed to explore, in a series of case studies, how these two types of religious experience encountered each other in the past. This exploration was descriptive (or, if one prefers, phenomenological), but for most participants there was the expectation that such an enterprise would eventually be useful to the contemporary dialogue between the world religions in philosophical and theological terms, notably the dialogue between Judaism and Christianity on the one hand and Hinduism and Buddhism on the other.

As was to be expected, this typology was sharply criticized in the course of the seminar and some of the participants (including the chairman, who first proposed it) were prepared after a while to abandon it. All the same, there was agreement that the typology, however flawed, did indeed refer to empirically valid phenomena. Since no agreement was reached on a new or modified typology, the originally proposed typology was left as the organizing principle of the seminar, and it is so left in this volume. The commentary of the chairman which follows discusses some of the problems of the developing discussion.

The papers are here arranged, not in the order in which they were presented, but by subject matter. Part I deals with the polarity in the Jewish, Christian, and Muslim traditions, Part II with the same polarity in the contexts of Hinduism and Buddhism. Part III contains an account of the discussion and a commentary on it.

Special thanks are due to Rabbi Steven Shaw, of the Radius Institute, and to Avery Brooke for her unstinting support and collaboration.

PETER L. BERGER

Part I

The Polarity in Monotheistic Traditions

PETER L. BERGER

The Other Side of God— Problem and Agenda

The papers collected in this volume revolve around one basic question: How can two types of religious experience, tentatively called "confrontation" and "interiority," be reconciled with each other? The question is, ultimately, philosophical or theological, but the book does not presume to deal with the matter on this ultimate level. Rather, it has a more modest aim—namely, to undertake a number of case studies in order to explore how this particular polarity was dealt with by specific individuals or groups in different religious traditions. In other words, this book is an exercise in the comparative phenomenology of religion rather than a philosophical or theological undertaking. All the same, there was the expectation that such phenomenological clarification might eventually be useful to those willing to go beyond it to a consideration of the truth claims of various forms of religious experience.

Wherever typologies are made, it is certainly not in heaven. The less than heavenly character of this particular typology becomes evident very early in the book and before long virtually everyone was quite ready to abandon it. At the same time, there was also general consensus that the typology, however inadequate, did refer to real differences in the history of human religion. Also, no generally agreed-upon substitute for the typology emerged. For this reason, as well as simply for the sake of convenience, it was retained throughout the seminar, as it has been retained in this volume, though mental quotation marks have now come to be attached to its two terms. There is, of course, nothing to be deplored in that. Typologies are intellectual constructs, usually of partial and temporary usefulness, and perhaps their major usefulness is manifested in the process by which they are demolished. The classical statement of this fact may be found in Max Weber's theory of "ideal types." It pertains to *any* application of intellectual constructs to the fluid and intrinsically anarchic reality of human experience. That part of human experience commonly designated as religion is no exception.

Still, the original typology must be understood if the work of the seminar is to make any sense.[1] It was originally proposed as a sort of working hypothesis, as follows: There are two distinct forms of religious experience, to be found in different places and at different times in the history of religion. In the first, the divine is encountered as a reality utterly transcendent with reference to the human, confronting the human from the outside; put differently, in this experience the divine and the human are sharply polarized. In the second form of religious experience, the divine is discovered within the depths of human consciousness itself (with which, in the extreme case, it may be identified). It was also hypothesized that, although both types may be found cross-culturally, they occur in, as it were, different frequency distributions. The first, confrontational, type is most characteristic of the monotheistic religions deriving from western Asia, epitomized in scenes of such power as that of Moses confronting the burning bush, Paul encountering the risen Christ on the road to Damascus, or Muhammad receiving the Quran on Mount Hira. The second, interior, type is most characteristic of the religious traditions deriving from the Indian subcontinent, epitomized once and for all by the Buddha experiencing enlightenment under the bo tree, though adumbrated in every variety of mysticism, no matter where it might occur; indeed, roughly speaking, the second type coincides with the category of mysticism, as the interior path to the divine or to ultimate reality.

This typology can hardly claim originality. It is at least implied in every attempt to delineate the phenomenon of mysticism over against other forms of religious experience, from William James on. A by now classic formulation of the typology is the one by Friedrich Heiler, in his great study of the forms of prayer.[2] Heiler designates the two types as "mysticism" and "prophetic piety," and discusses Teresa of Avila and Luther as, respectively, outstanding representatives of the two types. Mysticism is understood as the form of religious experience in which both world and self are radically denied, and in which the self is dissolved in the unity of the divine. By contrast, prophetic piety is "personality-affirming" (a term Heiler took over from Nathan Söderblom), active, demanding, ethically oriented. A considerable part of Heiler's work is devoted to the detailed comparison of the two types in terms of experience, of the conception of God, of ethics and attitude toward the world. Another well-known work of the same period, Friedrich von Hügel's study of Catherine of Genoa as a prototype of mystical experience, makes similar distinctions.[3] A more recent statement of the same dichotomy, this time designated as "mystical" and "numinous" religion, is by Ninian Smart.[4] Others could readily be added. If nothing else, perusal of the literature fortifies the idea that there is an empirically available polarity in the accounts of human religious experience; needless to say, it is another question whether the terms "interiority" and "confrontation" are best suited to designate it.

On balance, the answer is probably negative. The main reason for this is that the typology confuses two aspects of religious experience—namely, the *mode* and the *content* of the experience—or, in phenomenological terms, its noetic and noematic aspects. In the type called confrontation here the two aspects usually coincide, but this is not necessarily the case with interior modes of religious experience. Thus it is hardly conceivable that, say, Moses or Muhammad would have experienced the divine encountered in their respective moments of revelation as being ultimately identical with their innermost selves. In other words, the confrontational mode of encounter coincided with the confrontational (that is, utterly transcendent) content of that which was encountered. However, there are interior or mystical modes of

religious experience which, nevertheless, maintain or even rein-
force the polarity between the divine and the human. Taking
Heiler's prototypical case of Luther, for example, one may certainly agree that Luther represents a "prophetic piety" sharply
antithetical to Teresa's mysticism; yet Luther's religious experience centered from the beginning on *conscience,* an interior phenomenon *par excellence.*[5] And in this volume Howard Kee
makes the case that Paul's allegedly confrontational "Damascus
experience" may well have been an essentially mystical one—
though, again, Paul was hardly ever tempted to *identify* himself
with the divine as encountered in Christ.

If one wanted to focus on the noematic rather than the noetic
aspect of religious experience, a typology of "unity" and "differentiation," as proposed by Ewert Cousins, is probably to
be preferred. Cousins argues for a threefold typology, adding to
"unity" and "differentiation" a third, distinct, type of "unity in
difference," which roughly corresponds to experiences of "emanationism" (as in the Neoplatonic tradition) and which cannot
be seen as simply an intermediary case between the other two
types. Be this as it may, there are clearly two poles of religious
experience—one sharply differentiating the divine and the
human, the other tending to understand their relation as one of
ultimate unity. It is also clear that, while these poles do indeed
appear in the history of religion in virtually pure form (say, as
between the religious experience of ancient Israel and that of the
Upanishads), there are many intermediary cases (as, typically, in
various forms of mysticism originating in the context of monotheistic traditions). But the task of elaborating a typology that
would do justice to both the noematic and the noetic aspects of
religious experience cannot possibly be undertaken here. Suffice
it to say that the confrontation-interiority typology in this volume will be more useful if it is understood in a noematic sense;
that is, if the focus is on the content of the religious experiences
at issue rather than on the psychic modes by which such content
is arrived at. Thus confrontation refers to a highly differentiated
content, interiority to one tending toward unity.

Also, these papers have further clarified the cross-cultural
scope of the two types. While it may still be possible to say that
confrontation is the normative form of religious experience in the

monotheistic traditions deriving from western Asia, this can probably not be said of interiority in the religious history of India and the Far East. John Carman's work on Hindu bhakti and Robert Thurman's on Mahayana Buddhism make this point very persuasively. In other words, however the polarity is to be finally understood, it cannot be seen as neatly corresponding to an east-west axis.

Why should anyone be interested in this matter?

Butterfly collectors can excite each other to the point of ecstasy by exchanging and arguing over ingenious classification schemes; the ordinary person is unlikely to be greatly moved. Is this not another instance of an obscure taxonomic dispute? Not exactly—not, that is, if one has any interest at all in the truth claims of religion. For behind the just-outlined question of how a certain polarity in the history of religion may or may not be designated there lurks another, much more important question: Where are the boundaries of truth and illusion in the widely scattered accounts of human religious experience? Where specifically, for example, is the truth and the illusion in the religious accounts of, respectively, ancient Israel and ancient India? And, even closer to home, where are these boundaries in the various conflicting affirmations of religious faith in the world today? There are two groups of people for whom there is no problem in any of this. Those who are persuaded that *all* human religion is, in the final analysis, an illusion—be it an illusion *tout court*, or a symbolic projection of immanent human concerns of psychic or social provenance—those, clearly, have no problem here. If so inclined, they can classify and reclassify religious phenomena as a matter of intellectual interest, but no great passion is likely to be attached to the enterprise. On the other hand, there is no real problem for those who are firmly convinced that *only one* of the many religious traditions bears truth—say, the orthodox or neo-orthodox Christian, or the totally committed Buddhist. For such a Christian, the "interiority" traditions of Asia are, at best, a pale adumbration of the truth of biblical revelation—and, at worst, idolatry. For the totally committed Buddhist, on the other hand, the biblical texts and the entire stream of Judeo-Christian experience deriving from them are commonly perceived as records of man's spiritual childhood, relating to the great truths of Buddhism as a child's drawings relate to Michelangelo. May those *beati possedentes* of certainty enjoy their condition! Others, not so blessed, are faced with a problem of vast proportions: If the religious history of the human race cannot be viewed as a long story of error and illusion—and if no rocks of unshakable certitude can be discovered in that history—how is it conceivable that there is truth reflected even in the seemingly contradictory accounts of man's relations with the divine? Or, put more concretely: If neither the Bible nor the Upanishads can be dismissed as gigantic mistakes, in what sense could both be seen as containing truth?

Putting the question in this way implies a presupposition that ought to be explicated—namely, that what is commonly called religion is primordially an *experience*—or, more accurately, a *set of experiences.* This presupposition is at the root of the phenomenological approach to religion.[6] It means, among other things, that religion is *not* primordially a matter of reflection, theories, or intellectual constructions of any kind. And, indeed, most religious individuals, from the great figures in the history of religion to the ordinary worshipers, have had very little interest in the theoretical systems associated with their faith. In this respect, religion may be compared to music—neither Mozart nor the contemporary listener to Mozart's music must have an interest in the theories of the musicologists—and it is even possible that such an interest is detrimental both to the composition and to the enjoyment of music.

This presupposition has important consequences for anyone who would compare different types of religion, such as those at issue here. It is, of course, possible and thoroughly valid to compare the theoretical or ethical systems engendered by different religious traditions—say, Thomas Aquinas and Nagarjuna, or the Talmud and the Confucian corpus, and so on. But comparisons on this level cannot deal with the religious perceptions without which these theoretical and ethical systems would not have arisen in the first place. The phenomenological approach necessitates an effort, however difficult that may be, to penetrate through the levels of theoretical and ethicopractical articulation down to the level of the primordial religious experiences. In the case of Buddhism, for example, there is indeed the interesting possibility of simply studying the vast body of Buddhist philosophy, much of it still unknown in the West, and comparing it with the western philosophical tradition—or of studying the ethical precepts of Buddhism and their social ramifications in various Asian societies. But, from the viewpoint of the phenomenology of religion, such studies are quite different from the exploration of the question of just what it was that the Buddha experienced under the bo tree—and what it is that is experienced today by Buddhists at any stage of their alleged journey toward enlightenment. As long as one moves within the phenomenological frame of reference, such exploration is merely descriptive; that is, the effort is made to describe as precisely as possible the structure of the experience as reported by those who went through it, *without* passing any judgment on the ultimate veridical claims of this experience. In phenomenological parlance this means that the exploration takes place within brackets—that is, the ontological status of the experience is left undecided. Any passage from phenomenology to theology will mean that the brackets are removed; that is, some judgment will have to be made on the veridical claims of the experience. Thus the phenomenologist, if at all successful in his undertaking, will be able to say: *"This is the structure of Buddhist experience."* The theologian (or religious thinker) will eventually want to say: *"This experience is—or is not—true."* The papers collected in this volume are, very clearly, of the first rather than the second kind, though, as previously observed, there was an interest from the beginning in being helpful eventually to the second kind of undertaking.

It is obviously not possible here to go into the complex questions as to how religious experience is to be defined in distinction to other forms of experience, and how are to be envisaged the processes by which religious experience is reflected upon, articulated in bodies of theory, and eventually embodied in traditions and institutions that seek to bind both the thought and the behavior of masses of people.[7] But it does not require great philosophical sophistication to see very quickly that the phenomenological approach by itself faces great problems—even if one leaves aside for the moment the truly formidable problems one faces if one wishes to go beyond it to any assessment of truth in religion.

A key problem is how one is to distinguish religious *experience* from the *interpretations* of such experience.[8] This distinction is by no means easy in other areas of human life: how can one distinguish, say, between the experience of being in love and the various interpretations of love into which individuals are socialized in a particular culture? In the case of religious experience, precisely because of its extraordinary and *ipso facto* fugitive character, the distinction is all the more difficult. Yet, if one is to remain faithful to the phenomenon studied, the effort must be made. The position that religion is *nothing but* a set of interpretations of the world simply will not do; it is an intellectualization (very characteristic, incidentally, of nineteenth-century scholarship) which distorts the religious phenomenon very severely: whatever else he may be, *Homo religiosus* is not a "primitive philosopher."

At the same time, it may be stipulated that there is no "pure experience" in religion any more than in any other area of human life. All human experiences, even those directly of the senses, are influenced by and mediated through socially learned interpretations; thus there is evidence that even physical pain is experienced differently by individuals from different sociocultural backgrounds. It is clear, then, that no imaginable method will be able to present a "pure Buddhist experience," sterilely separated from the overlay of religious and other culturally derived interpretations of that experience. Yet it is possible to differentiate between experiences (such as those of Buddhist meditation) in which there is an immediate and overwhelming sense of reality and the various bodies of theories *about* these experiences. It is important to point out that this possibility has always been insisted upon by those claiming to have had such experiences. Indeed, the aforementioned sense of *immediacy* (analogous to what William James called the "accent of reality") is the most plausible criterion by which the primordial experience of anything can be distinguished, however imperfectly, from the interpretations of that experience. The same criterion would seem to be the only possible one if certain interpretations are to be characterized as false—that is, as not adequate or faithful to the experience as reported. (The question of whether one might also be able to speak of "false *experiences*" is not negotiable within the phenomenological frame of reference; it becomes crucial, of course, the moment phenomenological brackets are removed, but the problems of this passage cannot be taken up here.)

Human religious experience, it hardly needs saying, is not all of one piece. There are enormous variations between experiences of total certainty and intuitive, hesitant appropriations of something dimly perceived as real. This distinction was expressed by Max Weber when he talks about the "religious virtuosi" as against the "religion of the masses." All variants of religious experience must be taken account of by a phenomenological approach, but the experiences of the "virtuosi" are obviously more interesting (for the same reason that Mozart is more interesting for the student of music than the latest pop hit). And, again, the distinction must be made between the modes of experience and the structure "intended" by the experience—that is, between the aforementioned noetic and noematic aspects of religious experience. Yet, with all these complications in mind, it is still possible to make some tentative statements about the structures of religious experience relevant to the problem at issue here.

There are good grounds for thinking that there is a cross-cultural history of human consciousness deriving from a set of common primordial experiences (leaving aside the question of whether these experiences are grounded in the constitution of human consciousness itself or in the metahuman structures of reality). Of great importance in these common experiences is the one called mythological. Recognized as distinctive since classical antiquity and analyzed in modern times in various ways since Friedrich Schelling, this experience of the world as a mythological entity shows surprising similarities in different culture areas, to the point where it makes sense to talk of a common *mythological matrix* for all religious traditions (and, for that matter, of the history of human consciousness as such).[9] Perhaps the most succinct formulation of this experience may be found in the exclamation of Thales of Miletus: "The world is full of gods!" In other words, this experience is polytheistic, in that the divine manifests itself in a plurality of forms. The term "polytheistic" is misleading, though, if it is understood as implying a pantheon:

as Gerardus van der Leeuw insisted, the gods are latecomers in the history of religion. A better term (used repeatedly by Diana Eck in the seminar) is that of *plenum;* that is, the world is experienced as a plenitude of divine forces and beings. Now, an essential quality of this primordial experience is the interpenetration of the divine (or, if one prefers, the supernatural or the sacred) with all empirical zones, including the empirical human self. Rudolf Bultmann correctly perceived this quality as central to what he called the "mythological world view"; earlier, Lucien Lévy-Bruhl had referred to the sense of "mystical participation" of primitive man—a sense of reality in which the boundaries between the natural and the supernatural, and also the boundaries between self and world, are exceedingly fluid (especially when compared with the modern perception of these boundaries). In recent work in this area, it has been among the important contributions of Mircea Eliade and Eric Voegelin to show how this view of reality shapes entire human cultures (Voegelin's term "cosmological civilizations" is very apt here): in such cultures there is a sense of *continuity* between man and cosmos on the one hand, and between the cosmos and the divine forces underlying it on the other hand. One may also say that such a view of reality provides a place for man in the universe that is greatly more secure than, certainly, the place of man in the universe of modernity: it is not only that the world is full of gods, but that man is embedded in this world, and thus is embedded in the divine. This, as it were, ontological benefit of the mythological universe probably goes far in explaining its persistent attractiveness.

The mythological matrix can be called "primitive" in the sense that as one begins to go back in time in every known human culture, one comes upon its familiar features. This does not mean, however, that it is always unsophisticated or is incapable of theoretical articulation. One could argue that every "emanationist" theory of the divine, including the most sophisticated versions of Neoplatonism and its Asian parallels, may be seen as a reiteration of the primordial mythological experience on the level of theoretical reflection. One might even say (following Karl Barth's suggestion) that every notion of an "analogy of being" between man and the divine stands in the same stream of mythological experience and reflection. Be this as it may, the mythological matrix has never been left behind once and for all. In every religious tradition it has resurfaced over and over again, even in contexts that were profoundly inimical to it, as in the Judeo-Christian tradition. Thus Gershom Scholem has shown the dramatic reappearance of mythological forms in Judaism, for which he coined the term "remythologization."[10] One may say that if this can happen within the Jewish tradition, perhaps the antimythological tradition *par excellence* in religious history, then no tradition can be immune to such resurgences (and, one may add, neither is secularized modernity, as the history of twentieth-century ideologies has shown very clearly). In view of this, it is relevant to restate the phenomenological assumption that what is at issue here is not simply a particular interpretation of reality, a world view, that may be superseded and annulled by more "mature" interpretations, but rather a primordial human experience that cannot be ruled out by this or that intellectual development. The plenum was not only present at the beginning, but it reasserts itself, is "available," throughout human history; there is no reason to believe that it has ceased to be "available" today.

In the course of history (or, if one prefers, during the history of human consciousness) this primeval order of gods, men, and world was breached in several places and at different times. Eric Voegelin, rather dramatically, called these ruptures "leaps in being"; one may leave aside here the proposition, made by Karl Jaspers in his conception of the "axial" period, that all or most of these ruptures took place around the same time, between the eighth and sixth centuries B.C. In any case, some of these ruptures are only indirectly related to the religious polarity under consideration here. Thus, as Voegelin discussed in great detail, there was a Hellenic rupture, in which the mythological order was breached by means of the discovery of autonomous reason; he suggests that a comparable rupture took place in China with the advent of the Confucian system of order. But crucial for the present discussion are two ruptures in the mythological order: the *monotheistic rupture,* centered in western Asia, and the *mystical rupture,* not so clearly centered though very strongly present in the religious history of India.

Once again, it should be emphasized that these two ruptures

are experiential before they are theoretical. That is, what happened here was the appearance of new forms of human experience, which only later came to be articulated theoretically. The monotheistic rupture, then, is rooted in a monotheistic *experience*—to wit, the experience of the utterly transcendent, personal, speaking and acting God. In this experience, the world of the mythological matrix fades into insignificance and finally into irreality—the gods, as it were, fade out—and the divine and the human are sharply polarized. The historical roots and the geographical scope of this "leap in being" are not fully known; thus it is not at all clear what roles were played in this drama by monotheistic developments in Egypt and by the as yet imperfectly understood phenomenon of Zoroastrianism in Iran.[11] But there can be no doubt that the rupture was manifested most cataclysmically and with the vastest historical consequences in the religious history of Israel. And, of course, it is this religious experience that has formed the common ground for the three great monotheistic traditions arising in western Asia.

The mystical rupture is very different in character, though it is comparable at least in this one respect, in that it too breaches the mythological matrix. And in the case of mysticism it may be less necessary to insist that it is *experience* rather than speculation that lies at its root. This is not the place to enter into the long controversy over the proper definition of mysticism, a controversy that has recently gained new liveliness.[12] For the present purpose it should suffice to say that mystical experience is an inner path toward the divine or toward ultimate reality—that is, human consciousness turns inward (typically in a systematic, disciplined way, though there are also spontaneous and unplanned mystical experiences), and in this new world of interiority a profound linkage and, in the most radical cases, an ultimate identity between the self and the meaningful core of the universe is discovered. Here too the mythological matrix fades away; at the most, it now comes to be understood as a system of metaphors, useful on lower levels of the development of insight. In other words, here too the plenum of the gods vanishes into irrelevance if not illusion. It is important to insist that there are varieties of mystical experience, and concomitant varieties in the interpretation of this experience. Thus it would be thoroughly confusing to equate such different experiences as those of the pure and isolated self of Jainism, of "nature mysticism" in various forms, of the Upanishadic *atman-brahman* identity, and of the various Theravada and Mahayana versions of *nirvana*. As to the last, the universal Buddhist proposition that the self is an illusion (*anatta*; *shunyata*) should preclude such simplistic equations. Nevertheless, all these experiences are properly categorized as mystical in the aforementioned sense, and thus different from either the experiences of the mythological matrix or those of monotheistic encounter (though one might argue that so-called nature mysticism is close to the experience of the plenum).

This book has monotheism as its focus—more specifically, the relation of monotheism to the mystical experiences initially intended by the concept of "interiority." As the book progresses (and particularly at the insistence of Diana Eck), the relation of monotheism to the primordial plenum becomes another focus of attention. The interest throughout is on the manner in which those who reflected about these discrepant experiences either succeeded or failed in coming to terms intellectually with the discrepancy. Different papers, of course, deal with different aspects of this problem, but it is important to keep in mind that all the papers revolve around this one underlying issue, otherwise the volume will appear as a collection of disjointed exercises in religious scholarship. It is appropriate, then, to look *seriatim* at the way in which the different papers carried the discussion further.

Michael Fishbane's paper gives a vivid picture of the rupture effected by ancient Israel in the mythological universe of the Near Eastern civilizations—"a cosmos perceived as a plenum, interlocking and interconnected in substance," "a cosmic continuum, . . . a monism of divine life which finds expression or individuation in and through the plenum of nature." The mythological figure of Atum masturbating catches this experience of reality graphically indeed, as do the various maternal figures of Near Eastern sacred sexuality. Against all this, there is the revelation of divine *will*, experienced antithetically to the divine *life* of the cosmos and (perhaps necessarily) expressed in

paternal rather than maternal images. Against the cosmic security of the mythological matrix, Israel indeed "reopened the
abyss." But Fishbane also stresses the ongoing struggle between
the two religious structures: The austere Yahwism of the core
Israelite tradition did not win once and for all, but continued to
compete for centuries with the divinities it sought to replace.
The plenum, in other words, continued to be both available and
seductive.

Contemporary feminists, both Jewish and Christian, have
raised the theological question whether the paternal and antima-
ternal symbolism of the Hebrew Bible is necessary to the religious core of the latter, or whether alternatively this symbolism
may be dismissed (and, today, corrected) as a sexist accretion to
be ascribed to religiously irrelevant sociocultural forces of a by-
gone era. This question has far-reaching importance, and not
only for the biblical tradition, because it raises the further question of whether there are indeed necessary or "natural" symbols
in religion, or whether alternatively symbols are entirely the result of sociocultural history and thus may be freely replaced.
This question cannot be negotiated here. But the seminar, and
particularly Fishbane's paper, raises a more immediate question:
Could it just possibly be that the sharp antithesis experienced by
the Yahwists of ancient Israel was, so to speak, a bit of an exag-
geration? Or, put more graphically: Does Elijah's stance on
Mount Carmel, in his historic contestation with the priests of
Ba'al, require some revision? Fishbane cannot answer this question either, but he observes that there are "polarities seemingly
irreconcilable for the interpreter, but easily harmonized and sustained by the living religious consciousness." If so, then the recurrent resurgences of the mythological plenum, in Christianity
and Islam as much as in Judaism, might be seen, *not* as atavistic
aberrations, but rather as much-needed restorations of balance in
overly radicalized traditions.

Howard Kee's paper, quite apart from its intrinsic interest, is
very useful in refining the initial typology. Kee argues that the
confrontation-interiority typology does not pertain to the religious experience of Paul, in that the experience is at least in part
of the interior sort. Indeed, the dramatic encounter on the road
to Damascus may also fall under the interior category of "Christ

in me" (*en emoi*). Kee agrees with Gershom Scholem that Paul's religious experience is a case of Jewish "throne mysticism," at least in form. There are two possible consequences to this demonstration. One would be, as previously suggested, to change the typology in terms of a continuum of unity-differentiation; in that case, of course, Paul's religious experience is far toward the differentiation pole. Or, alternatively, the initial typology may be retained, with the added explication that it refers to the noematic rather than the noetic aspect of religious experience; in that case, Paul's experience, however mystical or interiorized in its noetic mode, must continue to be classified as confrontational in its noematic intention. In either case, Paul is certainly *not* a case of syncretism between the Yahwist tradition and the old plenum, as, among other instances, his attacks on the Corinthian compromises show. Put simply, Paul is unambiguously on Elijah's side.

Elaine Pagels shows that, at least in part, the split between orthodox and Gnostic Christianity was a matter of confrontation versus interiority. Thus, in the Gospel of Thomas, the Kingdom of God is an interior reality, identified in turn both with Jesus and with the disciples. The contrast with Paul is instructive here: in the Gnostic case, interiority applies to both the noetic and the noematic aspects of the religious structure. Of necessity, then, Gnosticism had to dehistoricize the tradition, thus reversing the original biblical transformation: where ancient Israel historicized the cosmic symbolism of the mythological matrix, Gnosticism remythologized the historical symbols of the Judeo-Christian tradition. In short, eschatology becomes mythology once again. In this reversal, Gnosticism is prototypical of other religious revolutions within the context of monotheism (such as various movements of Jewish, Christian, and Muslim mysticism).

Ewert Cousins' paper shows very persuasively not only that Christian mysticism challenged the orthodox tradition in terms of experiences of unity hard to reconcile with monotheism (Meister Eckhart is a classical case of this), but that there have been other mystical movements that put the challenge in terms not of divine-human unity but of a resurgent plenum. If one prefers, mysticism has posed both polytheistic and pantheistic challenges to the monotheistic traditions. Thus Francis was a clear instance of the "nature mystic." Not only is there no experience

of any quasi-Upanishadic absorption into God, but there is no interiority as such: the *external* world is the locus of the religious
experience. Cousins suggests that it was Bonaventure, a "speculative mystic," who introduced elements from the interiority traditions of Augustine and Bernard of Clairvaux into Franciscanism. Noematically speaking, both Francis and Bonaventure
must be deemed confrontational, but with important modifications: Against the sharp polarity between God and man of pristine Yahwism, God is now perceived as the source of a plenitude of manifestations in the world, a "fountain-fullness"
(*fontalis plenitudo*) which, one may imagine, would have
shocked Paul as much as Elijah. It is because of this that Cousins
suggests "unity-in-difference" as a third, distinct type alongside
unity and differentiation—as in Bonaventure's *coincidentia oppositorum*, a concept rooted in the emanationism of Christian
Neoplatonism. Again, it is important to stress that this rootage is
experiential as much as intellectual. If so, then Franciscanism
must be understood, not primarily as an ingenious reconcep-
tualization of Christian *ideas*, but rather as a reiteration of the
experience of the plenum in a Christian context.

Arthur Green's paper, on the other hand, presents a very clear
case of the primordial unity-differentiation antithesis—as if the
Upanishads in their most *advaita* form erupted in the midst of
the monotheistic milieu. Very interestingly, though, emanationist
conceptualizations were used to try to solve the antithesis—thus
challenging Cousins' suggestion that "unity-in-difference" is a
distinct type alongside the other two. Green's key proposition is
that Hasidism constituted a revolution in religious consciousness
and that this revolution posited such a threat to the very foundation of Judaism (to wit, its monotheistic foundation) that "at the
edge of this abyss, [Hasidism] retreated into safer expressions of
traditional Jewish piety."

Anyone familiar with Hindu and Buddhist language will sense
the, as it were, Sanskrit undercurrents in Green's materials. It is
as if these Jewish mystics were straining, sometimes desperately,
not to lapse into Sanskrit. Thus it comes as a shock when Green
recounts that, in the view of the Maggid, the first emanation
(*sefirah*) of God can be called "nothing" (*ayin*)—which is God
before the world, in himself. Or when Rabbi Epstein of Homel,

in a letter to another Hasid, uses profane Yiddish (rather than the sacral Hebrew) to say that "everything is God" (*Als iz Got*). The attempts to cope with this cognitive dissonance are fascinating—as, for example, the idea that God contracted within himself to allow the void to appear, and that consequently one aim of mystical experience is to return to the moment "just before" the creation of the universe, when the newly emergent void "waited" for the first word of God. But Green insists that the roots of these intellectual formulations are experiential, notably in "the experience of the negation or transcendence of self, and the discovery, in the wake of that experience, that it is only God who remains." This experience not only challenged the radical confrontationism of Jewish piety. It also challenged the very basis of Jewish existence: If God is everywhere, why not in the pig as much as in the cow? All of *halakha*, after all (and not just the dietary laws), rests on *differentiations*—and precisely such differentiations are, at the very least, relativized by this radical experience. *Mutatis mutandis*, the same challenge is to be found in Christian and Muslim mysticism: If God is everywhere, why particularly in Christ? If God is everywhere, why the Quran? As Green shows, virtually all the Jewish mystics drew back from these "anarchic" consequences; so did most Christian and Muslim ones. Those who did not (like Meister Eckhart or al-Hallaj) provoked violent reactions from the official guardians of the respective traditions.

As Gerhard Böwering points out, Islam is of strategic importance in the "topography" of the problem under consideration here. In terms of actual geography, if one thinks at all of an east-west axis in the history of religion, only Islam physically spanned the two centers of India and western Asia, Benares and Jerusalem, Sarnath and Sinai. In terms of the original typology explored by the seminar, the origins of Islam are indubitably confrontational, as is its continuing emphasis on the centrality of revelation; yet within Islam there developed the multiform traditions of Sufi interiority, "a vivid underground of rich religious experience." Nor is it irrelevant that some scholars (such as R. C. Zaehner) have argued for direct Hindu influences on Sufism.[13]

Böwering's case study, the Sufi author Sahl at-Tustari, shows very well the key tensions of such mysticism within the monotheistic context. God is understood as *both* utterly transcendent *and* omnipresent and therefore as penetrating man's innermost being; the intellectual problem is, once again, how these two aspects are to be reconciled—both, of course, being grounded in experience: the first in the daily exercises of Muslim piety, the second in the ecstasies of Sufi interiority. Here there is a striking parallel with the solution to the problem discussed by Arthur Green in the case of Hasidism: In mystical experience, according to at-Tustari, man is able to enter into an eternal "now" that takes him back to the so-called Day of Covenant, that moment before the creation of the world when all yet-to-be-created souls were summoned together and affirmed their allegiance to God. Once again, the "nothing" or "emptiness" of mystical experience is conceptualized as the silence preceding the creative word of God, thus establishing a hierarchy of experiences that safeguards the primacy of revelation. And, as with Jewish and Christian cases, emanationist ideas are used to conceptualize the relation between God, world, and man. There are many worlds of light in an "analogy of being" between God and man. God's light penetrates all reality, and there are various modes of participation in this light, but man can never participate in divine being as such; in this last insistence, there is again the hard line that recurs in all the monotheistic traditions. Böwering's discussion of at-Tustari does raise an interesting heterodox possibility—namely, that the utter transcendence of God may be a *transitional* quality, limited to the eon between the Day of Covenant and the Day of Resurrection, the same eon in which the phenomenal world exists. If so, such an understanding would be a far-reaching relativization of the God of revelation, reordering the hierarchy of experiences in a "Hinduizing" direction.

Diana Eck's paper is a very useful introduction to the consideration of Hindu and Buddhist cases, because it strikingly shows the similarities between the plenum of India and that of the ancient Near East. Many if not most of Eck's characterizations of the "organic ontology" of Hinduism could be transposed without serious changes to Michael Fishbane's paper. It would appear, then, that the idea of a cross-cultural mythological matrix is supported by these two cases (an important support, in view of their historical roles). One need not agree with Eck's position that the Hindu "biological world view" excludes transcendence in Rudolf Otto's sense, but it would certainly be a transcendence different from that experienced in monotheistic revelation. The basic question that Eck's paper raises is this: If there is indeed an underlying similarity, perhaps even equivalence, between the plenum in India and that in the Near East, what if any are the Indian equivalents of the Israelite rupture? Put in Eric Voegelin's terms, what were the "leaps in being" in India? Two answers would seem to be possible. The first, which could be developed out of Eck's presentation, would see at least an incipient rupture in all the "other shore" strands in Hinduism (presumably including the various forms of bhakti). The second answer would be in terms of the radical denials of the plenum, be it in the form of Upanishadic *advaita* (the plenum superseded by the *atman-brahman* unity) or of Buddhist enlightenment (the plenum negated by "emptiness," *anatta, nirvana*).

By using the term "theistic mysticism," John Carman subsumes Hindu bhakti under a cross-cultural category, allowing him to compare it with various western mystical traditions. Aspects of this are the dialectic of God's absence and presence, differentiation *and* unity in the experiences of the devotee, the paradoxical copresence of secrecy and the "open secret." Mysticism in all its forms is, by definition, a path of interiority. As Carman points out, though, the issue is the *goal* rather than the *method* of the mystic. This is another way of distinguishing the aforementioned noematic and noetic aspects of religious experience. Once the distinction is made, bhakti can be seen as a mystical method toward a goal of confrontation. Quite apart from its intrinsic interest, Carman's paper makes very clear that this latter goal is not limited to western monotheistic traditions but is very much a part of Hinduism. Indeed, if one looks at popular piety rather than at the "virtuosi" of Indian religion, it is very possible that bhakti is far more prevalent than any form of *advaita*. The question remains open to what extent bhakti may be understood as effecting a rupture in the mythological matrix; if the Gita is seen as a conceptualization of bhakti, for example, then the answer would presumably have to be positive, and the notion of the distinctiveness of the religious experience of western Asia would be further weakened.

The main thrust of Robert Thurman's paper is the elaboration of the point that both interiority and confrontation are present in Mahayana Buddhism, and further that complex conceptualizations have been developed in that tradition to account for this. To concede this point, one need not agree with Thurman that dichotomies exist only in the minds of intellectuals and that experience is always in some middle area between the monism-dualism dichotomy. Be this as it may, Buddhism has sought to solve the problem by its "two-reality theory," more specifically in the theory of the two bodies of the Buddha. This would appear to posit a hierarchy of experiences inverse to that posited by Gerhard Böwering's Sufis: the experiences of unity are those of the "body of truth" (*dharmakaya*), while all experiences of differentiation-confrontation are accorded a lesser status in the "body of form" (*rupakaya*). This same hierarchy allows Buddhists to be simultaneously tolerant and more than a little patronizing with regard to all monotheistic religions. *Mutatis mutandis*, incidentally, very similar attitudes may be found in sophisticated Hinduism. If one were to put this in an overly simplified form, one could formulate as follows: In a Jewish, Christian, or Muslim perspective, the experience of "emptiness" is the prelude to the confrontation with God's word; in a Buddhist or *advaita* Hindu perspective, all divine words (and indeed all gods) must pass away before the great silence of unity, though they may have all kinds of usefulness in the earlier stages of the journey toward truth. Or: For the Christian, Buddhist experience might be understood as *praeparatio Evangelii;* for the Buddhist, Christian experience could well be called *praeparatio nirvanae.*

Buddhism raises with particular gravity the problem of where to draw the line between religious experience and the interpretation of such experience: the very term "enlightenment," while clearly experiential in origin, already suggests propositional content—and indeed the Buddha himself, according to the traditional accounts, announced propositions in the immediate wake of the experience. There is, of course, the possibility (represented by Nagarjuna, also by the Zen masters) that any attempt to articulate ultimate reality in intelligible propositions is denied. Yet the very works in question show how persistent is the human urge to interpret these experiences, and even the most absurdist *koan* is, after all, a kind of interpretation.

Taitetsu Unno's paper, finally, presents another clear case of an attempt to integrate the two poles of religious experience in the context of Japanese Mahayana. If early Pure Land represents "confrontation" and Zen "interiority" (with its goal of the "non-dichotomous experience of reality"), then Shin is the attempt to combine these two poles in a "double exposure." Interestingly, a version of emanationism is once more employed to conceptualize the synthesis: "This Tathagata (the true body of the Buddha) fills the countless world, that is, permeates the hearts and minds of the ocean of sentient beings. Thus, it is taught that grass, trees, and land all attain Buddhahood." A central cognitive issue in this case must be the status of the Boddhisattva, the redeemer figure with which Shin (and all Pure Land) piety stands in a relation of confrontation. In Buddhist terms, does this figure of compassion arise from the true body, the *dharmakaya*, of the Buddha, or is it relegated to the lesser body, the *rupakaya*? Robert Thurman reports on Buddhist schools that take the latter option; Shin, according to Unno, takes the former option: the Boddhisattva, with his all-embracing compassion, arises from the ultimate reality, the *dharmakaya*, and thus cannot be understood as any kind of *praeparatio*. One sees here the two possibilities of hierarchization of experiences *within* Mahayana Buddhism; it is no wonder that early Christian missionaries to Japan perceived Pure Land as a strange form of their own faith.

It can be said with some satisfaction that the following essays have clarified the problematic with which we began. To repeat, such clarification remained strictly on the phenomenological level; that is, no attempt was made, or could be made in view of the methods employed, to move toward any kind of philosophical-theological assessment of truth claims. It would, therefore, make little sense to expect such a movement to follow directly from the work of the seminar. Yet the two avenues of intellectual enterprise are not unrelated: any assessment of truth claims in religion is helped by a clearer understanding of what different claims intend by way of a view of reality. The following observations on possible philosophical-theological next steps are meant to be highly tentative, but they are appropriate here since they were, however indirectly, stimulated by the work of the seminar.

The most promising procedure continues to appear an inductive one; that is, a procedure that has as its focus religious experience rather than (or before) the intellectual interpretations of such experience.[14] Such a procedure (whether called inductive or not) is often implied in various efforts at interreligious dialogue today.[15] There is a pretheoretical attitude presupposed by this approach: On the one hand, respect for the experiences of others; on the other hand, the determination to remain faithful to one's experience. Respect for the experiences of others means that one eschews interpretations that effectively negate or "nihilate" these experiences—as illusions, errors, "infantile" stages on the way of truth, or "anonymous" confirmations of one's own beliefs. But there is also the respect for one's own intimations of truth and insights into reality that may serve as a brake to the all too common "conversion-proneness" of modern individuals—in the West, a common readiness to denigrate one's own cultural and religious background, and to await *"ex oriente lux"* in a stance of uncritical expectation.

Only in such an attitude does the theoretical enterprise of philosophical-theological assessment hold some promise of progress. Yet it would clearly be foolish to expect that the great alternatives of man's religious quest will ever be resolved by any theoretical enterprise whatever. Religious affirmation will always be grounded in the *raison du coeur,* and not in the intellectual exercises of philosophers and theologians. It follows that, in the end, it will be an act of faith that will decide the issue for any individual. It also follows that the hierarchization of experiences discussed before is inevitable, and that the hierarchy eventually settled upon will itself be the result of an act of faith. In other words, both the understanding of Buddhism as a *praeparatio Evangelii* and of Christianity as a *praeparatio nirvanae* will be, respectively, the result of a Christian or a Buddhist act of faith. This may be faith in one's own experience (such as it may be) or in the experience embodied in an authoritative tradition; the difference between the two should not be exaggerated, since even the religious "virtuoso" has the problem of interpreting his own experience on the morning after it took place.

Taking one's position, in faith, in the context of the Judeo-Christian tradition, the problematic of the seminar would appear to point to two philosophical-theological areas, respectively concerned with the experience of the plenum and with the experience of mystical unity. The first area would call for a new theory of the divine fullness, of what Christian theology has called the *pleroma*. Such a theory would have to account for the entire, vast plenitude of divine manifestations in the world religions, without thereby losing the core insights of the monotheistic experience. It is hard to see how such a theory will be able to dispense with some version of emanationism or, if one prefers, with some version of Neoplatonist thought.[16] It is also likely that such a theory will have to be developed in close attention to the developments of modern philosophical anthropology and to the philosophical implications of modern physical science.[17] The second area would call for a theory of "emptiness" in Judeo-Christian rather than Hindu-Buddhist terms. The following papers indicate the extent to which the concepts developed by Jewish, Christian, and Muslim mystics may be useful to such an end. But it will not do to limit oneself to comparative mystical experience here, under some motto like "Mystics of all traditions unite, you have nothing to lose except your differentiations." It is precisely these differentiations—*non*mystical, most sharply brought out in the confrontational experiences of western monotheism—that must be taken into account: What is the status of nothingness in a world of being created by God, who is also the *ens realissimum*? How does God's speech relate to God's silence? And, on the most practical level, how can one both pray and meditate? These questions may at first appear impossible of any propositional answers; yet, it may be argued, an effort to answer them will be of paramount urgency if the historic monotheistic faiths are to cope with the great encounter with the faiths of Asia that is now beginning to appear on the horizon.

This leads to a final observation: The concerns of the papers collected in this volume could well appear to some readers as exceedingly specialized, even esoteric. This perspective changes abruptly if one takes seriously the possibility that Asian religion is today *ante portas*, especially in America, in a historically unprecedented way. There are, of course, many signs of a new

Asian religious presence in the West.[18] It does not follow from
this with logical necessity that this Asian religious presence will
force an agenda of dialogue on American Christians and Jews.
Very little in history follows with necessity. It is possible to envisage any number of scenarios, international as well as domes-
tic, which would obviate any need for interreligious dialogue—an
era of increasingly violent international conflicts, the erection of
new iron curtains between societies in different parts of the
world, an isolationist and "nativistic" America, and so on. All
these scenarios are more or less catastrophic. There is still
ground for restrained optimism. In that event, however, it is very
likely indeed that the age now beginning will be an age of
deepening contact and conversation among the great world religions, and particularly between western monotheism and the
religious worlds of eastern Asia. In such an age the concerns expressed here will be very far from esoteric. Indeed, they may
turn out to be practical in the extreme, for ministers of religion
as much as for thinking people in the pews.

NOTES

1. The seminar took as a starting point (no more than that) the typology
formulated in Peter Berger, *The Heretical Imperative: Contemporary Possibilities of Religious Affirmation* (Garden City, New York: Anchor Press/
Doubleday, 1979), pp. 168 ff.

2. Friedrich Heiler, *Das Gebet* (Munich: Ernst Reinhardt, 1923).

3. Friedrich von Hügel, *The Mystical Element of Religion, as Studied in
St. Catherine of Genoa and Her Friends* (London: Dent, 1923, 2 vols.).

4. Ninian Smart, *Reasons and Faiths* (London: Routledge & Kegan Paul,
1958).

5. For a classical discussion of Luther's "religion of conscience," cf. Karl
Holl, *Luther* (Tuebingen: J. C. B. Mohr, 1932), pp. 35 ff.

6. In terms of intellectual history, the father of this approach is Friedrich
Schleiermacher. But in this century Rudolf Otto, Friedrich Heiler, and Gerardus van der Leeuw are the major authors who elaborated the approach.
Needless to say, agreeing with their methodological presuppositions in no
way necessitates agreement with the details of their several elaborations.

7. For an attempt to deal with these questions in terms derived from Rudolf Otto and Alfred Schutz, cf. Berger, *op. cit.*, pp. 32 ff.

8. For an interesting discussion of this problem, cf. Steven Katz (ed.),
Mysticism and Philosophical Analysis (New York: Oxford University Press,
1978).

9. For a useful overview of theories of mythology, cf. Karl Kerényi (ed.), *Die Eroeffnung des Zugangs zum Mythos* (Darmstadt: Wissenschaftliche Buchgesellschaft, 1967).

10. Gershom Scholem, *Zur Kabbala und ihrer Symbolik* (Frankfurt: Suhrkamp, 1977), pp. 117 ff.

11. Cf., respectively, Erik Hornung, *Der Eine und die Vielen: Aegyptische Gottesvorstellungen* (Darmstadt: Wissenschaftliche Buchgesellschaft, 1971), and Walther Hinz, *Zarathustra* (Stuttgart: Kohlhammer, 1961).

12. Cf. R. C. Zaehner, *Mysticism Sacred and Profane* (Oxford: Clarendon Press, 1957); Frits Staal, *Exploring Mysticism* (Berkeley: University of California Press, 1975); Geoffrey Parrinder, *Mysticism in the World's Religions* (New York: Oxford University Press, 1976).

13. R. C. Zaehner, *Hindu and Muslim Mysticism* (New York: Schocken, 1969).

14. Cf. Berger, *op. cit.*, pp. 125 ff.

15. Cf. John Hick (ed.), *Truth and Dialogue in World Religions* (Philadelphia: Westminster, 1974); Raimundo Panikkar, *The Intrareligious Dialogue* (New York: Paulist Press, 1978); George Rupp, *Beyond Existentialism and Zen* (New York: Oxford University Press, 1979); Wilfred Cantwell Smith, *Faith and Belief* (Princeton: Princeton University Press, 1979). Also, cf. the special issue on Panikkar's work of *Crosscurrents* magazine, summer 1979.

16. Cf. Ewert Cousins, *Bonaventure and the Coincidence of Opposites* (Chicago: Franciscan Herald Press, 1978), pp. 229 ff. A similar position, of course, was taken by W. R. Inge.

17. Max Scheler had the former "correlation" in mind, while the latter concern was developed by Alfred North Whitehead, Pierre Teilhard de Chardin, and contemporary "process theology."

18. Cf. Harvey Cox, *Turning East* (New York: Simon & Schuster, 1977).

MICHAEL FISHBANE

Israel and the "Mothers"

Introduction

A recurrent feature of deliberations on the nature of religious experience has been the fact that the conceptual polarity of confrontation vs. interiority, as well as other formulations along these lines (e.g., differentiation vs. nondifferentiation), has been in need of modification. The questions arise as to whether such typologies reflect fundamentally different religious structures of experience, or whether they introduce and perpetuate methodological distortions of the experience. Do such polar conceptualizations of religious experience project a dominant historical configuration found within a world religion upon the whole of that religion? Do these polar conceptualizations actually disclose fundamental truths of religious experience, or are they artificial reconstructions of the latter? And finally, are these polar conceptualizations, however irreconcilable they seem to us, nonetheless reconcilable within the same historical religion?

To test these matters, this paper will study the conceptual polarities present in two different religious cultures: Israel and Canaan. No religious polarity would seem so fundamentally at odds as that between Elijah and the prophets of Ba'al. The broad outlines of this religious antogonism must first be drawn in order to appreciate the dialectic involved. Since little evidence of

Canaanite religion remains, it will be necessary to view Canaanite religious features within the larger and more amply documented spectrum of ancient Near Eastern religions.

I

The cumulative evidence of ancient Near Eastern religions presents us with a fairly stable and certainly identifiable mythic structure. By this structure I have in mind a cosmos perceived as a plenum, interlocking and interconnected in substance. This substance is a unity—insofar as nature is perceived as an unbroken continuum pulsating with divine life. Indeed, it is the very power and vitality of the gods which constitutes this chain of natural being. The world is not merely the garment of the gods, it is also their very body and substance. As one distinguished writer on ancient Egypt has ventured to put it: "There was . . . a continuing substance across the phenomena of the universe, whether organic, inorganic, or abstract . . . to the ancient Egyptian the elements of the universe were consubstantial."[1]

And why is this so? One reason is certainly rooted in the intuition that the distinguishable divine powers which make up this world constitute moments of emergence or differentiation from within one primal and inchoate element. Cosmogony is the final result of theogony: first there is the productive and repeated commingling of this divine element until the various gods are born; and then occur the subsequent antagonisms and redistributions of power among these gods from which results the world as we find it. The myths which conceptualize these intuitions differ greatly and cannot be reduced one to the other. In Mesopotamia, theogony and theomachy (as in *Enuma elish*) are often successive features resulting in cosmogony and anthropogony; in Canaan, by contrast, theogonic elements are found in one genre of texts while theomachy and cosmogony appear in others (such as the Ba'al and 'Anat Cycle); whereas in Egypt emanationist configurations from a primordial godhead sometimes set the pattern of theogony and cosmogony (as in the creation by Atum), and these are generically separate from combats between the resultant gods (such as Horus and Seth).[2] But however these myths differ, they commonly underscore the notion of a cosmic continuum, of a monism of divine life which finds expression or individuation in and through the plenum of nature. Perhaps an old myth about Atum, preserved in the Memphite tradition, best summarizes this matter in its crudely profound way when it refers to the origin of all things in a divine act of masturbation. The gods are the all-in-all; there is nothing which they are not, for their totality is wholeness itself.

In this world view, the gods are immanent and near, and there is a deep harmony linking man and god and world. This harmony is truly ontological. And how could it be otherwise? Do not man, god, and world share the same substance? Is not mankind created out of the very bodies of Tiamiat's cohorts in *Enuma elish*, even as the world is itself carved out of her desiccated hulk? The same energies flow throughout all being; indeed, there is a macrocosmic-microcosmic homology: all is linked, and every level of being ontologically "mirrors" all others. The cosmic *organum* is thus redolent with "sympathies" and correspondencies; an intricate and eternal network of correlations links gods and men, gods and nature, men and nature. Within this mythic monism, man could always say: "I am *also* that."

As S. Giedion has reminded us, in his great studies of prehistoric art and the beginnings of architecture: "Only if we understand the religious conviction that no discrimination was conceivable within the realm of animate matter can we comprehend that an insignificant insect and the cosmic godhead could be one and the same."[3] For, indeed, in ancient Egypt the god of creation (Atum) was identified with a lizard, and the sun-god (Ra) with a dung beetle. The transmutation of deities into animals, and animals into deities, was expressive of the ontological intuition that the bond of life was—for all its diverse manifestations—unbroken. Throughout this ancient world the life forces enlivening the biocosmic continuum were embodied in perceptible forms—the very forms of nature and its processes. And they were also embodied in figures and representations. These images—be they the signata of the sun, the figures of thunder-hurling storm gods such as Ba'al, or the nurturant features of mother goddesses such as Qudshu-Asherah-Astarte—brought to archetypal expression the divine powers which link all realms of existence one to the other: the gods were in and of nature, and so was mankind.

The iconic forms of the public and private cults gave concrete representation to the energies embodied in the world. These icons are truly gods and truly their representation.

The divine powers which constitute the depth and breadth of this entire nurturant and sustaining cosmos may be termed "the Mothers"—for all their diverse personifications and genders. And humankind, which has emerged from this engendering body as flesh of its flesh, remains dependent upon it as to the source of life itself. The "sympathies" and homologies between gods, men, and nature are also the sources of human meanings. The unified web of things rendered everything potentially ominous, potentially an omen by which to divine the will of the gods. This will is expressed in the stars and in the planets; in the entrails of sheep and in chance sounds; in the dreams of mankind by night and in their physical monsters by day. Experts studied the occurrences together with their correlations, checked them against events, and deepened their wisdom as to the inner nature of things. Revelation of divine will was thus not independent of "creation" or nature; divine will did not transcend the substance of the natural world. And this was equally true for the relationship between law and nature. In ancient Egypt *ma'at*—the principle of order, harmony, and justice—is a feature in and of the very structure of things. The pharaohs embodied this principle and through their rule and legal dicta humanized it for mankind in society. In ancient Mesopotamia, too, the principles of justice are embedded in the cosmic structure of things. It is the *me* of justice—as general principle—which the god Shamash allows Hammurapi to perceive, and so establish, concretely, *kittu u mesharu* (justice and right) on earth.[4]

But the "sympathies" and homologies between gods-men-nature/world are most fully present in the rhythms of life itself. It is here that the deepest needs and anxieties of humankind are "acted out" and projected onto the nature of things. Let us recall the simple and profound—but so often overlooked—insight of the great photographer F. Sommer, who observed that it is not nature which is "alive" but we who give it life. We animate nature by our personifications of its processes. In the ancient world, too, nature came alive as a pattern of dying and rebirth, of waning and waxing, of disappearance and emergence, and of desiccation and envigoration. The combats between divine forces (Seth and Osiris; Mot and Ba'al), the search for the powers of life (Isis and 'Anat), and the wailing and the celebrations (for Dumuzi; for Ba'al), all gave dramatic expression to what was deeply felt and everywhere seen. The mythic narratives on one level, like the dramatic mimes on another (cf. the *Min* and *Akitu* festivals; or the fertility rituals in Ugaritic texts) sympathetically sought to envigorate the processes of life and death. The waning and waxing of the moon, the cycles of seed time and harvest, the impregnation and gestation of wombs, are all homologies of one another.[5]

Mankind lives in the rhythms of nature, and so ritual expressions (such as the *hieros gamos*, and sacred prostitution, such as the defeat of the forces of disorder and sterility) participate in the cycle of life and help regenerate it. Life and death form an unbroken bond; the body of the underworld god Mot is, in Ugaritic literature, winnowed and enters the earth like seeds for new life. Death, hidden like seeds in the soil, is pregerminative. The substance of nature is one—mankind included. Salvation is cyclical; it is in and through the rhythms of nature. And if mankind is called upon to imitate the gods, and to reiterate their patterns, this is because the biocosmic energy is one; this is because human *eros*, in all its desires and urges, partakes of the *eros* of the gods. Man is made in the image of the gods, and his life is one profound *imitatio dei*. The dramas of ritual only make this explicit and focused in his consciousness.

II

It was against this awesome insight into the teeming vastness and unity of natural life that ancient Israel made its leap of consciousness. The concordance of all-in-all was ruptured; a hierarchy of natural differentiations, separated and ordered in accordance with a supernatural divine will, was spoken in Gen 1–2:4a. This creation account reflects the mature vision of a new religious orientation. Leo Strauss, in his penetrating essay on Jerusalem and Athens, aptly noted the subtle but marked accent in this document toward a religious anthropology.[6] The focus is on man and man's world; the heavenly bodies serve as time references for human life; plant and animal life are under his domain. There is, then, a shift away from heaven and any divinization of the forces of nature. Elohim is unengendered; there is neither theogony nor combat. Indeed, for all the mythic vestigiality of man made in the image of God,[7] or of a postscript referring to the *toledot* of heaven and earth (2:4a; *toledot* refers literally not to history but to "generation"), there is no panerotic or pandivine aspect to the orderly creation by Elohim. Later psalmists would underscore this vision with their emphasis that creation ever praises God, and that his creative spirit enlivens and nurtures all life (cf. Ps 104:24–30; 145:10, 16). But such a god is distinct from nature, which neither contains him nor exhausts his power. It is "will" which characterizes such a god. Such a one, says Gerardus van der Leeuw, is a Father—beneficent perhaps—but not a Mother.[8]

Such a religious vision was achieved at a great cost and required a fundamental spiritual transformation. The "great cost" involved is not so much the many remarkable attempts to absorb, reformulate, or otherwise integrate the mythic patterns, images, and values of Canaanite and ancient Near Eastern religions —though they are significant attempts and not to be minimized. The "great cost" is that this cataclysmic *Götterdämmerung*, or *Göttervernichtung*, opened an awesome abyss between God and man-world/nature. Let us not forget in this connection that the monotheistic revolution of ancient Israel—like that of Islam in its own time—is, from the viewpoint of the history of religions, a devolution. The phenomenon of a sky god who is an impartial sovereign and source of all law and order for the world, and who often becomes otiose or is replaced by the youthful vigor of the gods of nature (his sons and children), is widespread and well known. It is, indeed, a phenomenon found in the ancient Near East as well: e.g., Anu is replaced by Enlil; El is replaced by Ba'al. The gods of nature come closer to mankind, and sustain it. Israel reopened the abyss.

The chasm which separated God and man was crossed from two sides: it was crossed by the word of man in prayer and by the will of God in revelation. God's word expressed his will and confronted its recipients with demands: the patriarchs were confronted, Moses was confronted, and so were all the prophets.

These prophets were successively addressed by the holy one of
Sinai, whose presence and whose will confronted the Israelites in
the desert. At Sinai, in fact, a fundamental spiritual transformation occurred: it was now divine will which correlated all
the spheres of existence. In the words of later covenantal formulations, obedience was to be blessed with the fruits and fertility
of nature, disobedience with drought and a cast-iron sky; blessing brought with it social order and peace, while curse doomed
the people to war and exile. All was linked to the condition "If
you obey my Commandments" (cf. Deut 11:13–25; 28:10–69).

No power could be more embracing, no god more omnipotent,
than the nameless, imageless God of Israel. No guarantee of the
beneficent life of nature could exceed the promises of the covenant, spoken by One who was not seen—cannot be seen. Deut
4:12–19 drives this point hard in its homily on the imageless god:
it takes up the very hierarchy of forms created in Gen 1:2–4a
and denies them all representational equivalence with the Revealer. The Creator and Revealer are one God—who is neither in
nor of nature. And so revelation is also not grounded in nature.
The source of the Law is supernatural. And yet observance of
this Law—and it alone!—guarantees rain in its season.

The fundamental gulf which opens up between this mythos of
an omnipotent and transnatural divine will and the created, natural world is thus bridged by the covenant law. But not by this
alone. For the divine will also appears within the sphere of
human history and transforms it. Now it is true that several
Mesopotamian gods do respond to and determine the fate of
human history. But history is not a privileged mode of their appearance, insofar as they remain essentially grounded in the natural plenum of things. By contrast, the God of Israel is free of all
forms and substances, and remains free to exercise his will however he chooses. And he chooses to do so in history. Indeed, history and time are given new meaning as the expression and
mode of manifestation of a god of omnipotent will. Historical
time becomes the dimension and record of such a god's activity.
Such a modality of time is not linked to natural cycles; it is not
cyclical. Indeed, such a modality of time is solely a reflex of an
unconditional and unqualified divine will. *Imitatio dei* is thus
not the representation or reiteration of primordial acts of the

gods which have their eternal reflex in the natural cycle; *imitatio dei* is rather obedience to the divine will and imitation of certain divine attributes (e.g., Ex 22:24-26).

In the Bible, the category of history also determines the way older natural rhythms are assimilated and relived: the harvest festivals memorialize moments in Israel's historical destiny (they are moments of manifest divine will); the Sabbath is no longer a term designating a moment in the lunar flux, but transcends the natural cycle. The correlation of festivals with the new and full moon is no longer emphasized. Natural bounty becomes occasions for historical credos (cf. Deut 26); the seasons of life benefit from observance of the law (cf. Deut 28). The conditional grace of a rewarding Father replaces the unconditioned love of Mother Nature. A new consciousness has clearly set in. God and the gods are not as near or as real as one's body and the earth. The God of Israel is an incomparable god in heaven; but his law can be as near as one's mouth and heart (Deut 30:11-14). Alienation from nature and from God is overcome by obedience: the law of God mediates and regulates all things.

III

The foregoing discussion would thus serve to pit Cosmos vs. History, the gods of Nature vs. the God of Omnipotent Will, as mutually exclusive religious options. Indeed, official Israelite theology in its various genres—historiography, psalmody, prophecy—is fundamentally rooted in this bifurcation. From the official covenantal perspective, cultic involvement with the gods of the ancient Near East is the arch sin and a central reason for divine wrath and punishment (e.g., Judg 2:11-23; II Kings 17:7-23). But it is just here that a most fundamental paradox arises, one which bears significantly on the theoretical problem outlined at the outset of this discussion. For side by side with the official historiographies, historiographical additions, etc., and indeed in dialectical relation with them, another form of ancient Israelite worship emerges. The apparent contrast between the religions of cosmos and a religion of covenant, between religions in which god, man, and world are fundamentally nondifferentiated—i.e., they partake of the same cosmic "substance"—and the official religion of Israel in which God is wholly other than man-world, is radically contradicted by a fully evidenced and long-enduring syncretism.

The paradox is not that Cosmos vs. History is an improper juxtaposition, but rather that it is most proper. As opposed to the viewpoint most fully articulated in the *later* covenantal theology, in which obedience to the will of the God of Israel will bring on nature's benefits, sources from earliest times suggest a popular discontent with the notion that a transcendent God of history rules nature. Moving from a seminomadic to an agrarian environment, there was the tendency among ancient Israelites to prefer the local nature gods. After all, YHWH had simply not proved himself an agrarian diety. Thus, to whatever degree the divine promises to the patriarchs, or the conquest account itself, were intended to impress the notion that YHWH was the true Land-Lord (Ba'al) of Canaan, many remained unimpressed. From the very first, Israelites were involved in orgiastic fertility rituals (as at Ba'al Peor, Num 25:1–9) and build altars to Ba'al with sacred trees devoted to Asherah (El's wife) attached thereto (Judg 6:25, 28, 30). In an ironic touch which underscored the *Kulturkampf* involved, Gideon trampled his father's altar to Ba'al with a young bull—this latter being an old iconic representation of Ba'al's fertile force.

It is one of the peculiarities of official Israelite religious literature that it so insistently preserves the record of national apostasies. All the same, this record provides an invaluable index of the depth and breadth which bull imagery and Canaanite fertility practices infiltrated ancient Israelite religious life. Figures of bulls were set up in the tenth century B.C.E. by Jeroboam at the shrines of Dan and Beth-el (I Kings 12:28 ff.); and two centuries later Hosea still refers to practices associated with them (8:5 f.). The form of the bull is probably a reflection of the belief in some circles that YHWH had absorbed the properties of the Canaanite god El.[9] This would have been one path whereby various Canaanite practices would have found their point of entry into official Israelite worship. Thus pillars to Asherah were even set up in the Temple itself (II Kings 21:3); and official fertility votaries began to appear (I Kings 15:11 f.). An echo of a violent reaction against these practices by the Jerusalemite priesthood may be found in the portrayal of the orgiastic episode connected with the worship of the Golden Calf (Ex 32) for it has been well observed that the language of this text has been significantly influenced by the depiction of Jeroboam's apostasy.[10] From this perspective a later inner-priestly polemic was anachronistically retrojected into Israel's earlier history. Be the truth of this as it may, the literary juxtaposition of the Sinaitic theophany with the Golden Calf episode is richly symbolic of ongoing tensions and confusions in ancient Israelite religion.

The extent of the syncretism knew no bounds. From early times on, royal circles introduced and sanctioned Canaanite personnel and elements (e.g., I Kings 16:29–34; II Kings 10:18–29), and the people moved back and forth as their religious focus and needs required. Indeed, this is just the point of Elijah's remarks against the people in the ninth century B.C.E.: "Why do you hop back and forth on two branches?" The ordeal between Elijah and the prophets of Ba'al portrayed in I Kings 18 was expressly stated as a judgment as to who was the real God: YHWH or Ba'al (v. 21). It seems that most Israelites doubted that YHWH could bring rain, health, and fertility. For well beyond the specific ordeal on Mount Carmel, the various hagiographic legends of Elijah (and his successor Elisha, too) all pivot around such life issues. At one point, in fact, Elijah excoriates King Ahaziah for beseeching the oracle of Ba'al Zebub (god of healing) in his sickness with the words: "Is there no god in Israel that you go to beseech Ba'al Zebub, god of Ekron?" (II Kings 1:3; cf. vv. 6, 16).

Elijah's God, the God of the patriarchs (I Kings 18:36) was in the end victorious and did bring on the rains (vv. 38–45)— despite the ecstatic practices of the prophets of Ba'al and Asherah.[11] But it is the sequel to this event in I Kings 19 which is even more instructive. Fleeing to Mount Horeb as a Moses *redivivus*, Elijah received a theophany from his god.[12] In the depiction of this event the polemic between YHWH and Ba'al, the *numen* in and of the storm, is sharply cast: YHWH, the text says, was not in the storm or the wind; he was not in nor of any of the phenomena of nature (vv. 11–12). YHWH transcended them all. His appearance was but a silent timbre: a paradoxical voiced silence. The God of Israel is not to be identified with the forces of nature, the text implies; and yet nature is responsive to his will, and his alone.

But this protest notwithstanding, the situation in the eighth century B.C.E. was hardly different from the one which preceded it. Nevertheless, several new facets appear and are of interest. In Hos 4–13 we hear over and over again how the Israelites partook of Canaanite practices. For example, they celebrated and sought to influence the forces of fertility by practicing ritual sex at festival occasions, and on the threshing floor at harvest time (4:14; 9:1–2). In these and a myriad other ways they served Ba'al in Dan and Beth-el. Whether YHWH could bring the bounty of nature seems again at issue. And indeed, it is just this point which is highlighted in Hos 2:7. The prophet says that the people have forsaken YHWH for Ba'al, not knowing that it is YHWH (who took them out of Egypt, v. 15) who brings this boon (vv. 10–11). In future days the Israelites will not call him "my Lord" (lit., "my Ba'al"), or call on any of the ba'als (vv. 18–19). They will experience a covenant that YHWH will make for them with all of nature (v. 20). For it is he alone who can make nature "respond" with providential fertility (vv. 23–24). (And lest the prophet's pun be lost, let us simply observe that this fertile "responsiveness" of nature is conveyed by a verb playing on the name of the Canaanite fertility goddess 'Anat.[13]) YHWH will be Israel's husband; her former sexual alliances with Ba'al will be replaced by new covenantal vows (vv. 21–22). Israel's ritual dalliance with Ba'al is thus transformed by the imagery of a covenantal marriage. Fertility rites will be replaced by obedience to the divine will. The erotic was sublimated by a covenantal *hieros gamos*.

Syncretistic practices continued throughout the seventh to sixth centuries B.C.E. and continued to cut across official and popular spheres. Thus, e.g., the prophet Jeremiah refers to involvements in Canaanite fertility practices (2:20–25), to oaths to Ba'al (5:7; 12:16) and to prophecies in his name (2:8; 23:13). Doubts as to YHWH's power to bring rain continued to exist, as we can see from cultic statements to the contrary (Jer 14:22); and a cult to Ishtar, Queen of Heaven, is referred to (Jer 7:18), as well as cults to other cosmic powers such as the sun, moon, and zodiac (Jer 19:13; II Kings 23:5; Zeph 1:4–5, 8). Ezekiel, Jeremiah's contemporary, also refers to rituals to the sun (8:16) and to Tammuz, the Mesopotamian numen of the grain (8:14). Concern with the powers of fertility is also expressed in the numerous figurines of naked women found in Israelite archaeological strata of this period[14]; and the iconic images of the sun and moon are also represented there.

Lest we assume that these practices had no official standing, let us note that Ezekiel reports icons and pagan rites in the Temple (8:10–12); and during the same period, under royal direction, worship of Ba'al, Asherah, and various astral deities was set up throughout the land and in the Temple precinct itself (II Kings 21:3–7; cf. 23:4–6 and Ezek 8:4, 16).[15] There were even dormitories for the hierodules in the Temple, "where women wove garments for Asherah" (II Kings 23:7). Accordingly, the contemporary prohibitions in the Book of Deuteronomy against setting up an Asherah in the shrine, or receiving a hierodule's fare therein, were based on existing practices (Deut 16:21; 23:18–19). One can hardly doubt that any of these practices could have existed in the Temple without the support of the official priests of YHWH. Indeed, an explicit reference in this regard may be found in Ezek 44:6–12.

IV

What are we now to make of these syncretistic products of Israelite and Canaanite religious worship? For does all this evidence not raise fundamental doubts as to whether Yahwism and Ba'alism are mutually exclusive religious configurations? It seems quite evident that the position of religious purism was a restricted ideology at best, even if it was the ideology of those who in fact edited the Hebrew Bible. Nevertheless, it must be stressed that the religious impulses which erupted to create pure Yahwism were truly revolutionary when seen against the mythic structure and stage of development of regional religions of the time. These impulses contained religious intuitions which theoretically drove an impassable wedge between the God of Sinai and the gods of nature. This much is certain.

But it is equally certain that the gulf was crossed—although here our vision is obscured by the dark glass of polemical texts.

It is irritatingly unclear just how syncretistic notions developed in ancient Israel and how they were maintained in religious consciousness. Should we say that this syncretism was a paradoxical development and that the new Yahwistic phenomenon sought to absorb the entire plurality of nature gods (as the very divine name Elohim—literally "gods"—suggests)? Did Israel try to integrate fertility gods like Ba'al, and so serve YHWH in some Ba'alistic forms, only to find that these rituals so split their consciousness that they soon served powers other than YHWH, at least for some matters? Or is this prophetic perspective a distortion due to the pressures of purism? Some texts make it appear that the struggle to integrate a high God of Heaven and history with the near gods of nature and cosmos was never quite successful. If this is so, many Israelites must have felt that there were two types of power in heaven: YHWH and the gods of Canaan. Was YHWH considered by such persons just one—albeit favored and with special attributes—god in the pantheon? Was the attempt to portray YHWH as fully transcendent to the cosmic plenum, as ontologically unique, never quite common coin?

We must not shrink from such a possibility, as one often overlooked text makes quite clear. For were it not for Jer 44, we might assume that Israelite worship of cosmic powers and the like was often nothing but worship of YHWH via natural representations and expressions of his creative power (in much the same way as the iconic image of Phoebus Apollo on the sixth-century B.C.E. mosaic floor of the Beth Alpha synagogue has been interpreted).[16]

In chapter 44 we find a remarkable clash of explanations among the exiles of Judea. Jeremiah excoriates the exiles for worshiping "other gods" in Egypt when it was for just such practices that YHWH destroyed Jerusalem and the cities of Judea (vv. 1–10). Undaunted, the husbands—who knew their wives to be engaged in cult practices to other gods—the women, and the whole exile in Egypt answered the prophet that when they were in Judea, offering incense to the Queen of Heaven, pouring her libations and baking cakes, all was well. It was only when they ceased, presumably in response to prophetic demands, that she became upset and the ill of exile befell them. They therefore decided to fulfill their vows to the Queen of Heaven and perform her cult service (vv. 15–19, 25).[17] This was in the sixth century B.C.E. A century later the Elephantine papyri indicate that the Queen of Heaven had a temple in Syene, and that Jews swore by a goddess named Anatyahu.[18] In any event, the Judean exile to whom Jeremiah addresses himself clearly believed that the Queen of Heaven was capable of punishing her devotees with exile for ceasing her worship. No more could have been correspondingly said of YHWH, god of the cult of Jerusalem. Is there any reason to assume that these devotees believed YHWH to be differentiated from the natural plenum in a way that the Queen of Heaven was not?

Perhaps the following might be said: The explosion in religious consciousness which produced Yahwism introduced a fundamental split between Israel and the Canaanite religions of nature. Many believed that YHWH was differentiated from the natural plenum in a way that the gods of Canaan were not. As "other," he confronted man and world and guided them by his transnatural will. Accordingly the religious purists of Israel claimed that Yahwism and Ba'alism were antinomies and not to be homologized. The religious configuration these protagonists of a pure cult evolved was a self-confirming construct; religious experience and the strategies of purism reinforced the differences. But many could not yoke the "Mothers" to the Father's will. As a shadow side, worship of the numina of the cosmos struggled for independent existence. Their Israelite devotees gave them privileged place, so to say, at the right hand of YHWH. For such worshipers, the notion that Yahwism and Ba'alism represented irreconcilable phenomena was not an issue.

Thus, while such hermeneutical categories as differentiation and nondifferentiation do provide a valid heuristic for arranging religious phenomena, their value is limited: on the one hand, syncretism is a fact of religious life; on the other, such theoretical distinctions introduce polarities seemingly irreconcilable for the interpreter, but easily harmonized and sustained by the living religious consciousness.

V

The very concrete nature of "pure" Yahwism and "pure"
Ba'alism, and the concrete nature of the syncretistic practices
which developed, provides an intriguing point of departure for a
consideration of later phenomena in the history of religions. For
it seems to me that there is considerable truth to the observation
that religions often first produce concrete expressions or ob-
jectifications of their deepest religious intentions via myths and
cult practices, and that it is only at a later point that these intentions recur in spiritualized or interiorized forms.

One of the most arresting images of pure, concrete Yahwism is
the throne vision in Ezek 1. While this theophanic vision is a
complex blend of anthropomorphic, theriomorphic, and volcanic
imagery, there is nevertheless conveyed, through distancing
similes and exalted expressions, a depiction of the most transcendent god, YHWH. The ontological distance between God
and man-world is portrayed in all its awesome enormity. The vision confronts Ezekiel with thunderous otherness. It is no surprise, then, to find that the earliest expressions of Jewish mysticism build on this symbolic structure. The differences and
relationships within this ancient mysticism need not concern us
here. But what is to be noted is that via spiritual exercises and
pneumatic exegesis the adept could begin to ascend the infinite
and dangerous way to behold the very Throne of YHWH. This
mystical transport is highly spiritualized, to be sure; but no matter how interiorized this "ascension" to the "depths" of existence
is, there is never any qualification of the absolute transcendence
of God. He is not of this world, but is its Creator. Man and God
are never, even at the ultimate point of beatific vision and spiritual adhesion, of the same ontological "substance." In this fundamental sense, early throne mysticism preserves the pure theistic
dualism of the Hebrew Bible.[19]

The nature religions of ancient Canaan (Syria and Phoenicia)
also have an afterlife, taking on new dimensions in the mystery
cults of Hellenistic and Roman antiquity. For while these cults
carried over mythological and ritual programs from the ancient
Orient, they were nevertheless subjected to profound and

thoroughgoing spiritual reinterpretations. It is in this form that they provided the setting for personal mysticism. Thus it is that the mythic perception and ritual enactment of the ancient nature cults regarding the biocosmic unity of all things, and the salvific rhythm of the dying and rebirth of natural forms, provide the schema for sacramental mysteries of initiation and spiritual metamorphosis. The liturgical images of the Mithras mystery presented by A. Dieterich provide a particularly graphic illustration of how a series of ritual stages provide the outer skeleton of an interior journey, in which an initiate dies to his old self so as to be reborn as a new person (and indeed much currency was had of the verbal similarity between Greek "to be an initiate" and "to die").[20]

Whether the spiritual metamorphoses in the mystery religions express the inchoate intention and intuition of the old nature cults cannot be known. In any case, these nature religions were subjected to ever deeper spiritualizations, and many were affected by gnosticizing tendencies—a factor which helps account for initiates' concerns with ascensions to a spiritual source, with acosmic apotheosis, and the like. The profound reinterpretation of the old nature myth of Attis (in the Naasene treatise, the works of Porphyry, Sallustius, and the emperor Julianus) is a case in point. Attis, who turns away from the Great Mother toward the nymph, is identified with the Primal Man who falls into matter. After several episodes (including castration), Attis returns to the Mother, an event signifying rebirth and reunion with the divine world.[21] The adept relates all this to himself, so that the nature myth is exegetically sublimated into a framework for spiritual metamorphosis.

I have touched on these matters because the mythological speculations which Gnostics grafted onto archaic nature myths, such as the more philosophical speculations of Plotinus, share a vision of the cosmos as a great chain of being. All descends out of an absolute spiritual source, so that even the crudest depths of nature are not ontologically differentiated from this source, but rather retain sparks of the original pure light. Nothing would thus seem more fundamentally different than the throne mysticism which developed from "pure" Yahwistic dualism (God and man-world are differentiated), and the mysticism of the

"Mysteries," which developed from "pure" Canaanite monism (gods-man-world are not differentiated). And yet, without entering here into matters of historical influences and complex variations, the Jewish Kabbala presents us with a spiritual syncretism of these two mystical forms.

Over and over again we find Kabbalists taking positions on the relationship between the chain of emanations and the Emanator: Are the two consubstantial (no matter how subtly conceived), or is there a fundamental difference between them? Is all one unity —ontologically undifferentiated, while nevertheless differentiated in terms of the hypostases of the divine potencies? Or is there a hidden point of transcendence which is differentiated even from the divine life which fills "all the worlds"? It is quite clear that monistic annihilations of any ontological differentiation would run the risk of pantheism, whereas a theistic dualism would have to struggle with the meaning of the unity of God. Thus, the eruption of myth within mystical Judaism—an eruption which generated a new consubstantial unity among God and man and world through the realm of the divine emanations which filled all realms of existence in the form of a "Cosmic Tree" or Primal Man—could not ignore its own biblical heritage. These polar configurations had to again be syncretized.

The consubstantial nature of the divine world of emanations meant that all levels of existence could be homologized: thus man is a microcosm of the macrocosmic divine life and his ritual acts are of fundamental significance for maintaining its unity. The spiritual unifications which a mystic performs in the depths of his inner life have profound cosmic ramifications for the deepest unity of God. And as the potencies in this macrocosmic divine life are often hypostasized in masculine and feminine terms, a rich erotic symbolism fills the Kabbala. Man could act out and even initiate, at diverse spiritual and physical levels, events of *hieros gamos* within the Godhead. Rituals thus provide the outer structure for profound spiritual transformations, and are, so the Kabbala teaches, profound mysteries.

And, finally, the meaning of Torah undergoes a remarkable transformation within this Kabbalistic framework. Torah is not simply the mediating embodiment of a transcendent divine will; it is rather mystically one with the totality of divine life which

fills the universe. Revelation will now not have to cross an ontological abyss between God and man-world; it can occur repeatedly in the very soul of man. Torah is part of, indeed the very
fundamental structure of, the cosmic plenum itself (cf. Egyptian
ma'at; Greek *sophia*; and the like).[22]

We must stop here, for my concern is not to describe the
Kabbala but rather to indicate that the ancient *concrete syncretism* of Israel and the "Mothers" has its later reflex in the *spiritual syncretism* of the Jewish Kabbala. And yet it is a paradox
that just this spiritual syncretism may indicate the underlying intention of its earlier, concrete manifestation. I am inclined to
suppose that the accommodation of the "Mothers" within biblical monotheism reflects a distinct longing for direct and immediate contact with the primordial sources of divine power which
pulse throughout the cosmos; that it reflects a longing to overcome a felt alienation from God's concrete presence—from a god,
that is, whose very life might be experienced in the world, and
not only his will.

Given the transformative energy of syncretism in the history of
religions, and its profound consequences, we may, perhaps, conclude with the following question: Is there a line which a syncretism of originally distinct religious configurations may not
cross without changing the most fundamental intentions of the
religions involved? Posed thus, it may be productive to consider
the question of religious syncretisms, or of composite religious
modalities, as a case study of religious oscillations. One religious
pattern might absorb another, alien one and yet remain distinct
and identifiable to the extent that its primary intentions are not
lost and remain dominant. At this level one may find a practical
conjunction of what would be regarded, from a theoretical point
of view, as mutually exclusive religious modalities. But at the
point that a quantitative absorption of the alien patterns changes
the qualitative relation between the two religions, so that the
originally dominant configuration becomes the recessive one, the
originally dominant religion might die. Or this metamorphosis
may contribute to the rise of a new religion. Witness the origin
of Christianity.

NOTES

1. J. Wilson, *The Intellectual Adventure of Ancient Man* (Chicago: University of Chicago, 1946), 62–63.

2. Translations of these texts may be found in J. Pritchard, *Ancient Near Eastern Texts* (Princeton: Princeton University Press, 1955), 3–4, 60–72, 129–42. A Canaanite theogonic tradition is embedded in the eighth-century B.C.E. Aramaic Sefire inscriptions (I.A. 8–12), see *ibid.*, Supplement Vol., 1969, p. 659.

3. *The Eternal Present*, vol. II, *The Beginning of Architecture* (2 vols.; New York: Pantheon, 1964), 31.

4. Cf. the Code of Hammurapi xxvb 95 ff. ("I am Hammurapi . . . to whom Shamash has bestowed truths"); and the Inscription of Yahdun-Lim of Mari, in *Syria* 32 (1955), 4 (lines 1 ff.).

5. Cf. M. Eliade, *Patterns in Comparative Religion* (Cleveland and New York: Meridian, 1963), 315.

6. *Jerusalem and Athens: Some Preliminary Reflections* (City College Papers, 6; New York: City College, 1967), 8–9.

7. Apart from the oft-cited Mesopotamian parallels, the similarity between the mythic anthropomorphism in the *Egyptian Wisdom of Meri-Ka-Re* and Gen 1 is more remarkable. Cf. Pritchard (*ibid.*, 417); A. Volten, "Zwei altägyptische politische Schriften," *Analecta Aegyptiaca* IV, 1945, 73 ff.; and S. Hermann, "Die Naturlehre des Schöpfungsberichtes," *Theologische Literaturzeitung* 86 (1961), 413–24.

8. *Religion in Essence and Manifestation* (2 vols., New York: Harper & Row, 1963), I, 178.

9. See F. Cross, *Canaanite Myth and Hebrew Epic* (Cambridge, Mass.: Harvard University Press, 1973), 73 f. The bull was undoubtedly the pedestal of the imageless YHWH, but it is a short step from there to a perception of it as a *numen* transfigured by his immanent "power." On the question of aniconism in Phoenicia, see S. Moscati, "Iconismo e aniconisme nelle più antiche stele Puniche," *Oriens Antiquus* 8 (1969), 59–67.

10. M. Aberbach and L. Smolar, "Aaron, Jeroboam and the Golden Calves," *Journal of Biblical Literature* 86 (1967), 129–40.

11. See the discussion of R. de Vaux, "The Prophets of Baal on Mount Carmel," in his *The Bible and the Ancient Near East* (Garden City, New York: Doubleday, 1971), 238–51.

12. For the typological links with Moses and a thorough "tradition-history" analysis, see R. Carlson, "Elie à l'Horeb," *Vetus Testamentum* 19 (1969), 413–39.

13. See A. Deem, "The Goddess Anath and Some Biblical Hebrew Cruces," *Journal of Semitic Studies* 23 (1978), 25–30.

14. See J. Pritchard, *Palestinian Figurines in Relation to Certain Goddesses Known Through Literature* (New Haven: American Oriental Society, 1943; Krauss reprint, 1967).

15. Among moderns, W. Zimmerli accepts the veracity of Ezek 8 in his *Ezekiel* (Hermeneia; Philadelphia: Fortress, 1979), 236–46; M. Greenberg (in his prolegomenon to the 1970 Ktav reprint of C. C. Torrey's *Pseudo-Ezekiel and the Original Prophecy*, pp. 22 ff.) distinguishes between authentic reports of unofficial syncretism and inauthentic reports (projections of Manasseh's sins) of an official pagan cult. His argument has been contested (see n. 17, below).

16. Compare the remarkable prayer to Helios in the third-century c.e. magical text called *Sefer Ha-Razim*, where, however, this deity has exalted angelic status and no more; see the discussion of M. Margolioth, *Sefer Ha-Razim* (Jerusalem: Yediot Aharonot, 1966), 12–14 (Hebrew).

17. M. Smith, "The Veracity of Ezekiel, the Sins of Manasseh, and Jer 44:18," *Zeitschrift für die alttestamentliche Wissenschafft* 87 (1975), 11–16, has argued for a continuous royal-official cult to the Queen of Heaven.

18. For this oath, see B. Porten, *Archives from Elephantine* (Berkeley and Los Angeles: University of California, 1968), 154–55 and Appendix III. The Egyptian counterpart to Aramaic *malkat shemayin* (Queen of Heaven) is *nbt pt* (Lady of Heaven), an epithet applied to 'Anat on a jar of Prince Psammetichus; see B. Grdseldoff, *Les débuts du culte de Rechef en Egypte* (Cairo: 1942), 28 ff.

19. A basic description of throne mysticism in early Judaism can be found in G. Scholem, *Major Trends in Jewish Mysticism* (New York: Schocken p.b., 1961), 40–79.

20. *Eine Mithrasliturgie* (Leipzig and Berlin: Stuttgart-Teubner, 1966; reprint of 1923), 92–212. The Greek terms used are *teleisthai* (to be initiated or perfected) and *teleutan* (dying).

21. This synopsis follows Sallustius' *De diis et mundo*, IV; see the edition and translation by A. D. Nock, *Concerning the Gods and the Universe* (London: Cambridge University, 1926), 6–9.

22. On the various aspects of the Kabbala just alluded to, see G. Scholem, *On the Kabbala and its Symbolism* (New York: Schocken, 1965), chapters 2–4.

HOWARD CLARK KEE

The Conversion of Paul: Confrontation or Interiority?

The study of religious experience in early Christianity is made difficult by the fact that the primary and secondary material on the subject is limited in quantity, diverse in content and form, and of uncertain authorship. On the subject of the religious experience of Paul, however, our inquiry is facilitated by the relative abundance of primary and secondary material. Paul gives firsthand accounts of his conversion and of aspects of his subsequent religious experience. In the Book of Acts we have an extended account of one who implies that he has intimate association with and direct knowledge of the career of Paul from his conversion to his imprisonment in Rome. Our question as we review this material is whether the religious experience of Paul is to be understood under the model of confrontation or of interiority.

I

The author of Acts seems to have been fascinated by the conversion of Paul and was certainly convinced that his readers ought to be informed about the details—the antecedents, the conversion process itself, and the consequences. The centrality of this cluster of events is underscored by the author's first reporting them in detail, and then by having Paul recount them in public hearings twice over in the subsequent narrative. Paul (identified by his Semitic name, Saul) first appears in the narrative of Acts as an accomplice and ultimately a ringleader in the persecution of Christians taking place in Jerusalem, and throughout Judea and Samaria (Acts 8:1–3). Acts 9 details his conversion, which is reported as occurring in the vicinity of Damascus (Acts 9:3). A description of his earlier life as well as an account of his conversion is reported on the occasion of his arrest in Jerusalem by the Roman authorities, when he addressed his fellow Jews in Hebrew (Acts 22). On a similar occasion in Caesarea, in the presence of King Agrippa and his court, Paul is recorded as describing once again his background, his conversion, and his commissioning as the apostle to the Gentiles (Acts 26).

Curiously, the three accounts do not agree in every detail. Whether this was unintentional, or the result of the use of different sources, or whether it had some mysterious significance in the mind of the author is impossible to say. What is important for our purposes, however, is that there are features common to the three accounts. These are at least six in number: (1) the light shining from heaven; (2) Paul falls to the ground; (3) the voice from heaven; (4) the voice chastises Paul for his behavior toward the Christians, or, more specifically, for persecuting the one who is addressing him; (5) the speaker identifies himself as Jesus; (6) Paul is instructed concerning his future mission. The various accounts introduce interesting details. In Acts 26, the voice that addresses Paul is said to speak Hebrew, although that event is reported in Greek. There are puzzling features, such as what is specifically meant by the charge that Paul has been "kicking against the goads"—a metaphor of rebellion, clearly, but against whom and on what grounds? The implication that God has been trying to convey his purpose to Paul without success is apparent, but it is not possible to determine whether "Lord" is intended by the author as a polite form of address, the designation of God, or the Christian title of Jesus. The ambiguity is removed, of course, when the speaker identifies himself as Jesus. The central feature of Paul's conversion, therefore, is an encounter with Jesus (9:22; 22:8; 26:15).

Dramatic details heighten the narrative, especially in the first two versions. Paul is stricken with blindness (9:8–9) and has to be led by the hand into Damascus (22:11). The accounts cannot agree whether his companions heard the voice (22:9) or saw the light (9:7). But the extraordinary accompaniments of the conversion experience heighten the sense of awe. Indeed the phenomenon of visions serves to do this throughout the narrative of Acts: in 9:10 ff. Ananias is instructed through a vision to go to the stricken Paul in order to explain to him what God has commissioned him to do in carrying out the mission to the Gentiles. Similarly, in Acts 10 the visions of Peter and Cornelius are synchronized in order to prepare the Gentile for receiving the gospel and Peter for preaching it to him. The menagerie in the celestial sheet has to come down twice in order to convince the traditionalist apostle that the separation between Jew and Gentile is to be breached (Acts 10:9–16). This fascination with visions pervades not only Acts but pagan literature of the period as well. Perilous sea voyages, visits to shrines of world renown—such as those of Athens and Ephesus—miraculous deliverance from the jaws of death, apparitions of deities promising guidance and support to the faithful are to be found in the Hellenistic romances, such as the *Ephesiaca* of Xenophon.

The antecedents of Paul's conversion are described by the author of Acts in terms which are in part supplemental to, in part contradictory to the account we have in Paul's own writings. From Acts we learn that Paul was a native of Tarsus, that he was educated in Jerusalem "at the feet of Gamaliel" (Acts 22:3), and that the details of his life and training were well known among his fellow Jews. His zealous activity in persecuting the church is described briefly in Acts 8:1–3, and his reason for going to Damascus is to extend his extermination-of-Christians program in that ancient city as well (9:1–2). Later we shall note how Paul represents those preconversion experiences. The narrative in Acts 9 stresses the incredulity of the Jerusalem Christians that Paul had indeed been converted and their refusal to allow him to carry on evangelistic activity in the Jerusalem vicinity. The reader can sense the Jerusalem Christians' feeling of relief when he agreed to be sent off to Tarsus (Acts 9:30). Although these details are more important for sharpening the distinction between the territory of Jerusalem apostles (their city and nearby) and that of Paul (from Antioch toward Rome), the story as a whole underscores the encounter of Paul with God or Jesus and locates it on Gentile soil. Paul's plans to exterminate the Christians terminates in the confrontation near Damascus. That experience has public dimensions as the author of the Acts describes it, in that there are visual and aural accompaniments, apparent to others and with temporarily enduring consequences, as in Paul's blindness and necessity for being led about. The public nature of his conversion and the notoriety that emerges within the Jewish community as a result intensify the dramatic nature of the confrontation.

II

Before turning to Paul's accounts of his conversion and of subsequent religious experiences, it may be useful to examine the evidence that Paul provides in his letters concerning his own preconversion life. Of birth and residence in Tarsus, of education in Jerusalem, of instruction from Gamaliel, we read not a syllable in Paul. What we do learn is compactly stated and somewhat enigmatic. The most extensive autobiographical passage on his "former life in Judaism," as he describes it (Gal 1:12), is in Phil 3. There we learn that he was born and reared in a family that observed the Law ("circumcised on the eighth day"), that not only considered itself to be fully a part of Israelite tradition but even claimed genealogical links with Israel's heritage ("of the tribe of Benjamin"). It is not evident that most or even many Jews could trace their tribal links, other than those of Levi, in which case it was essential as a qualification for the priesthood. And Benjamin, the tiny buffer between the northern and southern tribes, is not a heritage that the impulse to inflate one's reputation or tradition would likely invent. Paul mentions this detail as part of the confirmation of the authenticity of his Hebrew heritage: "a Hebrew of Hebrews" (Phil 3:5)—which could mean "a thoroughgoing Hebrew," or "a Hebrew-speaking Jew," or it may have been intended to convey a meaning now lost. In any case, Paul wants to establish unequivocally his Jewish credentials.

Seemingly more specific is the claim of Paul that when it came to matters of the Law, he was a Pharisee (Phil 3:5). It would help us to understand Paul, to say nothing of our understanding of Jewish history in the period prior to the destruction of the Temple in 70, if we knew precisely what Pharisaism looked like in the middle of the first century. Jacob Neusner, in his more popular *From Politics to Piety*, as well as in his scholarly volumes, *The Rabbinic Traditions about the Pharisees before 70* (3 vols.), has traced the continuum of the movement of the Pharisees from their rise as a politically motivated group concerned for Jewish national independence in the second century B.C.E. to their emergence as circles of personal piety and group instruction that were given the Roman imperial *imprimatur* as the single legal instrument to carry forward the Jewish tradition after the fall of Jerusalem. Neusner has warned against reading back into the period before the first revolt the rabbinic and talmudic traditions of a later epoch. At the very least, Paul's Pharisaism would have included recognition of the wider canon of scripture (the prophets and writings, as well as the Law), a concern for the personal relevance of the scriptures rather than merely ritual participation in the cultus, and a keen sense of personal participation in the ongoing life of those who called themselves God's own people. Concern for religious identity is almost certainly what lay behind Paul's zeal to destroy the church, since the Christians would have represented for Paul an unwarranted claim on the promises and heritage of Judaism—claims which by their inclusiveness and negating of ritual and moral separateness constituted a major threat to the integrity of obedient Israel.

Neither in Acts nor in Paul's own letters is there an indication that Paul was harassed by a bad conscience or overwhelmed with guilt or moral failure. Indeed he asserts in Phil 3:6 that, as far as the Law was concerned, he was "blameless." It is tempting to psychologize this aspect of Paul, and infer that his zeal was a compensation for his guilt, but there is no hint of that factor in his letters. He comes through in the autobiographical passages as one who moved with efficiency and moral confidence in his efforts to extirpate this Christian movement that threatened his ancestral faith. He describes himself as having "advanced in Judaism beyond many of my own age" (Gal 1:14) in the matter of zeal for the traditions of the fathers. There is no trace of frustration or failure in Paul's religious life prior to his conversion.

Paul's use of the word "righteousness" in Phil 3 should probably not be understood as indicating that his major concern was with moral achievement or some kind of merit system. Those biblical interpreters who claim that the Greek word, *dikaiosunē*, connotes right relationship (i.e., with God) rather than superior moral qualities, are almost certainly correct. What Paul is maintaining, therefore, is that he was confident of his relationship with God, rather than that he was self-assured on the basis of his own meritorious achievements. The evidence of guilt is restricted to his postconversion evaluation of his activity in having persecuted the church of God (I Cor 15:9). He declares that his hostility toward the church calls into question his legitimacy as an apostle—although he would probably have been much annoyed if anyone else had raised similar doubts about his apostleship. What is of central importance for Paul is the question of personal identity in relation to the people of God. Prior to conversion, he stood firmly and, as far as we can determine, unambiguously on the ground of the Law and the traditions. That is the self-understanding which stands in sharpest contrast in Phil 3: his new locus is not "in Judaism," but "in Christ"; that is, in the new community of faith. The first place where Paul attacked the church, according to his own account in Galatians, is in Damascus. We must now turn to his description of what happened there.

III

Paul asserts unambiguously that he was "not known by sight to the churches of Christ in Judea" (Gal 1:22). It seems to me unthinkable that no one there would have known the man who was, according to Acts, the spearhead of the persecution of the churches in Jerusalem and its environs. If we assume that Paul is reporting the situation accurately—and it would have been to his disadvantage in the argument of Galatians to distort the record, since his argument was with the Jerusalem-based apostles who could dispute his word—we must conclude that Paul's base of operations for his destruction of the church was not Jerusalem but Damascus, since it is to that city that he returns (Gal 1:17). Obviously he could not speak of his "return" if he were going there for the first time, and the clear implication is that he was returning to the scene of his conversion following his stay in Arabia. He gives no hint as to how long he remained in Arabia. Since "Arabia" almost certainly means Arabia Petrea (modern Jordan) rather than the main part of the Arabian peninsula, a journey of a few hours and a stay of a few days or weeks are more likely than a protracted, long-distance withdrawal. The only time indications he offers relate to his later journeys: three years and fourteen years after his conversion or return he went to Jerusalem. The point of mentioning the long intervals is to declare his independence of the Jerusalem apostles; no clue is present about the time elapsed between conversion and return to Damascus. Although precedents for the withdrawal of religious leaders prior to launching or at midpoint in their public careers are abundant—Moses, Elijah, Isaiah, Jeremiah, and Jesus are obvious cases in point—it is idle to speculate how long Paul was in Arabia or what happened there. The details may be supplied by pious imagination or religious romanticism, but not by firm evidence.

Paul is remarkably succinct or even diffident about describing what we have come to call his conversion experience. In Gal 1, Paul declares that he received the gospel "by revelation of Jesus Christ" and that "he who had set me apart before I was born and called me through his grace was pleased to reveal his Son in me. . . ." The tradition of election for the prophetic role before birth is associated with Jewish prophets (Jer 1:5) as well as with figures such as John the Baptist and Jesus. But what are the details of the conversion experience proper? Apart from the assertions (1) that it was a "revelation," (2) that it took place at God's initiative, and (3) that the content of the *apokalypsis* was Jesus, Paul tells us nothing. The phrase "revelation of Jesus Christ" could be understood as subjective genitive, which would mean that Jesus had accomplished the revelation to Paul. But Gal 1:22 removes the ambiguity: God is the agent of revelation and the subject is Jesus. Paul's role is that of recipient. The same incident is referred to by Paul in I Cor 15, where he is transmitting the tradition about the resurrection of Jesus from the dead, and in the process enumerates the postresurrection appearances of Jesus. Although there are ways in Greek to depict the experience of seeing as an activity of the subject—as in English, "I saw . . ."—Paul here uses an idiom of circumlocution, which says literally, "The Lord was made visible to me." The same passive verb is used in the case of each of the appearances to the apostles and the other witnesses of the resurrection. The implication is one of passive reception rather than active participation.

Similarly, Paul might have said that God revealed his Son *to* me. Instead, he chose the somewhat awkward but, for that very reason, significant expression, "[God] was pleased to reveal his Son *in* me" (in Greek, *en emoi*). The inference we must draw is that the revelation is an inward experience, rather than a vision encountered from without. It is for Paul nonetheless real because it is inward; he in another context declares in a rhetorical question, "Have I not seen Jesus our Lord?" (I Cor 9:1), with the unmistakable claim that indeed he has. But when the revelatory experience itself is under scrutiny, as in Galatians, he uses the periphrastic expression about God revealing his Son in me, or in I Corinthians, "he became visible to me." There could scarcely be a more forthright claim of an interior religious experience.

What is missing from Paul's account of this experience will be obvious. There are no heavenly lights or voices, no attacks of blindness, no supporting visions from others, no falling to the ground, no scales dropping from the eyes. On the evidence that Paul presents, he was a resident of Syria all along, and known only by reputation in Jerusalem. He seems to have been living in Damascus at the time, since it is there that he returns after his retreat in the desert, which was of unspecified duration. No names are mentioned in connection with his persecution of or his subsequent participation in the Syrian churches. Later his base of operations was moved to Antioch-on-the-Orontes, the capital of the Roman province of Syria-and-Cilicia (Gal 2:11). Apart from the revelation itself, there are no supernatural features linked with Paul's account of his conversion. The focus is solely on Paul's inner experience.

IV

The same pattern of inner revelation is evident elsewhere in the Pauline corpus. Using the identical term linked with his conversion, Paul reports that his call on the Jerusalem apostles fourteen years later was "by revelation" (Gal 2:2). To underscore the nonspectacular, private nature of that event, he mentions that the whole conversation with the Jerusalem leadership was not a public event nor was it generally known in the Jerusalem church. His point in this passage is that he went up on his own initiative rather than in response to a summons by those whom he might have acknowledged as his superiors or at least as his predecessors in the faith. The force of his argument is to make it even more telling that the instigation for the call lies within Paul's own inner life and that such an activity is described by him as a "revelation."

Paul himself attests that these revelations were frequent occurrences. He confesses that he tended to feel unduly elated by "the abundance of revelations" (II Cor 12:7), so that we must conclude that they took place in his experience with great frequency.

Fortunately, Paul did not get around to acknowledging his spiritual pride on the matter of revelations until after he had described one in brief but vivid detail (II Cor 12:1-4). And the detail corresponds with what we know from other sources of the period which depict Jewish mystical experience. The passage begins with mention in the plural of "visions and revelations," so that the reader is notified that what is about to be described is by no means a unique event. Indeed the whole argument turns on the assumption that Paul has kept quiet about these revelations, frequent though they are, but now feels driven to acknowledge them because of the boastful claims that others are making for their superior spirituality. Since the main thrust of the particular revelation which he describes was to remind him of his weakness and hence his dependence on divine grace, he feels that it is not yielding to pride to tell his story.

The account begins diffidently, however, since Paul at first speaks of the subject of the revelatory experience in the third person and anonymously: "I know a man in Christ. . . ." By the end of the paragraph, however, it is evident that he is describing what happened to himself, even though for a time he keeps up the anonymous posture. The fact that he mentions that the event occurred "fourteen years ago" has led some interpreters to assume that he is talking about his conversion experience, which took place fourteen years before he made his second visit to Jerusalem. The interval is the same, but there is no indication that the events are identical. Further, the content of this revelation has to do with the meaning of Paul's own suffering, not the identity of Jesus as God's Son (Gal 1:16). For our purposes it is important to observe the detailed comment offered in passing, that Paul does not know whether this vision of transport occurred in the body or out of the body. He is emphatic about that: God alone knows the circumstances of the revelatory experience. Paul does know its locale, however: it took place in the third heaven, above the first heaven where the birds fly and the second heaven where the sun and moon and stars move.

As Gershom Scholem has noted in his classic study, *Major Trends in Jewish Mysticism,* we have here a classic instance of throne mysticism. Deriving from the experiences of Isaiah and Ezekiel in their visions of the throne of Yahweh (Is 6; Ezek 1), a stylized pattern of mystical experience emerged according to which the suffering righteous one is granted a vision of the divine throne, during which the garments or appearance of the visionary become radiant in the presence of the divine glory. The message conveyed through the vision is that the faithful one will be vindicated by God, and that he is therefore to accept suffering in tranquil confidence, awaiting divine vindication in God's own time. This mystical phenomenon is present in Dan 10, where the faithful remnant are assured that, in spite of the restrictions and threats uttered by the pagan rulers, God will vindicate them and establish his rule in the earth. In the apocryphal work the *Testament of Job,* Job confides to his friends toward the end of his life that he had been enabled to endure the trials and sufferings through which he had passed because earlier on he had been granted a vision of the divine throne, his garments had become radiant—as did those of Daniel, Moses, and others in this tradition—and he had been promised divine vindication. The

same tradition probably lies behind the story of the transfiguration of Jesus in Mk 9.

We are presented, therefore, with a concise report by Paul of
an experience fundamentally similar to these other mystical
transports. And the point is in each case the same: suffering is
not to be regarded as a divine punishment, but rather is to be
endured in the assurance of ultimate divine vindication. It is in
those terms that Paul is to regard the "weaknesses, hardships, in-
sults, persecutions, and calamities" (II Cor 12:10) that he is un-
dergoing. As we have seen to be characteristic of his religious
life from his conversion on, these experiences are not dramatic
public events, nor even charismatic displays that occur in the
public context of the worshiping Christian community. They are
private revelations that Paul confesses reluctance even to report:
"If I must boast, I will . . ." (II Cor 11:30). It would be interesting to know what it was that he referred to as a "thorn in the
flesh," which was given him to minimize his spiritual elation.
Scholars have conjectured that it was epilepsy or an eye ailment,
but we have no clues. All that is certain is that, like the revelations that fostered his elation, it was an inward experience. In
what is probably his latest surviving letter, Philippians, Paul depicts his inner striving for spiritual discipline, which is centered
on the knowledge *of* (not concerning) Christ and the participation in his sufferings and death, motivated by the hope of
sharing in the resurrection. Paul advances no external proofs or
signs of this participation; his confidence rests on eschatological
hope and the striving for mystical knowledge.

Conclusion

The difference between the account of Paul's conversion in
Acts and his own report of it in his letters is more than merely
conceptual or reportorial. Paul is describing what happened to
him against the background of the apocalyptic, charismatic, mystical traditions of Judaism. He was obviously deeply influenced
by the pervasive Hellenistic culture of his time, as is evident in
his regular use of Stoic virtues when outlining the specifics of
Christian moral responsibility. The seemingly chance linguistic
event that led to *nomos* as the Greek translation for Torah in the
Septuagint and other Jewish documents opened the way for an

understanding of the Law of Moses as akin to and consonant with Stoic natural law. Paul makes a significant place for conscience in his ethical system, even though it has no counterpart in Torah. Yet in spite of these accommodations to Hellenistic culture, Paul's basic life-world is that of postexilic Judaism, or more specifically of post-Maccabean Judaism: a three-storied heaven; conflicts of angels and demons; expectation of the end of the age and of eschatological vindication; God actively at work in human history to achieve his purposes; persons specially endowed by God to be his instruments in the accomplishment of those purposes; special revelation granted to the elect to understand the divine plan. This is the life-world implicit in the apocalypses of the period, in the Dead Sea documents, and—with certain modifications—in the Pauline corpus.

In contrast with it at crucial points, in spite of some basic similarities, is the life-world represented in Luke-Acts. The imminent end of the age is no longer expected. There is a world to be evangelized, but its culture is not to be rejected. Its religious aspirations are to be affirmed, in spite of their inadequacies (Acts 17). Its love of beauty and its longing for universalism are to be heeded and responded to positively, as the distinctive narratives and parables of Luke attest. Its author believes in exploiting the literary traditions of the Greco-Roman world in order to get his message across, as is evident from his use of the styles of Hellenistic historiography and romance. Above all, he is responsive to the early Roman world's fascination with divine confrontation, with miracles of deliverance and disaster, with visions and displays of the supernatural. These propaganda strategies are employed with great effectiveness in both parts of his two-volume work, not least in his repeated accounts of the conversion of Paul. He accommodates the Hellenistic attraction to the confrontational model of religious experience by describing nascent Christianity in those terms.

There are other religious models at work in the world of that time as well, and Judaism was by no means immune to their influence. The inscriptions preserved at shrines of Asclepius and of Isis, as well as the vestiges of the mystery religions that have come down to us, bear testimony to the wide appeal of the religions of participation. They had their rough counterparts in

Judaism, as the documents depicting throne mysticism attest.
Unlike the mystery cults, in which the divine agent of mystical
communion was a purely mythical figure, Paul believed that the
historical person, Jesus—"born of woman, born under the Law,"
as he phrased it (Gal 4:4)—was the subject of God's revelation
and the locus of mystical participation: "in Christ" (*passim*).
The distinction of the analyst of religion between the religion of
confrontation and that of interiority does not work for Paul.
There is a sense in which revelation takes place through divine
initiative, but its locus for Paul is "in me." I suspect that if one
were to explain the terminological distinction to Paul and then
ask him, "Was your religious experience a matter of confrontation or interiority?" Paul would answer, "Yes."

ELAINE PAGELS

The Orthodox Against the Gnostics: Confrontation and Interiority in Early Christianity

For several years, while working on the Gnostic Christian sources discovered at Nag Hammadi in 1945, I have been asking myself the question, What differentiates the gospels canonized in the New Testament collection (and so sustained in orthodox tradition) from those excluded and branded as "heresy" and "blasphemy against Christ"?

Before the discoveries at Nag Hammadi, New Testament scholars tended to assume that the canonical gospels represented the earliest—and hence the most authentic—traditions concerning Jesus. Tradition ascribed the gospels to disciples (*John* and *Matthew*) or to followers of disciples (*Mark* and *Luke*). Since the nineteenth century, however, scholars have recognized that such attributions were unprovable, and probably unhistorical. Further, the evidence indicated that many other gospels circulated in the early Christian communities before A.D. 200. In the

1890s, indeed, archaeologists had discovered a few fragments of a gospel of *Thomas* in a manuscript dated approximately A.D. 100. Irenaeus, bishop of Lyons (c. A.D. 180), had, indeed, indicted the heretics for being "utterly reckless" because "they put forth their own compositions, boasting that they possess more gospels than there really are . . . what they have published . . . is totally unlike those which have been handed down to us from the apostles," which, he insists, alone are "true and reliable" (*Adv. Haer.* 3.11.9). Some other sayings attributed to Jesus were known from papyrus fragments, and from writings of the church fathers. Apart from these, however, virtually the only direct evidence of noncanonical gospels comes from later centuries—usually the fourth century and later.

The discoveries at Nag Hammadi changed the whole picture, challenging traditional accounts of the origin of Christianity. This discovery included writings called "gospels," revelations, and apocrypha attributed (like the New Testament gospels) to Jesus' disciples and their followers. Dating the texts is problematic: in all likelihood, they vary in date over about a two-hundred-year range. Yet some scholars—notably Professor Helmut Koester of Harvard University—now suggest that some of the traditions they offer (specifically, some sections of the gospel of *Thomas*) date back to A.D. 50–100, as early as—or earlier than—the gospels of the New Testament. Several of the texts discovered at Nag Hammadi (e.g., the gospel of *Thomas* and the *Dialogue of the Savior*) apparently use sources that they shared in common with the synoptic evangelists; others may have derived their sources from the synoptics.

What, then, differentiates the Gnostic writings from the accounts accepted into the New Testament canon? I am the first to admit—even to emphasize—that the answer to that question will not be a simple one. But, reflecting on Peter Berger's proposed typology of religious experience in terms of *confrontation* and *interiority*, I began to suspect that it contained a clue. With appreciation for the warnings against oversimplification that Ewert Cousins and Robert Thurman give in their essays, I suggest the following: The gospels which came to be accepted as orthodox generally interpret the Jesus traditions in *confrontational* terms;

Gnostic gospels tend instead to interpret the same (or similar) traditions in terms of *interiority*.

For the purpose of illustrating this hypothesis, let us restrict ourselves to examples from both orthodox and Gnostic sources that seem to work from common traditions. These include sayings and parables attributed to Jesus, as well as such events as the crucifixion and resurrection.

The theme that dominates the earliest known texts from both orthodox and Gnostic traditions (the New Testament gospel of *Mark*, c. A.D. 50–90 and the gospel of *Thomas* from Nag Hammadi, c. A.D. 50–120) is that of the Kingdom of God. *Mark* describes Jesus' first proclamation as one of confrontation with the Kingdom of God:

After John was arrested, Jesus came into Galilee, preaching the gospel of God, and saying, "The time is fulfilled, and the Kingdom of God is at hand: repent, and believe in the gospel." [*Mk* 1:14–15]

Both context ("after John was arrested") and formulation ("the time is fulfilled") indicate that, according to *Mark*, Jesus announces the Kingdom as an event about to occur in history, shattering historical time. And that event is coming soon: Jesus declares that some of his disciples, to whom is given "the secret of the Kingdom of God" (4:11) themselves "will see the Kingdom of God come with power" (9:1). When they ask him when it will happen, Jesus answers that other events must first take place—war, earthquakes, famines—but that the disciples are not to despair of the Kingdom's arrival. Facing death, he vows that he will not drink wine again "until that day when I drink it new in the Kingdom of God" (14:23). According to Rudolf Bultmann, this indicates that Jesus

clearly expected the irruption of God's Kingdom as a miraculous, world-transforming event—as Judaism, and later his own Church, did. . . . Both . . . the eschatological proclamation and the ethical demand direct man to the fact that he is thereby brought before God, that God stands before him; both direct him into his Now as the hour of decision for God. [*Theology of the New Testament*, I:21–22]

The gospel of *Luke*, as many scholars have observed, interpreting the Jesus traditions perhaps a generation later than *Mark*, renders Jesus' proclamation of the Kingdom in more ambiguous terms. The disciples are given the "secrets (*mysteria*) of the Kingdom of God" (8:9). This is not, as in *Mark*, the single "secret" of its near approach, but, *Luke* implies, many divine "secrets" which it represents. And from Jesus' declaration that the disciples during their lifetimes will "see the Kingdom of God" (9:27), *Luke* apparently omits the final phrase ("come with power"). This may suggest that the disciples, through faith, perceive the Kingdom in a spiritual sense, rather than witnessing its actual realization on earth. *Luke's* account of Jesus' refusal to predict the exact time of the Kingdom's arrival contains a similar ambiguity:

Being asked by the Pharisees when the Kingdom of God was coming, he answered them, "The Kingdom of God is not coming with signs to be observed, nor will they say, 'Lo, here it is!' or 'There!' For behold, the kingdom of God is among [*Entós*] you." (*Lk* 17:20–21)

The preposition (*Entós* = within, among) has allowed for various translations: one interprets that the Kingdom is "within" the disciples, another that it is "among" them through Christ's presence.

The gospel of *Thomas*, while containing many parallels to sayings recorded in the synoptic gospels, offers two different versions of the saying—versions that move in the same direction as *Luke's* spiritualizing interpretation, but are considerably more radical. According to *Thomas's* account, Jesus ridicules the idea implied in *Mark*, that the Kingdom of God is to be expected to occur in the dimension of space and time: "Rather, the Kingdom is inside of you, and it is outside of you." *Thomas's* version allows none of the ambiguity that has perplexed scholars in *Luke* (between the Kingdom understood as an eschatological event and as a spiritually perceived reality), for Jesus goes on to explain that

When you will come to know yourselves, then you will become known, and you will realize that you are the sons of the living Father. But if you will not know yourselves, then you will dwell in poverty, and you *are* poverty. [*Thomas*, Logion 3]

According to *Thomas's* conception, it is not the hostile Pharisees, but the ignorant disciples who persist in mistaking the Kingdom for a future event:

His disciples said to him, "When will the Kingdom come?" Jesus said, "It will not come by waiting for it. It will not be a matter of saying, 'Here it is,' or 'There it is.' Rather, the Kingdom of the Father is spread out upon the earth and men do not see it." [*Thomas*, Logion 113]

In the gospel of *Thomas*, the Kingdom symbolizes a transformation in spiritual consciousness: it has become an interior reality.

If we go on to compare how *Mark* and *Thomas* characterize Jesus himself, we discover a similar contrast between *Mark's* view of Christ as the one who inaugurates that new reality, the "inbreaking of God's Kingdom," and *Thomas's* view of Christ as the symbol of one's true interiority. *Mark* relates, for example, that when Jesus questions his disciples ("who do people say that I am?") they reply that most people assume that he is one of the prophets whose presence requires that the nation of Israel encounter the presence of God. But Peter recognizes the truth: "You are the Messiah," the one chosen to inaugurate the new age (*Mk* 8:27–29). *Matthew* adds to this that Jesus blessed Peter for the accuracy of his recognition and declared immediately that the church shall be founded upon Peter, and upon his recognition of Jesus as the Messiah (*Mt* 16:16–20). One of the earliest of all Christian confessions states simply, "Jesus is Lord!" But *Thomas* tells the story differently:

Jesus said to his disciples, "Compare me to someone and tell me whom I am like." Simon Peter said to him, "You are like a righteous angel." Matthew said to him, "You are like a wise philosopher." Thomas said to him, "Master, my mouth is wholly incapable of saying whom you are like." Jesus said, "I am not your master. Because you have drunk, you have become intoxicated from the bubbling spirit which I have measured out."

And he took him and withdrew and told him three things. When Thomas returned to his companions, they asked him, "What did Jesus say to you?" Thomas said, "If I tell you one of the things which he told me, you will pick up stones and throw them at me, and a fire will come out of the stones and burn you up." [*Thomas*, Logion 13]

What Jesus said to Thomas, apparently, is too secret to be written even in this secret gospel. On the basis of analogy with esoteric traditions, scholars have suggested that the three sayings may be something like the following: "I am God"; "You are God"; "I am thou." Such suggestions receive some confirmation in saying 108:

Jesus said, "Whoever will drink from my mouth will become like me. I myself shall become he, and the things that are hidden shall be revealed to him."

Here, as the two become one, Jesus himself (or the divine being he represents) *becomes* the interiority of the disciple.

The form of the New Testament gospels differs in an analogous way from that of Gnostic traditions. *Mark, Matthew, Luke,* and *John* each narrate a series of confrontations. Jesus confronts his family; John the Baptist; the presence of Satan manifested in sickness and demonic possession; his disciples; the Pharisees; the Romans. The story of these encounters with Christ is the story of "the gospel" as the evangelists tell it. The gospel of *Thomas* and the *Dialogue of the Savior,* on the other hand, primarily consist of lists of sayings attributed to Jesus. Often, in these sources, he is responding to the disciples' questions; but the sole point of the interaction is to elicit Jesus' *words* (not, for example, his intervention, his healings, or other deeds). The special tradition of *Thomas* (that is, the traditions not paralleled in the New Testament gospels) describe the process of discovering the divine as one that takes place *within the disciple himself*:

Jesus said, "If you bring forth what is within you, what you bring forth will save you. If you do not bring forth what is within you, what you do not bring forth will destroy you." [*Thomas,* Logion 70]

Who, then, is this Jesus? Besides being the one whom the disciple discovers within himself, he discovers him also outside, in all of being:

Jesus said, "It is I who am the light which is above them all. It is I who am the All. From me did the All come forth, and unto me did the All extend. Split a piece of wood, and I am there. Lift up the stone, and you will find me there." [*Thomas,* Logion 77]

The latter two sayings refer, apparently, to forms of mystical union that Stace describes, respectively, as introverted and extroverted mysticism. Note again that both of these sayings derive from a tradition unique to *Thomas,* not paralleled in the synoptic gospels.

To find a third example of the contrast between orthodox and Gnostic interpretations of Christ, let us compare how the two traditions describe the way that the disciple receives revelation. According to the New Testament gospel of *John,* God encounters man uniquely in Christ. This account, like the synoptic gospels, narrates a series of encounters with Christ. As Rudolf Bultmann points out, each signifies a moment of crisis (*Krísis,* literally, "decision"). Whoever meets Christ receives condemnation and judgment, or else blessing, depending on how he responds to that challenge:

God so loved the world that he gave his only Son, that whoever believes in him should not perish but have eternal life. For God sent his Son into the world, not to condemn the world, but that the world might be saved through him. Whoever believes in him is not condemned; whoever does not believe in him is condemned already, because he has not believed in the name of the only Son of God. And this is the judgment, that the light has come into the world, and men loved darkness rather than light, because their deeds were evil. . . . But whoever does what is true comes to the light, that it may be clearly seen that his deeds have been wrought in God. [*John* 3:16–21]

So when, in *John,* Thomas asks Jesus how the disciple can find the way to him, Jesus replies that he himself is the only way: "I am the way, the truth, and the life; no one comes to the Father, except through me" (*John* 14:6). In the gospel of *Thomas,* on the other hand, the same question receives a different answer:

His disciples said to him, "Show us the place where you are, since it is necessary for us to seek it." He said to them, "Whoever has ears, let him hear. There is light within a man of light, and he lights up the whole world. If he does not shine, he is darkness." [*Thomas,* Logion 24]

The *Dialogue of the Savior* recounts the following:

They said to him, "What is the place to which we shall go?" The Lord said, "The place which you can reach, stand there!" [*Dial. Sav.* 142:16–19]

Both Gnostic accounts indicate that "the way" involves not so much confrontation with Christ, but the discovery of interiority. One must discover the "light within"; one must find the place that one can reach oneself.

This follows naturally from the view that Christ, rather than standing *over against* the disciple, is to be recognized as the divine principle within him. Like *Thomas,* then, the *Dialogue of the Savior* stresses not the disciples' differences from Christ (as the unique Son of God) but their identification with him. The Savior came to "open the way"—but the way leads through the discovery that the disciple and teacher are essentially identical. When the disciple asks "Who is the one who seeks, and who is the one who reveals?" Jesus, refusing to distinguish between them and himself, replies that the two are the same: "The one who seeks is also the one who reveals" (126:5-10). He declares that he carries burdens, as they do, along "the way" to the "place of life" (139:7-8). When Matthew asks a question, Jesus replies that he has not heard the answer to it himself, "unless [I hear it] from you" (140:3-4). In the passage cited above (when Jesus tells the disciples to find "the place which you can reach"), Mary Magdalene is distressed not to have received more specific instruction. So she asks whether "everything that is established is seen in this way"—that is, not by authoritative teaching, but by self-discovery. To this question, Jesus simply replies, "I have told you that the one who seeks is the one who reveals" (142:20-24). When Matthew asks Jesus to grant him to see "the place of life," Jesus responds that "every one of you who has known himself has seen it" (132:15-16). Finally, Mary Magdalene asks the Lord why she has come into human existence—"to benefit, or to suffer loss?" That is, has the disciple come into this world to gain spiritually, or to suffer purgation? Jesus replies that the answer is neither of these, but "because you reveal the greatness of the revealer," for "the living God dwells in you, and you dwell in him" (137:22-140:18).

Many of the same themes occur in the *Gospel of Truth,* an evocative, poetic meditation on the significance of Christ's coming. Here again, as in *Dialogue of the Savior,* Jesus comes as a teacher who "showed the way. And the way is the truth which he taught them" (18:19-21). This Gnostic gospel offers moving accounts of the crucifixion; unlike *Mark* or *Matthew*, it does not interpret Jesus' death as an atonement for sins, the penalty that must be paid to remove the barrier that separates God from humankind. Here, instead, the image of the crucifixion becomes a metaphor for interior self-discovery. It is that which discloses the essential identity of those who are spiritual with Christ himself. "Nailed to a tree," Jesus becomes the fruit of a *new* tree of knowledge. While the tree of the garden of Eden brought destruction upon those who ate of its fruit, the "tree of the cross" bears Christ, and so becomes for those who eat of his body and blood (i.e., in the eucharistic feast) a source of joy

in the discovery. For he discovered them in himself, and they discovered him in themselves, the incomprehensible, inconceivable one, the Father, the perfect one, the one who made everything, since everything is within him, and has need of him. [18:24–35]

What Christ comes to accomplish, then, is not to confront humanity with the coming Kingdom of God (so *Mark*) nor to confront humanity with himself, as the one in whom each person must encounter God's presence (so *John*). Neither does he come to teach the way of righteousness, nor to save those who fail it from sins by his sacrificial death on the cross (so *Luke* and *Mark*). Rather, he is the one who discloses the disciples' own true identity, previously obscured by ignorance and illusion; and he reveals that that identity is, simultaneously, in the divine presence within. This may be the symbolic significance of the title of the gospel of *Thomas*, attributed to Didymus Judas Thomas— Thomas the twin, who appears in the New Testament as well. But here, as the Gnostic *Book of Thomas the Contender* explicitly states, "the twin" is *Jesus'* twin brother. According to the gospel of *Thomas*, Thomas is the one disciple who, unlike Peter and Matthew, recognizes Jesus not as the Messiah, teacher, or master, but as his twin—his true, spiritual "other self." The title of these texts implies, I suggest, that "you, the reader, are the twin brother of Christ." Jesus' words to Thomas, then, are addressed to the reader:

Since it has been said that you are my twin and true companion, examine yourself that you may understand who you are, in what way you exist, and how you will come to be. Since you are called my

brother, it is not fitting that you be ignorant of yourself. And I know
that you have understood, because you had already understood that I
am the knowledge of the truth. So while you accompany me, although
you do not understand [it], you have already come to know, and you
will be called, "The one who knows himself." For whoever has not
known himself has known nothing, but he who knows himself has at
the same time already achieved knowledge about the depth of all
things. [*Thomas the Contender* 138:7–18]

As the *Gospel of Truth* transforms the crucifixion from the historical event narrated in the synoptic gospels (without *denying*
its historicity) into an image for the discovery of one's spiritual
interiority, the Gnostic *Treatise on Resurrection* does the same
for the resurrection. What the New Testament gospels and Acts
describe as the most astonishing event in world history—an event
that confronts humanity with the miraculous power of God—the
Treatise interprets as an event that occurs *within the disciples'
inner consciousness*: "The resurrection is the revelation of what
is, and the transformation of things, and a transition into
newness" (48:34–37). So, the author urges his student, "Why not
consider yourself as risen, and already brought to this?"
(49:22–24)

As Gnostic authors can interpret the Kingdom of God, the person of Christ, the crucifixion, and the resurrection as symbols of
the internal experience of the disciple, so they can also interpret
Jesus' parables and sayings. The *Gospel of Truth,* for example,
interprets the parable of the lost sheep in a way characteristic of
Valentinian Gnosticism—and very different from the version
Luke offers. According to *Luke,* Jesus tells this parable in response to Pharisees who malign him for eating with disreputable
people. He replies by telling of the shepherd who has lost one
sheep out of a flock of a hundred, and spends great effort retriev-
ing it. After the parable, he explains that there is "more joy in
heaven over one sinner who repents than for ninety-nine righteous people who need no repentance." Here again, as in the account of the crucifixion, the context is that of alienation between
God and humankind, sin and the need for repentance, and reconciliation which takes place only through the Savior. Apart
from his ministration, the "sheep" would be irretrievably lost.

The author of the *Gospel of Truth,* on the other hand, uses common Christian language to describe how the Savior

became a way for those who were lost . . . a discovery for those who are searching . . . He is the shepherd who left behind the ninety-nine sheep which were not lost. He went searching for the one who was lost. [31:35–32:3]

According to this Gnostic author, however, the lost one wanders, not in sin, but in oblivion, which is ignorance of God—and hence of himself. Christ

gave life to the sheep, having brought it from the pit, *so that you may know interiorly*—you, the sons of interior knowledge . . . Say, then, from the heart that you are the perfect day, and in you dwells the light that does not fail . . . For *you are the understanding that is drawn forth.* [32:20–33:9]

This author explains that the ninety-nine, here taken as the numerological symbol for utter deficiency, indicates that as long as one remains oblivious of that "interior knowledge," one remains, whatever else one has, wholly deficient. But when one finds that knowledge, then the whole being is transformed and fulfilled, "and thus the number becomes one hundred," the symbol of completion. So, he continues,

It is within Unity that each one will attain himself; within knowledge [*gnosis*] he will purify himself from multiplicity into unity, consuming matter within himself like fire. . . . [25:10–16]

The author explicitly refers his image to direct experience: "These things have happened to each one of us." Those who come to this knowledge no longer need to search for truth, for

they themselves are the truth; and the Father is within them and they are in the Father, being perfect, being undivided in the truly good one, being in no way deficient in anything, but . . . set at rest, refreshed in the good. [42:25–33]

What kind of knowledge, then, is this *gnosis*? Many scholars have said that the Gnostics were interested in theoretical speculation, in elaborate cosmologies, and in building theological systems. Some, of course, were; but the Christian Gnostics whom these texts represent were not. The author of the gospel of

Philip criticizes simultaneously the views of naïve Christians *and* the conception of Christian *gnosis* as some kind of intellectual "knowledge." He explains that the language of religious discourse can be "very deceptive": words "divert our thoughts from what is accurate to what is inaccurate." He explains that when people hear such words as "God," "the Son," the "Holy Spirit," often they "do not perceive what is accurate but what is unaccurate." Specifically, they reify these names, regarding their referents as "things" like other worldly phenomena. But religious language, the author continues, differs essentially from ordinary language, in that its referent is entirely symbolic:

> Truth did not come into the world naked, but it came in types and images. One will not receive truth in any other way. [*Philip* 67:9–12]

What differentiates *gnosis* from ordinary perception, then, is that ordinary perception involves what is external to the perceiver: "in the world" a person "sees the sun without being a sun, and sees the sky and the earth and all other things, but he is not these things" (*Philip* 61:24–26). But the characteristic of spiritual perception—*gnosis*—is that it transforms the one who perceives it:

> You saw the spirit, you became spirit. You saw Christ, you became Christ. You saw the Father, you shall become the Father . . . [What] you see [is] yourself, and what you see you shall become. [*Philip* 61:29–35]

Most believers, the author explains, only appropriate Christian language as if it described things—and beings—external to themselves. Only the Gnostic Christian who recognizes them in terms of interiority, becomes "no longer a Christian, but a Christ" (*Philip* 67:26–27).

This preliminary attempt to apply the confrontation-interiority typology to early Christian sources offers, then, a way of analyzing the criteria used to set the boundaries of Christian orthodoxy. Put most simply, those sources that presented Christ and his message in confrontational terms tended to be accepted as orthodox; those that presented them exclusively in terms of interiority were rejected.

This is not to deny, of course, the great diversity of sources and viewpoints that still remained *within* orthodox tradition. The gospel of *John*, for example, despite its affinity with the synoptics, is the only one of the New Testament gospels that clearly moves toward interiorizing the Christian message. The letters of Paul, too, contain many statements that tend toward interiority ("I am crucified with Christ; nevertheless I live; yet not I, but Christ lives in me"). Precisely for this reason, apparently, the Johannine and Pauline writings are those the Gnostics loved best —and, indeed, claimed as genuinely *Gnostic* Christian writings.

Although orthodox Christians rejected as heresy many sources that took such tendencies further, Ewert Cousins' research will remind us that Christians throughout the history of their tradition have recognized the potential for interiorizing the Christian message, and often have done so. The continual re-emergence of expressions of interiority within Christianity—despite a selection of canonical sources biased against it—may confirm the validity of our typology. The two poles of religious experience seem necessarily to imply—and require—one another.

Let me state my conclusions, then, more carefully. If some of the canonical sources of Christian tradition—Paul's letters and John—include references to both types of religious experience, others, such as *Mark, Matthew,* the *Pastoral Letters,* and *Revelation* tend to present Christ and his message exclusively in *confrontational* terms. But the opposite does not occur. Early Christian sources that present Christianity exclusively in terms of *interiority*—like the gospels of *Thomas* and *Philip,* the *Treatise on Resurrection*—or even primarily in these terms, like the *Gospel of Truth*—are rejected from orthodox tradition as dangerous heresy, "blasphemy against Christ."

EWERT H. COUSINS

Francis of Assisi
and Bonaventure:
Mysticism and
Theological Interpretation

In our search for case studies of mysticism in the monotheistic religions, the choice of Francis of Assisi has much to commend itself. Francis was one of the most striking and widely acknowledged Christian mystics of the high Middle Ages, a period in which mysticism flourished. Although he left few writings, his prayers and especially *The Canticle of Brother Sun* reflect the quality of his religious experience.[1] Also, we have an enormous amount of biographical material, gathered shortly after his death, which has been painstakingly edited by scholars over the last eighty years.[2] In fact, we have more biographical data on Francis than on any other medieval Christian saint. Furthermore, this data is of a personal nature, transmitted by his intimate companions and by members of the Franciscan Order who knew him personally or who had close contact with the early traditions. The biographical data reaches its climax in the most widely acclaimed Christian mystical experience of the Middle

Ages: Francis's vision of the six-winged Seraph in the form of the Crucified in September 1224, on Mount La Verna in Tuscany, during which he received the stigmata. Not only the vision itself, but also Francis's psychological state during it is described in detail in the accounts. Subsequently the vision of La Verna was depicted by Giotto and numerous other artists and became a major force in the widespread diffusion of devotion to the passion of Christ in western culture.

The case of Francis commends itself from the standpoint of the typology of religious experience. Francis's experience is thoroughly confrontational in the sense that he clearly distinguishes between God as Creator and Lord, on the one hand, and himself and the phenomenal world, on the other. Even in his ecstatic states there is no hint of his being absorbed into God to the point of losing his ontological identity. However, he emphasizes the confrontation of love and joy rather than that of fear and judgment. He experiences a union of himself with nature that is unique in Christian history, so much so that he has emerged as the classical example of a nature mystic among Christian saints. Furthermore, he was a great visionary mystic, whose life was guided by dreams, voices, and visions; from the time of his conversion when he heard the crucifix speak to him in the church of San Damiano until his climactic vision at La Verna. Most of these visions were of Christ and the cross and, together with his life-style of Gospel simplicity, led to a progressive identification with Christ. Again he was not absorbed into Christ to the extent of losing his own identity; yet his assimilation into Christ reached such a point that it expressed itself in the appearance of the marks of Christ's suffering in his body. In the Middle Ages this was looked upon as a miraculous sign of the intensity of his union with Christ and led to the claim that in all Christian history he was the one who most closely imitated Christ.

Francis is also significant because of what is lacking in his type of mystical experience. In his own writings and in his biographies, there is no testimony that he experienced God within himself. This is not merely to say, as we did above, that his personal identity does not become absorbed into God, but rather that he does not even turn to his inner experience as a locus for contacting God. Francis does not find God in interiority; he does not travel the inward way. In Rudolf Otto's typology in *Mysti-*

cism East and West, he is a mystic of the unifying vision, not of introspection.[3] Feeling united with creatures, Francis moves through the external world to God, not through the depths of his soul. In this he is unlike Augustine, who sees Christ as interior teacher, shining as the light of truth within his soul.[4] And he is unlike Bernard of Clairvaux, who sees Christ as interior lover, the bridegroom of the Song of Songs, who lovingly embraces his soul as bride.[5] For Francis the allegorical imagery is reversed and transposed. His soul is not the bride or Christ the bridegroom; rather, according to a medieval tradition, Francis himself is a bridegroom who, in imitation of Christ, marries Lady Poverty.[6] For Augustine and Bernard, Christ is primarily the Logos who is the ground of the soul; for Francis he is primarily the historical Jesus, who suffered and died and whose external life serves as a model to be imitated, even in radical literalness.

Bonaventure and Francis

To add Bonaventure to our case study brings an important dimension to our research. For he provides an example of how the mystical experience of Francis was integrated into the traditional body of Christian theology and spirituality. Francis was by no means a technical theologian or a psychologist of mysticism. He was the epitome of simplicity and spontaneity—one might say the epitome of pure religious experience. Several decades after Francis's death, Bonaventure, one of the leading intellectuals of the thirteenth century, situated Francis's mystical experience within an elaborate speculative structure which included theological, philosophical, and psychological dimensions.[7]

Bonaventure represents the intellectual wing of the new Franciscan Order. Trained at the University of Paris, he was heir to the rich theological tradition that came from the Greek Fathers to the West through the Pseudo-Dionysius, whose writings were translated into Latin in the ninth century by John Scotus Erigena. Another line of the tradition flowed from Augustine, Bernard of Clairvaux, and the Victorines into the early Franciscan school at the University of Paris. The basic elements of this theological tradition are the principles of what can be called Christian Neoplatonism. Derived from Plato through Plotinus and his disciples, these principles consisted of emanation, exemplarity, and knowledge by participation and illumination. In the hands of Christian theologians, these principles were transposed into a Christian key by being drawn into the doctrines of the Trinity and the Incarnation, where emanation, exemplarity, and illumination were seen to be grounded ultimately in the Trinitarian processions, from which they were reflected in creation and salvation history. It was into this tradition that Bonaventure integrated the religious experience of Francis; but this did not involve merely providing a theological frame for the picture of Francis. On the contrary, the spirit of Francis permeated the entire structure, injecting new energy and drawing out new dimensions.

The relation between Francis and Bonaventure is more complex than that between experience and interpretation. For one thing, Bonaventure adds to the mystical experience of Francis by tapping the interiority traditions of Augustine and Bernard of Clairvaux. Yet he does this in the spirit of Francis and in keeping with the latter's implicit principles. In contrast, he draws experiential elements from the Pseudo-Dionysius's *Mystical Theology* which Francis did not express as such and which may not harmonize with the latter's mystical experience. But more significantly, Bonaventure himself may be classified as a mystic, although we have no explicit testimony that he had ecstatic experiences. If he were so classified, he would rightly be called a speculative mystic, that is, one whose mystical experience is of a highly intellectual character. In other words, the very principles of emanation, exemplarity, and illumination which Bonaventure uses to give a theoretical foundation for Francis's mystical experience may well have been experienced by him mystically.

Plan of Case Study

Our case study will proceed in a twofold manner, exploring (1) Francis's mystical experience and (2) Bonaventure's integration of this experience into the Christian theological tradition. Our method will be phenomenological and philosophical-theological. Basing ourselves on texts that have been established by critical-historical research, we shall employ the method of phenomenology to the mystical experience of Francis expressed in these texts. This indicates that we are taking "phenomenological" here to refer not to the study of phenomena as perceived by sense perception, but to the study of states of consciousness. In dealing with Bonaventure, we shall use chiefly the methods of philosophy and theology; however, we shall also employ phenomenology here since, in keeping with our position stated above, the contents of both philosophy and theology can be grasped in mystical consciousness.

In treating Francis, we will explore first his nature mysticism as expressed in *The Canticle of Brother Sun* and then his visionary mysticism, in the vision of the six-winged Seraph at La Verna, as described by his biographers. In dealing with Bonaventure, we shall base ourselves chiefly on his treatise on contemplation: *The Soul's Journey into God,* which derives its inspiration and plan from Francis's vision of the six-winged Seraph. We shall include material from Bonaventure's other writings, where he develops his positions on emanation, exemplarity, and illumination within the context of the doctrines of the Trinity and the Incarnation.

Our conclusions will indicate that both Francis and Bonaventure fall into the confrontation class, but with decided emphasis on the encounter of love. Although Bonaventure assimilates and Franciscanizes the interiority traditions of Augustine and Bernard of Clairvaux, the soul remains always the image of God and his bride—never absorbed to the point of losing its identity. In the case of creation's relation to God, the same is true. God has left his imprint on creation; although the world reflects God in a myriad of symbols, it never melts into the sea of the divinity. The phenomenal world never fades into illusion before the Absolute. Granted this, I would nevertheless propose that we introduce a distinct category to deal with the Franciscan experience. Between the nondifferentiation of monism and the radical differentiation of certain strands of monotheistic religions, I would place a third class: namely unity-in-difference, where the difference of the monotheistic religions would be maintained, but a unity experienced that establishes a mutually affirming complementarity between the poles of difference. In this class of mystical experience, there is an interpenetration of the divine and the human soul, of Creator and creation, which constitutes a *coincidentia oppositorum.* It is through this *coincidentia oppositorum* that a major strand of the Christian tradition has dealt with mystical experience. I believe that the *coincidentia opposi-*

torum is found in the experience itself and is not merely a product of reflexive consciousness in its philosophical-theological interpretation. My final conclusion, then, will be that this type of unity-in-difference mysticism is not foreign to Christianity as a monotheistic religion, but indigenous to it; consequently it can surface spontaneously and harmoniously in the religious experience of great saints like Francis of Assisi and find its appropriate theological context in the intellectual tradition represented in Bonaventure.[8]

Francis's Nature Mysticism

In the recent past certain authors have felt compelled to approach Francis's nature mysticism with caution by disclaiming any trace of pantheism. For example, Johannes Jörgensen writes: "Nothing would be more unjust than to call him a pantheist. He never confounded himself or God with nature, and the pantheist's alternations of wild orgies and pessimistic melancholy were quite foreign to him. Francis never, like Shelley, wished to be one with the universe."[9] G. K. Chesterton distinguishes Francis from the age of Byron and Scott, which saw nature as a vague background; for Francis individual creatures were luminescent in the foreground.[10] "St. Francis was a mystic," Chesterton says, "but he believed in mysticism and not mystification. As a mystic he was the mortal enemy of all those mystics who melt away the edges of things and dissolve an entity into its environment. He was a mystic of the daylight and the darkness; but not a mystic of the twilight."[11] This polemic tone is a reaction against the Romantic period, evoked by the fear that Francis might be swallowed up in the romantic reconstruction of the Middle Ages. Hopefully, at this point in the twentieth century, supported by extensive research into the psychology of mysticism and the history of religions, we can proceed with a phenomenological exploration of Francis's nature mysticism without being caught in the tension between nineteenth-century Romanticism and early-twentieth-century apologetics.

What is the focus of Francis's mystical consciousness in relation to nature? Or, in more phenomenological terms, what is that toward which his consciousness tended? His mystical consciousness encompassed nature as a whole, but focused on specific creatures: e.g., the sun, the moon, and the stars. It focused on the inorganic kingdom and the realm of plants and animals, with a special predilection for birds. Animal stories abound in the biographies: his preaching to the birds, his advice to a cricket, his protection of earthworms, his taming the wolf of Gubbio. Although he loved all animals, he had a special affection for those which Scripture singled out to serve as symbols of Christ. Writing not primarily as a theologian but as a biographer, Bonaventure describes Francis's attitude toward creatures:

When he considered the primordial source of all things he was filled with even more abundant piety, calling creatures, no matter how small, by the name of brother or sister, because he knew they had the same source as himself. However, he embraced more affectionately and sweetly those creatures which present a natural reflection of Christ's merciful gentleness and represent him in Scriptural symbolism. He often paid to ransom lambs that were being led to their death, remembering that most gentle Lamb who willed to be *led to slaughter* (Isa. 53:7) to pay the ransom of sinners.[12]

Note two elements in Bonaventure's description: the single source, God, and Francis's feeling of belonging to the family of creatures. Francis's nature mysticism includes a consciousness of God, with the appropriate religious attitudes of awe and gratitude. That Francis should see God in relation to nature would be expected since this is a common awareness in the sacred books of Judaism, Christianity, and Islam. What is original with Francis is his sense of belonging to the same family as inorganic nature and plants and animals. He calls creatures his brothers and sisters and speaks to them with a warmth and affection characteristic of the intimacy of a family. In his major biography of Francis, Bonaventure collects the animal stories in a chapter devoted to the virtue of piety (*pietas* in Latin). This is the old Roman family virtue, so highly praised by Virgil in the *Aeneid*, which includes much more than the English *piety:* namely, love, devotion, affection, reverence, kindness, fidelity, and compassion. Note Bonaventure's use of the term *piety* in the quotation given above, suggesting that at the base of Francis's consciousness of nature is a "family feeling," grounded on the fact that God is the common source, hence by analogy the parent or Father of all creatures, including himself.

The Canticle of Brother Sun

The classical text of Francis's nature mysticism is *The Canticle of Brother Sun*,[13] composed in the spring or summer of 1225, some six to ten months after he had received the stigmata. The place of composition is most likely San Damiano, at that time the convent of the Poor Clares, where a small hut had been set up for him.[14] At that period Francis was in poor health, almost blind. The immediate circumstances are described as follows in the *Scripta Leonis, Rufini et Angeli*: "He could no longer see in daytime the light of day, nor at night the light of the fire, but always remained in the house and in the little cell in darkness. Moreover, he had great pain in his eyes day and night so that at night he could scarcely rest or sleep." The account goes on to describe a further problem: "There were many mice in the house and in the little cell where he lay . . . The mice ran backwards and forwards over him and around him, and so did not let him go to sleep."[15] The mice plagued him both night and day, interfering with his meals and even with his prayer. One night, feeling deeply distressed and sorry for himself, he said inwardly: "Lord, come to my help and look on my infirmities so that I may be able to bear them patiently."[16] Then he heard a voice assuring him that he would receive an immense reward for all his sufferings; the voice concluded with the following statement: "Therefore, brother, rejoice, and rather be glad in your infirmities and tribulations, since henceforth you are as secure as if you were already in my kingdom."[17] The next morning when he arose, he told his companions that he should rejoice in the midst of his sufferings and be grateful that God has assured him of eternal salvation. He then composed his *Canticle of Brother Sun* and planned that Brother Pacificus, his accomplished troubadour, and some of the other friars be sent out to sing the Canticle "as minstrels of the Lord."[18]

The text of the Canticle is given below, in the original Umbrian dialect and English translation.[19] The verse on forgiveness (lines 23–26) was composed by Francis shortly after, on the occasion of a dispute between the bishop and the podestà of Assisi. The verse on Sister Death (lines 27–31) was composed by him during his final illness not long before his death.

IL CANTICO DI FRATE SOLE

1 Altissimu onnipotente bon signore,
2 Tue so le laude la gloria e l'honore et onne benedictione.
3 Ad te solo, altissimo, se konfano
4 Et nullu homo ene dignu te mentovare.

5 Laudato sie, mi signore, cun tucte le tue creature,
6 Spetialmente messor lo frate sole,
7 Lo qual'è iorno, et allumini noi per loi.
8 Et ellu è bellu e radiante cun grande splendore,
9 De te, altissimo, porta significatione.

10 Laudato si, mi signore, per sora luna e le stelle,
11 In celu l'ài formate clarite et pretiose et belle.

12 Laudato si, mi signore, per frate vento,
13 Et per aere et nubilo et sereno et onne tempo,
14 Per lo quale a le tue creature dai sustentamento.

15 Laudato si, mi signore, per sor aqua,
16 La quale è multo utile et humile et pretiosa et casta.

17 Laudato si, mi signore, per frate focu,
18 Per lo quale enn'allumini la nocte,
19 Ed ello è bello et iocundo et robustoso et forte.

20 Laudato si, mi signore, per sora nostra matre terra,
21 La quale ne sustenta et governa,
22 Et produce diversi fructi con coloriti flori et herba.

23 Laudato si, mi signore, per quelli ke perdonano per lo tuo amore,
24 Et sostengo infirmitate et tribulatione.
25 Beati quelli ke 'l sosterrano in pace,
26 Ka da te, altissimo, sirano incoronati.

27 Laudato si, mi signore, per sora nostra morte corporale,
28 Da la quale nullu homo vivente pò skappare.
29 Guai a quelli, ke morrano ne le peccata mortali:
30 Beati quelli ke trovarà ne le tue sanctissime voluntati,
31 Ka la morte secunda nol farrà male.

32 Laudate et benedicete mi signore,
33 Et rengratiate et serviateli cun grande humilitate.

THE CANTICLE OF BROTHER SUN

1   Most high omnipotent good Lord,
2   Yours are the praises, the glory, the honor and all blessing.
3   To you alone, Most High, do they belong,
4   And no man is worthy to mention you.

5   Praised be you, my Lord, with all your creatures,
6   Especially Sir Brother Sun,
7   Who makes the day and through whom you give us light.
8   And he is beautiful and radiant with great splendor,
9   And bears the signification of you, Most High One.

10   Praised be you, my Lord, for Sister Moon and the stars,
11   You have formed them in heaven clear and precious and beautiful.

12   Praised be you, my Lord, for Brother Wind,
13   And for the air—cloudy and serene—and every kind of weather,
14   By which you give sustenance to your creatures.

15   Praised be you, my Lord, for Sister Water,
16   Which is very useful and humble and precious and chaste.

17   Praised be you, my Lord, for Brother Fire,
18   By whom you light the night,
19   And he is beautiful and jocund and robust and strong.

20   Praised be you, my Lord, for our sister Mother Earth,
21   Who sustains and governs us,
22   And produces various fruits with colored flowers and herbs.

23   Praised be you, my Lord, for those who give pardon for your love
24   And bear infirmity and tribulation,
25   Blessed are those who endure in peace,
26   For by you, Most High, they will be crowned.

27   Praised be you, my Lord, for our Sister Bodily Death,
28   From whom no living man can escape.
29   Woe to those who die in mortal sin.
30   Blessed are those whom death will find in your most holy will,
31   For the second death shall do them no harm.

32   Praise and bless my Lord and give him thanks
33   And serve him with great humility.

Experience Expressed in Canticle

Clearly the Canticle finds its place within the confrontational category of religious experience, on the side of the spectrum which is colored by gratitude, love, and joy. That it is confrontational is obvious from the first verse, where God is addressed in personal terms as the "most high omnipotent good Lord." He is omnipotent and good; to him are due praises, glory, honor, and all blessings. These belong to him alone as the Most High, and no man is worthy even to mention his name. This first verse could be cited as a classical example of Rudolf Otto's phenomenological description of the "numinous" experience.[20] For God is addressed by Francis as the "wholly other," the *mysterium*, with the attribute of majesty. Instead of his majesty revealing itself primarily as tremendous (*tremendum*, from the Latin *tremor*, meaning fear or dread), it manifests itself as "good," thus revealing the more positive side of the fascinating (*fascinans*) pole of the numen. Francis's response to the numen is classical, giving a quintessential expression of the "creature-feeling" described by Otto.[21] Toward God Francis responds in praise; toward himself, in abject humility. Not only is Francis on a different plane from God, but he and all men are not even worthy to mention the divine name.

Given Francis's positive experience of confrontation with the "wholly other," the question arises: Does he express in the Canticle an experience of unity with God through nature? The answer to this question is central to our concerns and will provide the object of our search as we examine the remainder of the Canticle. In the second verse, Francis turns to creation, singing: "Praised be you, my Lord, with all your creatures (*con tucte le tue creature*)." The picture of "all creatures" is then painted in a grand cosmic panorama, which reflects the creation account of the first chapter of Genesis. Francis calls upon the heavens—the sun, the moon, and the stars; then the four elements—air, water, fire, and earth. Both the suggestion of Genesis and the four elements from Greek cosmology evoke a vision of cosmic totality. Although the cosmic sweep is vast and comprehensive, Francis's tone is intimate and personal. He calls the sun his "brother" and the moon his "sister." He has an intimate sense of his union with the totality of creation, not in its abstract wholeness, but in its individual parts. Although Francis's Canticle is clearly indebted to the "Canticle of the Three Young Men" in the Book of Daniel (3:52–90) and to Psalm 148, nevertheless, it expresses a kinship with nonhuman creation that is beyond the biblical sensibility. For, as we stated above, Francis saw creation as a great family and felt that he himself was related to each of its elements as a brother.

How is God related to this family of nature? This is the crucial question for nature mysticism. Nature itself could be substituted for the Absolute; in this case, the Absolute collapses into the finite, stripping the mystical sense of its transcendent dimension. On the contrary, nature could become so completely absorbed into the Absolute that it would lose its ontological consistency, becoming mere illusion. As an alternative to these two positions, nature could stand apart from the Absolute, who is seen as Creator and Lord. This is the common position of the three great monotheistic religions: Judaism, Christianity, and Islam. Does Francis offer a middle position between the monotheistic doctrine of the separation of creature and Creator and the monistic experiences of nature mysticism which obliterate either God or the phenomenal world?

If we were to look to *The Canticle of Brother Sun* for an answer, it would hinge on the translation of the Italian preposition *per*, which occurs ten times in the piece; for example, "Praised be you, my Lord, for (*per*) Sister Moon and the stars." The Italian *per* can be translated by the English prepositions *for*, *by*, or *through*. In three of the instances, the *per* clearly means *by* or *through*, in the sense of instrumentality (lines 7, 14, 18). However in seven other instances, the *per* can be translated as *for*, *by*, or *through* (lines 10, 12, 15, 17, 20, 23, 27).[22] If we translate it as *for* or *by*, while not eliminating a mystical interpretation, it would not give evidence for it. If, however, we translated the *per* as *through*—meaning not merely a synonym for *by*, but "reflected through"—then we favor a mystical interpretation which would provide an alternative to the typologies described above and establish itself as a legitimate form of monotheistic nature mysticism.

If we were to translate *per* by the English *for*, the phrase would express gratitude: "Praised be you, my Lord, for [in gratitude for] Sister Moon and the stars." Francis would, then, be thanking God for all the blessings bestowed on him personally and mankind generally through the gift of creatures. For example, Mother Earth "sustains and governs us," enriching us with fruits, flowers, and herbs. Brother Sun and Sister Moon and the stars, as well as Brother Fire, delight us with their beauty; Sister Water is very useful; Brother Wind gives sustenance to creatures. The feeling of gratitude, which is a basic religious feeling, permeates the text whether or not we translate *per* by *for*. That Francis intended the hymn chiefly as an expression of gratitude is corroborated by the circumstances of its composition. According to the *Scripta Leonis, Rufini et Angeli,* immediately before composing the Canticle, Francis said: "I want for his praise and my consolation, and the edification of our neighbours, to make a new song of Praise of the Lord for his creatures, which we use daily and without which we could not live. In them the human race greatly offends the Creator and daily we are ungrateful for such grace, because we do not praise our creator and giver of all good things as we ought."[23]

If we translate *per* by the English *by*, the phrase would express agency: "Praised be you, my Lord, by [by the agency of] Sister Moon and the stars." In this interpretation Francis would be calling upon all creation to express the fundamental religious attitude of praise of God. In terms of Otto's phenomenology of religious experience, creatures because of their creature-feeling before the "wholly other" majesty of God should respond appropriately with a hymn of praise. This interpretation is supported by the final verse, which sums up the whole, combining the attitude of praise with that of gratitude: "Praise and bless my Lord and give him thanks / And serve him with great humility." It is corroborated by Francis himself, who wrote in his Letter to All the Faithful: "Let every creature which is in the heavens, on the earth, in the sea and in the depths render praise to God."[24] It is further corroborated by Francis's first official biographer,

Thomas of Celano, who states that when Francis "found an abundance of flowers, he preached to them and invited them to praise the Lord as though they were endowed with reason. In the same way he exhorted with the sincerest purity cornfields and vineyards, stones and forests and all the beautiful things of the fields, fountains of water and the green things of the gardens, earth and fire, air and wind to love God and serve him willingly."[25] When speaking directly of *The Canticle of Brother Sun*, Thomas states that after Francis received the promise of eternal life, "he composed the *Praises of Creatures* and inflamed them as much as he could to praise their Creator."[26]

A third way of translating *per* is by the English *through*, meaning not instrumentality but that God is reflected through all of creation. This is the exemplaristic interpretation, in which creatures are seen as symbols expressing God as their Exemplar. One striking witness to this meaning is given in the second verse of the Canticle itself: speaking of Brother Sun, Francis says that he "bears the signification of you, Most High One." This interpretation is corroborated by both Thomas of Celano and Bonaventure in their biographies of Francis. The former states of Francis:

In every work of the artist he praised the Artist: whatever he found in the things made he referred to the Maker. He rejoiced in all the works of the hands of the Lord and saw behind things pleasant to behold their life-giving reason and cause. In beautiful things he saw Beauty itself; all things were to him good. "He who made us is the best," they cried out to him. Through his footprints impressed upon things he followed the Beloved everywhere; he made for himself from all things a ladder by which *to come even to his throne* (Job 23:3).[27]

Writing on the same theme in his *Legenda major*, Bonaventure uses some of the above material verbatim in the passage below, which we will set in sense lines in order to retain the balance of Bonaventure's prose:

Aroused by all things to the love of God,
he *rejoiced* in all *the works of the Lord's hands*[28]
and from these joy-producing manifestations
he rose to their life-giving
principle and cause.

In beautiful things
he saw Beauty itself
and through his *vestiges* imprinted on creation
he followed his Beloved everywhere,[29]
making from all things a ladder
by which he could climb up
and embrace him *who is utterly desirable.*[30]
With a feeling of unprecedented devotion
he savored
in each and every creature—
as in so many rivulets—
that Goodness
which is their fountain-source.
And he perceived a heavenly harmony
in the consonance
of powers and activities
God has given them,
and like the prophet David
sweetly exhorted them to praise the Lord.[31]

I personally favor taking all three interpretations as simultaneously valid, since there is internal and external evidence for all three. Furthermore, such an interpretation is consonant with the vestige doctrine and the notion of God as fountain-fullness (*fontalis plenitudo*), which Bonaventure develops explicitly in relation to Francis's religious experience of nature. However, it is important to highlight the interpretation of *per* as *through,* meaning that creation reflects God. It is precisely this interpretation that is central to Bonaventure's whole system and that he develops in a technical way, grounding his vestige doctrine on the principles of emanation and exemplarism. Stated briefly, exemplarism maintains that the created world is an outer expression of inner perfections of God. If we contemplate creation in its depths, we can be drawn back to the archetypes within the divine mind. This position, which we will explore later in Bonaventure, provides a basis for nature mysticism within monotheism.

Francis's Vision at La Verna

Although Francis's nature mysticism is open to various interpretations, there is less room for controversy over his visionary mysticism. This is especially true of his climactic vision of the six-winged Seraph at La Verna. Since the reporting of details is important here, I will present the lengthy account of Thomas of Celano. In their accounts of the vision, the biographers Bonaventure and Julian of Speyer draw largely verbatim from Celano.

Two years before Francis gave his soul back to heaven, while he was living in the hermitage which was called Alverna, after the place on which it stood, he saw *in the vision of God* (Ezek. 8:3; 1:1) a man standing above him, like a seraph with six wings, his hands extended and his feet joined together and fixed to a cross. Two of the wings were extended above his head, two were extended as if for flight, and two were wrapped around the whole body. When the blessed servant of the Most High saw these things, he was filled with the greatest wonder, but he could not understand what this vision should mean. Still, he was filled with happiness and he rejoiced very greatly because of the kind and gracious look with which he saw himself regarded by the seraph, whose beauty was beyond estimation; but the fact that the seraph was fixed to a cross and the sharpness of his suffering filled Francis with fear. And so he arose, if I may so speak, sorrowful and joyful, and joy and grief were in him alternately. Solicitously he thought what this vision could mean, and his soul was in great anxiety to find its meaning. And while he was thus unable to come to any understanding of it and the strangeness of the vision perplexed his heart, the marks of the nails began to appear in his hands and feet, just as he had seen them a little before in the crucified man above him.

His hands and feet seemed to be pierced through the middle by nails, with the heads of the nails appearing in the inner side of the hands and on the upper sides of the feet and their pointed ends on the opposite sides. The marks in the hands were round on the inner side, but on the outer side they were elongated; and some small pieces of flesh took on the appearance of the ends of the nails, bent and driven back and rising above the rest of the flesh. In the same way the marks of the nails were impressed upon the feet and raised in a similar way above the rest of the flesh. Furthermore, his right side was as though it had been pierced by a lance and had a wound in it that frequently bled so that his tunic and trousers were very often covered with his sacred blood.[32]

This vision has clear characteristics of an ecstatic mystical experience: the powerful psychic energy of the vision, the mixed emotions and the extraordinary physical effects of the stigmata.

In fact, in the thirteenth century technical mystical terminology was applied to the experience. For example, Bonaventure speaks of Francis's being *in excessu contemplationis in monte excelso* (in the ecstasy of contemplation on the height of the mountain).[33] The term *excessus,* meaning literally a "going out," has the same type of Latin etymological roots as its Greek counterpart *ecstasis,* which means a "standing out." Bonaventure also uses a Latinized version of the Greek term and combines it with the indigenous Latin term: *ecstaticos excessus* (ecstatic going out).[34]

How should this ecstatic experience be classified typologically? From the evidence we have, it seems to be clearly a confrontational experience. At first glance, it does not even seem to touch God directly since the vision contains images of intermediaries between God and man: the angel and Christ. It is true that the Seraph belongs to the loftiest choir of angels, whose gaze is turned lovingly to God, and Christ is the God-man. Yet the focus is on the humanity of Christ, since the figure is in the form of a crucified man. In their accounts, Thomas of Celano focuses first on the human figure and Bonaventure on the Seraph. In either case, the drama of the event culminates in the tangible imprint of Christ's wounds on Francis's body. Christ here is not the Bridegroom of the Song of Songs; the effect is not mystical marriage, but the stigmata. There is no question of Francis's identity being absorbed in God. Although union with God might have accompanied the vision, it is not formally part of the visionary content of the experience. This leads us now to Bonaventure's interpretation of the vision and through this to his interpretation of Francis's religious experience in general.

Bonaventure on Francis's Vision

Our treatment of Bonaventure will contain two stages: (1) We shall explore his symbolic interpretation of Francis's vision in *The Soul's Journey into God.*[35] Here he interprets the vision as a symbol of seven stages of Christian contemplation, several forms of which Francis did not exemplify in his personal experience. In this way Bonaventure incorporates Francis's mystical experience into the larger body of Christian mysticism. (2) We shall study Bonaventure's theological-philosophical interpretation of both

Francis and the Christian mystical tradition. We can find this interpretation explicitly in *The Soul's Journey into God*, but will draw also from other sources in his writings.

In the fall of 1259, two years after he had been elected minister general of the Franciscan Order, Bonaventure retired to Mount La Verna, as he says, "seeking a place of quiet and desiring to find there peace of spirit."[36] His statement reflects the administrative problems he had to deal with as general, especially the tensions between factions within the order. Spiritually, his journey to La Verna seems to have been a search for his Franciscan roots. "While I was there," he says, "reflecting on various ways by which the soul ascends to God, there came to mind, among other things, the miracle which had occurred to blessed Francis in this very place: the vision of a winged Seraph in the form of the Crucified."[37] In this meditation Bonaventure grasped a symbolic meaning of the vision. "While reflecting on this," he says, "I saw at once that this vision represented our father's rapture in contemplation and the road by which this rapture is reached."[38]

For Bonaventure the six wings of the Seraph symbolize the six stages of the soul's journey into God. In his own words: "The six wings of the Seraph can rightly be taken to symbolize the six levels of illumination by which as if by steps or stages, the soul can pass over to peace through ecstatic elevations of Christian wisdom."[39] His basic pattern contains three major stages: the contemplation of the sense world, of the soul, and of God. According to the prophetic vision of Isaiah (Is 6:1–13), which is the biblical source of Francis's vision, each of the Seraphim have three pairs of wings: two covering their feet, two covering their faces, and with two they hovered aloft. For Bonaventure the two lower wings symbolize the contemplation of God in the sense world; the two middle wings, the contemplation of God in the soul; the two upper wings, the contemplation of God in himself. Each of these stages is subdivided into two, making a total of six. For example, the two lower wings symbolize first the contemplation of God in the exterior material world, then the contemplation of God in the internal activity of sensation. The second pair symbolizes first contemplation of God in the natural faculties of the soul, then in these same faculties reformed by grace.

The third pair symbolizes the contemplation of God as Being and as the Good. Bonaventure adds a seventh stage which corresponds to Francis's ecstatic experience on La Verna and in which the soul is lifted out of itself, beyond all symbols and concepts into a state of apophatic rapture.

Bonaventure developed this symbolic interpretation of the vision in his work the *Itinerarium mentis in Deum,* which I have translated as *The Soul's Journey into God.*[40] Written shortly after his meditation on La Verna, this brief treatise of about fifty pages presents in the condensed *summa* form of the thirteenth century a compendium of types of mystical experience. From one point of view, it can be seen as a typology of the major forms of mystical consciousness; from another, it can be seen as the map of the spiritual journey, in which these various forms of mystical consciousness are related to each other as stages on the way. Since the plan of the chapters provides the typology and the direction of the journey, it seems wise to list the chapter headings as Bonaventure presented them at the end of his prologue:

CHAPTER ONE
On the Stages of the Ascent into God and on Contemplating Him through His Vestiges in the Universe
CHAPTER TWO
On Contemplating God in His Vestiges in the Sense World
CHAPTER THREE
On Contemplating God through His Image Stamped upon Our Natural Powers
CHAPTER FOUR
On Contemplating God in His Image Reformed by the Gifts of Grace
CHAPTER FIVE
On Contemplating the Divine Unity through Its Primary Name Which Is Being
CHAPTER SIX
On Contemplating the Most Blessed Trinity in Its Name Which Is Good
CHAPTER SEVEN
On Spiritual and Mystical Ecstasy in Which Rest Is Given to Our Intellect When through Ecstasy Our Affection Passes Over Entirely into God[41]

Mystical Tradition Franciscanized

What has Bonaventure accomplished here? He has subsumed within Francis's nature mysticism the whole of the Christian medieval spiritual tradition. In so doing, he has extended the scope of Francis's nature mysticism to include the entirety of human experience; and he has given a unifying perspective to the varieties of mystical experience. He has Franciscanized the tradition and traditionalized Francis. In a certain sense, *The Soul's Journey* is Bonaventure's *The Canticle of Brother Sun*, but instead of seeing God only *through* (reflected through) the outer world, he sees God reflected also in the inner act of sensation, in aesthetic experience, in the activities of memory, understanding, and will, and in the contemplation of Being and self-diffusive Goodness. By plunging into the very metaphysics of the preposition *through,* he has integrated the mysticism of the inward way with the mysticism of the unifying vision; the nature mysticism of Francis with the soul mysticism of Augustine and Bernard of Clairvaux; the spontaneous mysticism of Francis with the speculative mysticism of the Pseudo-Dionysius; the cataphatic mysticism of *The Divine Names* of the Pseudo-Dionysius, with the apophatic mysticism of his *Mystical Theology.*

This integration can be seen by a systematic correlation of the chapters of *The Soul's Journey* with their sources in the tradition. Chapter One applies the vestige doctrine of Augustine to the nature mysticism of Francis: "From these visible things, therefore, one rises to consider the power, wisdom and goodness of God as existing, living, intelligent, purely spiritual, incorruptible and unchangeable."[42] Chapter Two contemplates the reflection of God in sensation chiefly in the aesthetic experience of harmony: "Augustine shows this in his book *On True Religion* and in the sixth book *On Music,* where he indicates the differences of numbers [harmonies] which ascend step by step from sensible things to the Maker of all so that God may be seen in all things."[43] Chapter Three bases itself heavily on Augustine's doctrine of the soul as image of the Trinity, with memory reflecting the eternity of the Father, intelligence the Son as truth, and the will the Holy Spirit as goodness: "See, therefore, how close the soul is to God, and how, in their operations, the memory leads to eternity, the understanding to truth and the power of choice to the highest good."[44] Chapter Four deals with the restoration of the soul as image of God after its fall into sin. Drawing from Bernard of Clairvaux, it describes the union of the soul with Christ its bridegroom: "Having recovered these senses [i.e., spiritual senses lost through sin], when it sees its Spouse and hears, smells, tastes and embraces him, the soul can sing like the bride the Canticle of Canticles, which was composed for the exercises of contemplation in this fourth stage."[45] Chapter Five reflects John Damascene and the general Aristotelian tradition that focuses on God as Being, and Chapter Six applies Pseudo-Dionysius's notion of self-diffusive goodness to the inner life of the Trinity: "Damascene, therefore, following Moses, says that *He who is* (Ex 3:14) is God's primary name; Dionysius, following Christ (Mk 10:18; Lk 18:19), says that the Good is God's primary name."[46] Chapter Seven presents the apophatic or negative way to God, basing itself on an extended text from *The Mystical Theology* of the Pseudo-Dionysius: "In this regard . . . little or no importance should be given to creation, but all to the creative essence, the Father, Son and Holy Spirit, saying with Dionysius to God the Trinity: 'Trinity, superessential, superdivine and supereminent overseer of the divine wisdom of Christians, direct us into the super-unknown, superluminous and most sublime summit of mystical communication.'"[47]

This rich heritage is drawn by Bonaventure into the universe of Francis as described in *The Canticle of Brother Sun*—thus bringing the range of human experience into the context of symbolic mysticism. Just as Francis's vision of the six-winged Seraph symbolized for Bonaventure the soul's journey into God, so all of creation and human experience symbolize God. Bonaventure expresses this universal symbolism through a cluster of images: the mirror, the book, the ladder, the stained-glass window:

. . . the entire world is a shadow, a road, a vestige, and it is also *a book written without.* (Ez. 2:9; Ap. 5:1) For in every creature there is a shining forth of the divine exemplar, but mixed with darkness. Hence creatures are a kind of darkness mixed with light. Also they are a road leading to the exemplar. Just as you see that a ray of light entering through a window is colored in different ways according to

the different colors of the various parts, so the divine ray shines forth
in each and every creature in different ways and in different properties; it is said in Wisdom: *In her ways she shows herself.* (Wis.
6:17) Also creatures are a vestige of the wisdom of God. Hence creatures
are like a kind of representation and statue of the wisdom of God.
And in view of all of this, they are a kind of book written without.[48]

Christian Neoplatonism

The Franciscan view of universal symbolism was given a theoretical foundation on the philosophical-theological structure of
Christian Neoplatonism. Once again, Bonaventure inherited this
tradition already richly elaborated by Augustine, the Pseudo-
Dionysius, the Victorines, and his teacher Alexander of Hales.
Developing it with his own genius, he integrated into it dis-
tinctly Franciscan dimensions. This Christian Neoplatonic tradition contains three principles, which impart to it its distinct
form: emanation, exemplarity, and knowledge by participation
and illumination. Bonaventure summed up his entire system with
the statement, "This is our entire metaphysics: emanation, exemplarity, fulfillment, that is, to be illumined by spiritual rays
and led back to the highest reality."[49] This text is found at the
center of a discourse on Christ the center, specifically on Christ
as Son of the Father in the Trinity. This indicates the strategy of
Christian theologians as they built these principles into their tradition. Although these principles are common to the pagan
Neoplatonists, the Christians reshaped them for their own purposes, integrating them into their belief in Christ and the
Trinity.

The principle of emanation was situated at the center of the
doctrine of the Trinity, so that it became expressed in the processions of the Son and Holy Spirit from the Father. For Christians
this emanation was consubstantial with the highest level of divinity itself and not subordinationist as it was in the case of
pagan Neoplatonists. According to the Nicene-Constantinople
creed, the Son and Holy Spirit were in every respect consubstantial with the Father. Within this context, Bonaventure develops
his notion of the Father as the fountain-fullness of the divinity
(*fontalis plenitudo*). In the Father the divinity possesses the
fullness of perfection, the fullness of fecundity, the fullness of

self-diffusing goodness. Drawing a principle from the *Liber de causis*, he applies it to the Father in the Trinity:

. . . but the more primary a thing is, the more it is fecund and the principle of others. Therefore just as the divine essence, because it is first, is the principle of other essences, so the person of the Father, since he is the first, because from no one, is the principle and has fecundity in regard to persons.[50]

Later Bonaventure applies to the Father in the Trinity the principle of the self-diffusiveness of the good, derived from the Pseudo-Dionysius.[51] Out of this transposition of classical Neoplatonism, Bonaventure produces a notion of God as boundlessly dynamic and fecund, eternally communicating his divine perfection in a flow of creativity and love that begins with the Father, flows through the Son, and is completed in the Spirit.[52] Such a doctrine of God harmonizes eminently with Francis's religious experience.

The principle of emanation leads to the principle of exemplarity. When the Father out of his fecundity generates the Son as his Image and Word, he produces within the Son the *rationes*, ideas, or archetypes of all that he can create. As Bonaventure says, "the Father generated one similar to himself, namely the Word, co-eternal with himself; and he expressed his own likeness and as a consequence expressed all the things that he could make."[53] Since this generation is eternal and the ideas are co-eternal with it, the world has an eternal existence in the divine mind, on the divine level itself. When God freely chooses to create, he selects from among these archetypes, producing creatures in space and time which express in a finite way the divine archetypes. Thus the Word in the Trinity is the Exemplar of creation. Just as the Word is the Image of the Father, so on the finite level, creatures are symbols of the Word. According to Bonaventure's imagery, the Word is the book written within the divinity, and the world is the book written without.

The generation of the divine ideas within the Word provides the ontological and theological base for the universal symbolism whereby creation reflects God. It is important to note that, in general, this principle of exemplarity forges a closer link between God and the world in the hands of Christian theologians than among their pagan Neoplatonic counterparts. For the Christians the Word is the consubstantial Image of the Father; but for the pagan Neoplatonists, the Nous is on a lower ontological level. Hence the material world is not so closely linked to the One as it is to the Father in the Trinity. Also even among the Christians, Bonaventure emphasizes the fact that God has ideas even of individuals and not merely of genera and species, thus providing an ontological base for Francis's love and concern for individual creatures, even the most lowly, like an earthworm.

This ontological exemplarism provides the basis for Bonaventure's doctrine of the vestige, which he derives from Augustine. The Latin term *vestigium*, meaning literally "footprint," was applied to the imprint of God on his creation. Since the act of creation proceeded from the Father, through the Son and was completed in the Holy Spirit, creation itself—because of emanation and exemplarism—bears the stamp of the power of the Father, the intelligibility of the Son, and the goodness of the Holy Spirit. Bonaventure sums up his vestige doctrine in the following quotation from *The Soul's Journey*, which we give in sense lines:

For these creatures are
shadows, echoes and pictures
of that first, most powerful, most wise and most perfect
Principle,
of that eternal Source, Light and Fulness,
of that efficient, exemplary and ordering Art.
They are
vestiges, representations, spectacles
proposed to us
and signs divinely given
so that we can see God.
These creatures, I say, are
exemplars
or rather exemplifications
presented to souls still untrained
and immersed in sensible things
so that through sensible things
which they see
they will be carried over to intelligible things
which they do not see
as through signs to what is signified.[54]

For the Christian Neoplatonists the entire created world is a vestige of the Trinity, but because of his subjectivity man reflects God more closely. This leads us to the doctrine of man as image of God and image of the Trinity and through this to the third Neoplatonic principle, namely, knowledge by participation and illumination. The epistemological counterpart to exemplarism is the Platonic doctrine of knowledge by participation and the Augustinian doctrine of illumination. According to the Platonic principle, our minds participate in the world of the forms; according to Augustine, God is reflected in the depths of our soul as the light of eternity, truth, goodness, and beauty. In Chapter Three of *The Soul's Journey*, Bonaventure bids us to enter into the temple of our minds. "Here," he says, "the light of truth, as from a candelabrum, glows upon the face of our mind, in which the image of the most blessed Trinity shines in splendor."[55] At the depth of memory, intelligence, and will, Bonaventure contemplates the reflection of God in the soul like light in a mirror. It is by turning to this light that one is assimilated into the likeness of the Exemplar; it is by following this light that one proceeds on the soul's journey into God. Although God's light is most intimate to the soul, penetrating the soul's very fibers, as it were, it always remains reflected light and the soul remains a mirror. The mirror of the soul is never absorbed into the divine light.

Conclusion

In looking back over the material presented, we can conclude that both Francis and Bonaventure fall, without dispute, into the confrontational class, on the side of love rather than dread. For these two Franciscans, God remains distinct from the world, and the soul retains its autonomy even in the face of the Absolute. In this respect, they differ sharply from those mystics who negate the distinction between God and the world, declaring the phenomenal world an illusion and themselves identical with God. For Francis and Bonaventure not only the theological interpretation, but the very mystical experience itself was not one of undifferentiated unity. Yet, although they were not monists, they were not radical dualists either. Instead of emphasizing the distance between creator and creation, they highlighted intimacy between God and even the most insignificant of his creatures. The key to this Franciscan intimacy between God and creation is the preposition *per* of *The Canticle of Brother Sun,* as interpreted exemplaristically by Bonaventure. Creatures are symbolic expressions of God because God himself is dynamic and expressive in his inner Trinitarian life. The Father eternally expresses himself in the Son, who is his Image and Word. This eternally flowing fountain-fullness of divine fecundity wells up in the free act of creation, providing a myriad of creatures in space and time which reflect the divine perfections. Whereas all creatures are intimate expressions of God, rational creatures share this intimacy more profoundly since they have God reflected as light in the depths of their souls. This multileveled intimacy is formulated by the three principles of Christian Neoplatonism: emanation, exemplarity, and illumination. I believe that these principles are not merely reflexive philosophical-theological interpretations, but reveal archetypal dimensions of the mystical experience itself. The archetypes of intimacy between God and creatures have been brought to light systematically not only by Bonaventure, but by the Christian Neoplatonic tradition as a whole, although Bonaventure's version was enriched by the power and spontaneity of Francis's mystical experience. Furthermore, I believe that the mystical experience of Francis and these archetypes contain within themselves the logic of the *coincidentia oppositorum,* which I have attempted to analyze elsewhere as a clue to the distinctive type of mystical experience involved.[56]

My final conclusion, then, is that Francis and Bonaventure provide an example of a specific type of mystical experience that finds a congenial home within the belief system of monotheistic Christianity. Should we introduce a special category to deal with this form of mystical experience? Perhaps. If so, I might suggest the category "unity-in-difference," which I used in my study of the *coincidentia oppositorum* in Francis and Bonaventure.[57] Whether we restructure our teminology or not is not the crucial issue. What is important, I believe, is the fact that much of the Christian mystical tradition has grounded itself in the very archetypes of Christian Neoplatonism, summoned by Bonaventure

to interpret the mystical experience of Francis. Emanation, exemplarity, and illumination have provided both the metaphysical
geography and the map of the soul's journey for many Christian
mystics who have found themselves drawn into an ever more intimate relation with God. This fact, I believe, must be taken into
account in any typology of religious experience. I hope, then,
that this case study of Francis and Bonaventure has not only
called attention to a significant historical moment, but in some
small way has also raised issues for discussion.

NOTES

1. Cf. the recent critical edition of Francis's writings: *Die Opuscula des
Hl. Franziskus von Assisi: Neue textkritische Edition,* edited by Kajetan
Esser, O.F.M., *Spicilegium Bonaventurianum,* cura pp. Collegii S. Bona-
venturae, Vol. XIII (Grottaferrata: Collegium S. Bonaventurae, 1976).

2. Cf. the critical texts of the biographies of Thomas of Celano, Julian of
Speyer, Bonaventure as well as other documents in *Analecta Franciscana,*
Vol. X: *Legendae S. Francisci Assisiensis saeculis XIII et XIV conscriptae,*
ad codicum fidem recensitae a patribus Collegii, editae a patribus Collegii S.
Bonaventurae, adiuvantibus aliis eruditis viris (Quaracchi: Collegium S.
Bonaventurae, 1926–46). Cf. also the critical text of the writings of early
companions of Francis: *Scripta Leonis, Rufini et Angeli, sociorum S. Francisci,*
edited and translated by Rosalind B. Brooke (Oxford: The Clarendon Press,
1970).

3. Rudolf Otto, *Mysticism East and West: A Comparative Analysis of the
Nature of Mysticism,* translated by Bertha L. Bracey and Richenda C. Payne
(New York: Collier Books, 1962), pp. 57–72.

4. Augustine, *De magistro,* XI, 38 ff.; *In Joan. Evang.,* tr. 20, n. 3; tr. 26,
n. 7; *Enarrat. in Ps. 118,* serm. 18, n. 4.

5. Bernard of Clairvaux, *Sermones super Cantica Canticorum.*

6. On Francis's relation to Lady Poverty, cf. the early work *Sacrum
commercium Sancti Francisci cum Domina Paupertate.* The theme of his
marriage with Lady Poverty is developed by Dante in *Paradiso* xi, and in
the fresco above the altar in the crypt of the Basilica di S. Francesco at Assisi.

7. For the critical text of the writings of Bonaventure, cf. *Doctoris
Seraphici S. Bonaventurae opera omnia,* edita studio et cura pp. Collegii
a S. Bonaventura, ad plurimos codices mss. emendata, anecdotis aucta,
prolegomenis scholiis notisque illustrata; X volumina (Quaracchi: Collegium
S. Bonaventurae, 1882–1902); to this should be added the updated critical
texts of his two biographies of Francis in *Analecta Franciscana,* vol. X,
referred to in note 2, above, and *Sancti Bonaventurae sermones dominicales,*
ad fidem codicum nunc denuo editi studio et cura Jacobi Guidi Bougerol,
O.F.M. (Grottaferrata: Collegio S. Bonaventura, 1977). The most impor-

tant collection of recent studies on Bonaventure is to be found in vols. I–IV of the five-volume series entitled S. *Bonaventura 1274–1974*, edited by Jacques Guy Bougerol, O.F.M. (Grottaferrata: Collegio S. Bonaventura, 1972–74); vol. V of this series contains the most comprehensive bibliography on Bonaventure, with entries from 1850 to 1973.

8. For a study of the logic of the *coincidentia oppositorum* in Francis and Bonaventure, cf. my book *Bonaventure and the Coincidence of Opposites* (Chicago: Franciscan Herald Press, 1978).

9. Johannes Jörgensen, *St. Francis of Assisi: A Biography*, translated by T. O'Conor Sloane (Garden City, New York: Image Books, 1955), p. 254.

10. G. K. Chesterton, *St. Francis of Assisi* (Garden City, New York: Image Books, 1957), pp. 86–88.

11. *Ibid.*, p. 88.

12. Bonaventure, *Legenda major*, VIII, 6; the English translation is my own from *Bonaventure: The Soul's Journey into God, The Tree of Life, The Life of St. Francis* in The Classics of Western Spirituality (New York: Paulist Press, 1978), pp. 254–55.

13. For the critical text cf. Esser, *op. cit.*, pp. 122–33.

14. Scholars recently have disputed whether the Canticle was composed at San Damiano, at the Vescovado or palace of the bishop of Assisi, or at La Foresta in the Valley of Rieti. For a summary of the arguments for all three locations, cf. Raphael Brown's Appendix VIII in Omer Englebert, *St. Francis of Assisi: A Biography*, translated by Eve Marie Cooper, second English edition, revised and augmented by Ignatius Brady, O.F.M., and Raphael Brown (Chicago: Franciscan Herald Press, 1965), pp. 445–57. Brown concludes that the evidence favors San Damiano.

15. *Scripta Leonis, Rufini et Angeli*, 43; English translation by Rosalind B. Brooke, *op. cit.*, pp. 163, 165.

16. *Ibid.*; Brooke, *op. cit.*, p. 165.

17. *Ibid.*

18. *Ibid.*; Brooke, *op. cit.*, p. 167.

19. The text in the Umbrian dialect is taken from the critical edition of Kajetan Esser, *op. cit.*, pp. 128–29; the English translation is my own, published in the Bonaventure volume of The Classics of Western Spirituality, *op. cit.*, pp. 27–28.

20. Rudolf Otto, *The Idea of the Holy*, translated by John W. Harvey (New York: Oxford University Press, 1958), pp. 1–40.

21. *Ibid.*, pp. 8–11.

22. For a statement of the problem and a survey of the literature on the subject, cf. Raphael Brown, in Englebert, *op. cit.*, pp. 442–45. However, Brown does not relate the translation of *per* by *through* to the exemplaristic meaning of *through*, as we will do here.

23. *Scripta Leonis, Rufini et Angeli*, 43; Brooke, *op. cit.*, p. 165.

24. *Epistola ad fideles* II; Esser, *op. cit.*, p. 211; the English translation is my own. Cf. Apoc. 5:13.

25. Thomas of Celano, *Vita prima*, 81; English translation by Placid Hermann, O.F.M., in *St. Francis of Assisi Writings and Early Biographies:*

English Omnibus of the Sources for the Life of St. Francis, edited by Marion A. Habig (Chicago: Franciscan Herald Press, 1973), pp. 296–97.

26. Thomas of Celano, *Vita secunda,* 213; Hermann, *op. cit.,* p. 533. Cf. also II Celano, 217 and Bonaventure, *Legenda major,* IX, 1.

27. Thomas of Celano, *Vita secunda,* 165; Hermann, *op. cit.,* pp. 494–95.

28. Ps 91:5.

29. Job 23:11; Cant 5:17.

30. Cant 5:16.

31. Bonaventure, *Legenda major,* IX, 1; Cousins, pp. 262–63.

32. Thomas of Celano, *Vita prima,* 94–95; Hermann, *op. cit.,* pp. 308–09. Cf. also Thomas of Celano, *Tractatus de miraculis,* 4; Bonaventure, *Legenda major,* XIII, 3; Julian of Speyer, *Vita S. Francisci,* 61–62.

33. Bonaventure, *Itinerarium,* VII, 3 (V, 312).

34. *Ibid.,* prol. 3 (V, 295); cf. also the title to chapter 7 (V, 296, 312), where Bonaventure uses the phrase: *De excessu mentali et mystico* (concerning spiritual and mystical ecstasy).

35. The critical text of the *Itinerarium* is found in vol. V of *S. Bonaventurae opera omnia,* 295–313; English translations of the *Itinerarium* will be taken from my version in The Classics of Western Spirituality, *op. cit.,* pp. 51–116; the other translations of Bonaventure will also be my own.

36. *Itinerarium,* prol. 2 (V, 295); Cousins, p. 54.

37. *Ibid.*

38. *Ibid.*

39. *Ibid.,* 3.

40. On the translation of the title, cf. the introduction to my Bonaventure volume in The Classics of Western Spirituality, *op. cit.,* pp. 20–21.

41. *Itinerarium, capitula* (V, 296); Cousins, p. 58.

42. *Ibid.,* I, 13 (V, 299); Cousins, pp. 64–65.

43. *Ibid.,* II, 10 (V, 202); Cousins, p. 74. Cf. Augustine, *De vera religione,* XL, 74–76; *De musica,* VI, *passim.*

44. *Itinerarium,* III, 4 (V, 305); Cousins, p. 84. Cf. Augustine, *De Trinitate,* VIII–XV.

45. *Itinerarium,* IV, 3 (V, 306); Cousins, p. 89. Cf. Bernard of Clairvaux, *Sermones super Cantica Canticorum.*

46. *Itinerarium,* V, 2 (V, 308); Cousins, p. 95. Cf. John Damascene, *De fide orthodoxa,* I, 9; Dionysius, *De divinis nominibus,* III, 1; IV, 1.

47. *Itinerarium,* VII, 5 (V, 313–14); Cousins, pp. 113–15; Dionysius, *De mystica theologia,* I, 1.

48. *In Hexaemeron,* XII, 14 (V, 386).

49. *Ibid.,* I, 17 (V, 332).

50. *I Sent.,* d. 2, a. un., q. 2 (I, 53); cf. also *I Sent.,* d. 27, p. 1, a. un., q. 2, ad 3 (I, 471). Cf. *Liber de causis,* prop. 1, 16, 17, 20.

51. *Itinerarium,* VI, 2 (V, 310–11). Cf. Dionysius, *De oaelesti hierarchia,* IV, 1; *De divinis nominibus,* IV, 1, 20.

52. For a treatment of the dynamic Trinity in Bonaventure, cf. my book *Bonaventure and the Coincidence of Opposites,* pp. 51–59, 97–103, 235–62.

53. *In Hexaemeron,* I, 16 (V, 332).

54. *Itinerarium*, II, 11 (V, 302); Cousins, p. 76.
55. *Ibid.*, III, 1 (V, 303); Cousins, p. 79.
56. Cf. note 8, above.
57. Cf. especially pp. 18–27. There I formulated it as "unity and difference," but now prefer the hyphenated form "unity-in-difference."

ARTHUR GREEN

Hasidism: Discovery and Retreat

The image of Judaism among the world's religions is one of
proclaimer of divine transcendence *par excellence*. The per-
sonified God of the Hebrew Bible, alone and bound by no order
except that of his own making, stands supreme over all his creation. He is Father (occasionally even Mother) and Judge, King,
and Lover. He has chosen Israel and entered into a covenant of
intimacy with her. However close he is to his loved ones, however, indeed however much he is to be found in their very midst,
his transcendence remains uncompromised; God stands over
against man and world, in love as he does in judgment.

This view of Judaism, recently restated with such elegance in
the 1975 Vatican guidelines for interfaith contact with Jews
(". . . the Jewish soul—rightly imbued with an extremely high,
pure notion of divine transcendence"), is of course not completely lacking in foundation. It is largely true for the Bible itself, and even may be said to characterize the dominant strand
in Jewish religion down through the ages. The fact that we shall
here study, within the very heart of a group that saw itself as
completely faithful to that heritage, formulations of experience
that seem entirely contradictory to whatever we think of as bibli-

cal-western understandings of God, should teach us as much about the history of religions altogether as it does about the particular case of Judaism.

Hasidism is a very late movement within the history of European Judaism; its first central figure, the Ba'al Shem-Tov, died in 1760, and most of the literature we are to study comes from the turn of the nineteenth century. Much has been made recently of the fact that socially Hasidism must be seen in part as a modern movement, an early reaction from within to the breakdown of the long-established social order. Be this as it may, Hasidism *religiously* must be viewed as a late postmedieval phenomenon. Its theological assumptions and limitations are (for the last time in Jewish history) those of the classic rabbinic-medieval world: the authority of Scripture, the inviolability of *halakhah*, the mysterious truth hidden in the teachings and parables of the Talmudic sages. The entire burden of tradition is to be borne with joy, and nothing in human experience may exist that will declare any part of it invalid.

Hasidism may be characterized as a movement of mystical revival; it was a popular phenomenon, embracing the lower classes and rapidly capturing the loyalty of vast numbers of Jews throughout Eastern Europe. As will be expected in such a movement, its leaders were not primarily theologians but preachers, its doctrinal formulations were loose and easily swayed by the situation in which they were uttered, and passion readily carried the day over caution in the ways one spoke of God. In good Jewish fashion, absolute "orthopraxy" was maintained (only the fixed hours of prayer were loosened), though this failed to stave off the rabbinic critics of the movement who raged relentless war against it for the first thirty years of its existence, and whose latter-day followers continue to sneer at Hasidism even to this day.

The main body of Hasidic literature, homiletical, devotional, and legendary (the oral tale was a classic Hasidic form), does not show an essential change in the typology of religious experience as recorded in the earlier Jewish tradition. Yes, there is much made of informal Yiddish conversation with the Master of the Universe, as well as of argument and even occasional chiding, but none of this was entirely new and should not concern us

here. Our interest is in the exception rather than the rule in
Hasidic literature, in expressions of religious experience that
seem utterly alien to the tradition out of which they emerge. A
number of figures in the early days of Hasidism flirted seriously
with such expressions, left striking record of them here and
there, and then retreated from them. Our interest is in the inner
movement in the history of Judaism to which such seeming
anomalies attest, in their appearance and the reaction it caused,
and in understanding the rapid retreat from them. Our contention is that Hasidism came to the threshold of a major break-
through in religious consciousness, but one that at the same time
threatened to destroy all that its Western legacy thinks is required for the preservation of the religiosocial order. At the edge
of this abyss, it retreated into safer expressions of traditional
Jewish piety.

The sort of material that we seek, formulations of experience
that cross the bounds into the realms of pantheism, acosmicism,
or mystical union, are by and large not to be found in the literature of Hasidic tales. There the religious expressions are more of
the orthodox variety: the tales were frozen into writing only
later, and were intended for mass consumption. The rabbis appear in the tales generally as loving children of the Father or as
loyal, if familiar, servants of the King. It is to the homiletical literature of Hasidism, and then only to that of its first few generations, that we must turn for the more unusual formulations. Even
there, it should be emphasized, they are often only half expressed or combined with metaphors more to be expected in
Jewish sources.

The generation of the Ba'al Shem-Tov himself left almost
nothing by way of written record. All that can be authenticated
as coming from the pen of the first great master himself seems to
be a single letter (though a very revealing one) and a commentary to one Psalm. There are, however, a great many quotations
from the Ba'al Shem-Tov contained in the writings of his various
disciples. Most prominent among these sources are the works of
Jacob Joseph of Polonnoye (d. 1784). We begin with one of
these quotations, couched in the seemingly "harmless" language
of the king and his son:

I heard from my teacher, of blessed memory, a parable that he spoke before the blowing of the *shofar*. There was a very wise king who, by means of optical illusion, made walls, towers, and gates. He commanded that he be approached through these gates and towers, and he ordered that the royal treasury be scattered at each gate. One went up to the first gate and returned, another etc. Finally his loving son struggled hard to reach his father the king. Then he saw that there was no separation between them, that it had all been optical illusion. The meaning is understood, and "the words of a wise man's mouth are gracious." [Eccles 10:12][1]

Minimally, the parable (recorded in typically clumsy and elliptical fashion) speaks of the dangers of being led astray in the course of mystical ascent. Some are so lured by the glitter of transcendental experience that they forget what the ascent was all about, returning to the world with mere illusory treasure. The truly faithful son does not have his head turned by riches; he thus comes to know that there is no real content to religious experience but the encounter with God himself.

That the Ba'al Shem was a person of such ecstatic "journeys" we know from the letter which has been mentioned: most of it is a description of just such an ascent. Here he seems to place himself over against a great deal of Kabbalistic tradition, heavily laden with detailed descriptions of the worlds above and the particular meaning of each stage of the journey.

Does the parable tell us more? Is the son also to realize that the world from which he has come is one of illusion? Is he to see that he too is nought, and that there is nothing but the king? I think not, or not yet. The phrase that would indicate the latter would be "there was no separation between them," and the Hebrew seems to suggest that intimacy is thus permitted, but not that they are actually one.

The existence of the phenomenal world is probably not at issue here, as it usually is not in the rather practically and devotionally oriented teachings of the Ba'al Shem-Tov. His concern is rather that of constructing a sort of mental monism, showing the disciple that in all his *thoughts,* wherever they may stray, there is nothing real but God. This teaching itself has rather far-reaching and potentially dangerous implications, especially since the Ba'al Shem was wont to apply it to thoughts of evil as well as to the meaningless glitter of spiritual titillations. An understanding of this will be our reward for following closely a typically abstruse bit of homiletics, the opening passage in his disciple's *Toledot Ya'aqov Yosef*, in which the teacher referred to is the Ba'al Shem himself:

It is said in the Talmud that Joseph was liberated from prison on the New Year, as Scripture says: "He set it as witness in Joseph when he went forth upon the Land of Egypt." [Ps 81:6]

To understand this we must recall the Tiqquney Zohar's comment on: "I the Lord have not changed" [Mal 3:6]—"In relation to the wicked God does change and hide Himself . . . in various garbs, veils, and shells . . . these are chaos, void, darkness, etc. Of these Scripture says: "I shall hide My face from them" [Deut 32:20]. But for those who are bound to Him and His *shekhinah*, He never changes." So there are various garbs and veils in which the Holy One, blessed be He, is hidden.

I heard from my teacher, of blessed memory, that where a person knows that God is hiding, there is no hiding. "All the workers of iniquity split apart" [Ps 92:10]. This is the meaning of: "I shall hide, hide My face from them" [Deut 31:18]; the verse means to say that He will be hidden from them in such a way that they will not know that God is there in hiding. I have also heard from him that the five words *'amar 'oyev 'eredof 'assig 'ahaleq* ["The enemy said: I shall pursue, catch, divide"—Ex 15:9] begin with five 'alephs: the Aleph of the universe is hidden there, just as in the name SamaEL . . .

Once a person knows this great principle, that there is no curtain separating him from his God, then even if distracting thoughts come before him while he is at study or prayer, being the garb and veils in which God is hiding—since he knows God is hiding in them, there is no hiding.

This is why *ha-shanah* ("the year") is numerically one more than *Satan*: add the one of the universal Aleph, for there too is He hiding. Now we understand why it was on the New Year that Joseph came out of prison. Once Joseph knew the *New Year* (lit.: "Head of the Year"), namely that Satan plus the One who stands at the head make the New Year, for He of whom Scripture says: "His kingdom rules over all" [Ps 103:19] is hidden even within the Satanic shells—then the shells are defeated and the year is renewed. When a person knows this, "all the workers of iniquity split apart"; they were the shells that formed the prison for the *shekhinah*. Thus was Joseph, now also in the corporeal world, freed from prison: through this knowledge he had broken the bonds . . .²

Translation: True liberation comes about through the realization that God is hidden even in the seeming forces of evil. Here the Ba'al Shem-Tov goes much further than he had in our earlier parable. Not only is it the illusory beauty of heavenly ascent that may keep one from God; it is also wayward and seemingly demonic thoughts that in fact may contain him! The references to Samael and Satan are crucial here. They remind us that Hasidism emerged from circles that had only of late cut away the Sabbatian and demonic elements in their mystical theology. We also see the intellectual-spiritual means by which this cutoff had been effected. Here the archons of the demonic universe, usually treated with such utter seriousness by the Kabbalistic sources, have no power over the one who sees through them, and perhaps have no existence at all outside the unliberated mind. More significantly, such liberation happens not only through ecstatic or transcendent experience. *Awareness* itself seems to suffice: once you *know* that God is hidden in evil, you have in fact found him. A kind of abbreviated hide-and-seek, if you will, in which you don't actually have to touch the quarry to declare him found. In the heights and in the depths of man's inner universe, the Ba'al Shem tells us, there is nought but God.

What then of the phenomenal world? The earliest sources of Hasidism, as we have noted, seem concerned less to question its existence than to assure the possibility of its conversion. The old Kabbalistic image of "the uplifting of sparks" became central here: wherever a person turns, whatever he may encounter, contains sparks of divinity that seek to rise to God through him. "Know Him in all your ways" (Prov 3:6) became a kind of watchword in early Hasidism, as did the Zohar's "There is no place devoid of Him." All, however, depended on awareness; "there is no place devoid of Him" really meant "there is no place or situation that cannot bring a person of awareness back to the presence of God." Hasidism had a penchant for extreme examples:

Through everything you see, become aware of the divine. If you encounter love, remember the love of God. If you experience fear, think of the fear of God. Even when in the toilet you should think: "here I am separating bad from good, and the good will remain for His service!"[3]

At this point we should stop to ask what it is in these Hasidic sources that makes them surprising to the western religious frame of mind. The notion that God is to be found everywhere? Surely the author of Psalm 139 would not be shocked. That the glories of the upper worlds and the terrors of death and the netherworld are nothing when seen from the perspective of one who has true faith in God? Again, one could find support for such a view in Scripture and tradition. No wonder that it has more than once been said of Hasidism that from a doctrinal point of view there is virtually nothing new in the movement. The *hasidim*, of course, would be the first to support this reading.

Not so quickly, however, shall we accept this point of view. Given the historical context of Jewish mystical thought, something important has already happened here. The reality of the Kabbalistic universe has begun to be called into question. The outer phenomenal world may remain relatively untouched by the earliest teachings of Hasidism, but the inner "world of truth," as the Kabbalists called it, had started to crumble. Seeking a religion in which personal piety and enthusiasm would be the highest values, the popularizing tendencies of early Hasidism found no room for the heavily arcane quality of the old Kabbalistic world view. Having turned against the aloofness of the rabbis for their Talmudic mental gymnastics, seemingly without value and beyond the reach of the common Jew, they could not but feel the same way about the infinitely complex structuring of the cosmos and the meditations on each and every of the countless spheres that had been promulgated by the post-Lurianic Kabbalists. Simplicity, wholeness of heart, personal awareness of the constant presence of God—these were to carry the day in the new movement, and intellectual mysticism would have to bow before them.

The mystics have discovered many meanings in each word of prayer. No one person can know them all. One who tries to meditate on the hidden meaning of the prayers can only perform those meditations that are known to him. But if a person joins his entire self to a word, *all* the hidden meanings enter of their own accord.[4]

Unable to openly deny the world of Kabbalistic gnosis (for this too had become orthodoxy), Hasidism here simply undercuts its value. The same will happen to all the basic areas of Kabbalistic doctrine; it is through the simplification and veiled destruction of the typically medieval multitiered universe of Kabbala that Hasidism creates a cosmology of its own and enunciates precisely those formulations that are of interest to us here.

This step is taken in the second and third generations of Hasidic development, most particularly in the school of Dov Baer the Maggid ("preacher") of Miedzyrzec. The Maggid was the second great leader of the Hasidic community, and the last single figure who commanded the loyalty of even most of the Hasidic groups. By both temperament and education a very different man from his predecessor, the Maggid brought to Hasidism an intellectual-theological sophistication that the movement had not known in its earliest days. An avid student of Kabbala long before he met and was "converted" by the Ba'al Shem-Tov, he in effect sought to offer a rereading of various key terms and symbols in that tradition in the light of the new ecstatic devotion by which he was so attracted. He built around himself a school of young followers, several among them major religious *illuminati* in their own right; almost all of the major works of Hasidic thought and schools of interpretation within the movement are somehow rooted in this circle around the Maggid.

We turn our attention first to the *sefirot*, the graded series of ten divine emanations that form the core of all Kabbalistic expression since the thirteenth century. These serve, it will be recalled, both as the stages through which the hidden God comes to be manifest in the revealed creation and as the steps the adept must follow in his journey toward God. They represent an inner structure of the universe believed to be repeated at every level of existence, including within the soul of man as microcosm. This latter fact allowed room for the emergence of a specifically Kabbalistic psychology, usually presented in a moralizing context. This psychology, a view of the inner life of man in terms of the sefirotic structure, gained importance from the sixteenth century, especially through the influence of Moses Cordovero's popular treatise *The Palm Tree of Deborah* (*Tomer Devorah*). It is always understood in these works, however, that the psychological import of the ten rungs is but a reflex of their role in cosmology.

In Hasidism, the sefirot have largely been relegated to the world of psychology alone.[5] The Maggid uses the old terms frequently, but almost always in discussions of the inner life of the *hasid*: *hesed* and *din*, the right and left sides of the cosmic balance in the Kabbala, have now become *love* and *fear* in the life of the worshiper. The "seven structuring days" in sefirotic cosmology now usually refer to the range of human emotions or moral qualities that must be perfected. In fact the old Kabbalistic cosmology has been vitiated, and only the *first* and *last* of the sefirot remain significant in the Maggid's view of the universe. The first is *hokhmah* ("wisdom"), also called by the name *'ayin* ("nothing"); the last is *malkhut* or *shekhinah*, taken here (as in rabbinic sources but not in classical Kabbala) to refer to the indwelling presence of God in the world.

What follows is one of the many statements in which this "abbreviated" Kabbala appears in the writings of the Maggid's school. Using the genre of the Kabbalistic tradition itself, and piecing together a number of symbols that are taken from the medieval sources, here Menahem Nahum of Chernobyl has turned Kabbala against itself. He speaks of the two divine names, YHWH and *'Adonay*, one representing the God beyond and the other the God inherent in all things:

All the worlds depend on this—the unification of the God beyond and the God below. Now when these two names are joined together with their letters interspersed in this way (YAHDWNHY), the combined name both begins and ends with the letter *yod*. "You have made them all in wisdom" (Ps 104:24), and *yod* represents *hokhmah*, the primal source of all the letters . . . *Hokhmah* is the ultimate prime matter; it is called by the sages *hyle*, from the words *hayah li* ("I had it"). All things were in it; from it they emerged from potential into real existence.

Even though the *'aleph* is the first of the letters (and thus one might expect that it should be used to designate this primal substance), the *'aleph* itself is constructed of two *yods* with a diagonal *waw* between them. The first *yod* refers to primal *hokhmah*, the prime matter in which all the worlds were included. The *waw* (shaped like an elongated *yod*) represents a drawing forth and descent, the bringing forth of that potential. Thus were all the worlds

created, finally forming the second *yod,* called the lower *hokhmah* or
the Wisdom of Solomon [*shekhinah*], the aspect of '*Adonay,* divinity
as garbed in all things and filling the world.

When a person does all his deeds for the sake of God, he draws all
things in the lower world near to the upper fount of *hokhmah,* the
Creator Himself who calls all the worlds into being. By means of his
awareness he fulfills "Know Him in all your ways" (Prov 3:6). This
"knowing" or awareness is a unitive force; it binds together the upper
yod and the lower *yod* so that the entire universe forms one single
'*aleph.* This is why God is called "the cosmic '*aleph.*"[6]

The cosmos ultimately consists of two *yods, hokhmah* and
malkhut, God before or above creation and God inherent in the
universe. The rest of the sefirotic world is merely the *waw,* the
extension or connecting link (*da'at*) by which they are joined together. Man's task is the cultivation of his own *da'at,* in the form
of awareness, so that he too may become a channel for drawing
together the God beyond and the God within.

The universe may be viewed from either of these two ends.
When seen from the point of view of *hokhmah,* the beginning of
emanation, the world is yet nothing. Here all is pure potential;
no separation from the One has yet taken place. *Hokhmah,* in a
well-known play on words, is *koah mah,* undefined divine energy
or potential. *Hokhmah* is a pure flow of *hiyyut,* the divine life
force, and nothing more. In fact, however, "potential" existence
here is conceived as already defined potential. The world as it is
to be, down to every final detail, already exists in *hokhmah.*

The tree is planted from seed, and that tree bears fruit. Surely the
tree, its branches, and its fruit were all there in the seed from the beginning, but in a hidden way.[7]

Though Hasidic sources refer to *hokhmah* by the Greek term
hyle, what they really have in mind is more pure form than un-
formed matter.

At the other end of the sefirotic process we find *malkhut,* the
presence of divinity in the things of this world. Here the physical
creation has already taken place; it is God within world rather
than world within God to which we now turn our attention. The
sense that the world is fraught with divine presence was the essential insight of the Ba'al Shem-Tov that the Maggid had found

so renewing. He, however, sought for it a more sophisticated cosmological setting. Yes, the world is filled with divinity. All things are enlivened, or in fact reified, only by the presence of the *hiyyut* within them. All other properties they have about them, including substance, extension, and so forth, are merely the "veils" that cover and hide the *shekhinah*, the only real thing about them.

God has made "something" (the ephemeral phenomenal world) out of "nothing" (*'ayin;* his own Self before manifestation). Man's essential devotional task, as the Maggid and his disciples frequently repeat, is to make "nothing" out of "something"—in their contemplative lives to so strip both self and world of corporeality that it is again as it was before the process of Creation began.[8] This "stripping," however, is really a matter of seeing through a veil of illusion—knowing that God is there in hiding. By this it becomes clear that in fact the *process* of emanation through the sefirotic world, from hidden potentia to the reality of being, is no process at all. Everything is in the end as it was in the beginning; the task of the devotee is to become aware of this sameness, to discover the hidden divinity within the world, and thus to see that Nothing, or God as he was before creation, is in fact all that exists. Traditional western emanation theology has thus been swept away and replaced by a very different type of religious claim: nothing but God is real, there is no duality of God and world, but only a false duality of God and illusion.

The issue of *zimzum,* or the contraction of the infinite God in order to allow for the world's existence, is treated by the Maggid in similar fashion. *Zimzum* was a major pillar of the new Kabbala elaborated by Isaac Luria and his followers in the sixteenth century, a system that, as Gershom Scholem has shown, originated partially in reaction to the cataclysm that had befallen Spanish Jewry in the preceding generations. Luria no longer accepted the old notion of graded emanations to explain the emergence of the multiform universe from the depths of the one and undivided God. He sought an explanation of a rather more dramatic and total sort. If God was alone before creation, he claimed, then God was and filled all; there was no empty space beside him. To claim that God existed alongside an eternal void would be to capitulate to an ultimate dualism, one that by implication might see evil as being co-eternal with God. Rather, he taught, the first step in creation was a contraction within the all-pervading God, one that allowed for a void within which creation could take place.

Scholem has shown how succeeding generations of Lurianists (his doctrine dominated Kabbalistic circles for some two hundred years after his death, and is still the path followed by Kabbalists of Near Eastern origin) could use this notion of *zimzum* in nearly either theistic or pantheistic ways.[9] For the Kabbalist who took *zimzum* literally, God indeed had vacated primal space, and creation was from without, the work of a transcendent God. Those who tended to pantheism claimed rather that full *zimzum* was impossible, that even in the divine act of withdrawal his presence was confirmed, and that the void was never truly empty of God at all. For them the creation from without was more an activation of the underlying divine presence (*reshimu*), and the God who inhered in the universe was central to their religious lives. It has also been demonstrated, primarily through the work of Isaiah Tishby, that the entire myth of *zimzum* is a myth of divine self-purification and of the origins of evil; the all-containing God contracts in purity before creation, leaving in the void those "roots" of evil that are to inhabit the universe there created.

The Maggid, as will be expected, follows those Kabbalists who do not take *zimzum* literally, those who believe in the continued presence of divinity in space even after the primal contraction. He goes further than his predecessors, however, reducing *zimzum* to a gracious act of a loving father-God who performs it in a semi-illusory way in order to allow psychological "room" for his child to exist.

Since it was the primal will of God that the righteous among Israel exist in each generation, He contracted His brilliance, as it were, just as a father reduces his mental level and speaks of childish things with his small child . . . *zimzum* took place for the sake of Israel, and it was love that brought it about.[10]

A teacher studies with his pupil. If the pupil is greatly concerned with what his teacher is saying and pays close attention to him, the teacher may open the gates and reveal his wisdom. Even though he may not be able to share all of his abundant wisdom with him, a student who is almost a peer can attain to nearly all that his teacher has to offer. If, however, the student is dull and slow to understand, the teacher has to contract his great wisdom and teach him on his own level. Were he to offer him too much, trying to reveal to him the most profound depths, the student would only become confused and turn aside from learning. Then he would not even acquire that bit which is within the range of his abilities. Thus must a teacher reduce his wisdom down to his student's level . . . *Zimzum* took place so that the world could properly exist. Without it we would not be able to bear the brilliance of His light, and our existence would be negated.[11]

The last phrase here will be of interest to us a bit further along, but for now we are interested in the change in *zimzum* itself. The concept has here been psychologized: it is the human *mind* that must be left room to exist alongside the great light of God, rather than the world itself that must perforce exclude him. Here the potential Gnostic sting of *zimzum* has been removed; we are no longer speaking of the world's origins and the roots of the demonic, but rather of God's abundant love and his patience with man's small-mindedness or his willingness to allow for our humanity. Once again, as with the *sefirot*, a myth that accounted for a degree of distance between God and man has been undercut, allowing for a full immediacy of divine presence. The father's mind, we must realize, is not *really* reduced to childish dimensions; it is rather by a willful act of compassion that he offers the child the appearance of proximity to the child's mental level. This is done, of course, in a pedagogic context: the father hopes bit by bit to expand his child's mind.

We have approached early Hasidism to this point very much from the perspective of its *theology*, seeing the development of doctrine as would the intellectual historian. Here we must say that such a point of view will not do for us. These changes in formulation of ideas accompany and reflect a change in the modality of religious experience of those who bear them. We shall not be so naïve as to try to define which of these changes first, the doctrine or the experience; here as elsewhere in the history of religion a good case could be made for either. But we must remember that Hasidic thought is promulgated against the background of an intense and ecstatic feeling of the all-pervading presence of God. The prayer-life of the earliest conventicles was denounced for its wild shrieks and uncontrolled jumping and shaking; there was about them an aura of spiritual frenzy that was compared (and not only by enemies) to both madness and drunkenness. We will do well to bear this *Sitz im Leben* in mind as we examine now some selections of teaching from the Maggid's school in which the horizons of western religious living seem most radically to be expanded.

We begin with a passage of devotional instruction:

The proper intention with which to recite the word "One" of the *shema'* ("Hear O Israel the Lord is God the Lord is One") is that there exist nothing in the entire world except for God, whose "glory fills all the world." The main intent is that man make himself into absolute nothing. There shall be nothing of him but his soul, which is "a part of God above." Thus is there nothing in the world but God who is One. This is where one's thoughts should be turned while saying "One": the whole world is filled with His glory and there is no place devoid of Him, be He blessed.[12]

This call for spiritual self-annihilation is of course common to many mystical literatures; by its very nature it also calls forth an immediate revision of traditional cosmology. If annihilation of self and world leads to a "higher" state, it must perforce also lead to a greater "truth" in understanding what the world really is. Devotion and cosmology (statements of "you should feel" and statements of "the world is") are often combined with one another in the sources:

This is a high rung: when a person constantly considers in his heart that he is near to his blessed Creator and is surrounded by Him on all sides. He should be so attached to Him that he has no more need to reassure himself that this is the case: he should rather see the Creator, blessed be He, with his mind's eye, and that He is the "place of the world." This means that He was before He created the world and that the world stands within the Creator, blessed is He. He should be so attached that his sight is chiefly upon God, rather than seeing the world first and the Creator only second . . . Such a person merits to have the "shells" fall away from him. It was they that had brought darkness, separating God from man and blinding the mind's eye from the sight of the Creator.

Think that the Creator, blessed be He, is endless and surrounds all the worlds, that His blessed influx flows downward from above by means of channels throughout the worlds. We are ever walking about in God, blessed be He, and we could not make a single movement without His influx and life-flow.[13]

Note that the language remains very much that of western theism: God is primarily referred to by the term "Creator," even though the world view here has rather little to do with that which is usually called Creation. The exhortation to ever concentrate our sight on God rather than on the world could easily be supported by passages of a more moralizing intent throughout medieval pietistic literature. The sense that every movement of the human body is controlled by God also has its well-known precedents in the philosophical (or antiphilosophical) literature of medieval Judaism and Islam. The full constellation, however, remains startling. Here the notion that all is God is approached with a radical enthusiasm that is previously unknown in Jewish sources.

The final statement of this, the "All is God" spoken plainly, is that which we should most be surprised to find within Judaism. The wide freedom of interpretation permitted within the tradition, combined with the various philosophical and mystical influences upon later Judaism, might eventually lead to a carefully guarded formulation that in fact meant nearly the same thing—but surely pious Jews could not say it out in just so many words. Even within the loose dogmatic structure of Judaism that would seemingly have to be perceived as heresy. It is especially interesting, then, for us to quote from a precious document that was never intended for publication, an early nineteenth-century letter from one important *HaBaD* Hasidic disciple to another, in which he outlines the real meaning of Hasidism and the reasons for its persecution. The letter reflects an inner controversy within that particular school, the details of which are not essential for our purposes here. The writer is Rabbi Yizhak Isaac Epstein of Homel (1780–1857):

> Listen, please, my beloved friend! Do not say that this is, God forfend, heresy and philosophy. . . . And all *hasidim* . . . have this faith. And it is generally sensed when reciting the Eighteen Benedictions. That is to say, after all the goodly meditations while reciting the

songs of praise and reciting the *shema*ʿ, with the higher and lower unification, then it is sensed that, in Yiddish, all is God. . . .

All *hasidim* share this faith. As for the opponents . . . they do not have this faith except in exceedingly great concealment, exactly as it was when Israel was in Egypt. Even though God to them also is the single object of faith, they have nonetheless no room for this faith that all is God.[14]

The letter is written in a thorough mixture of Yiddish and Hebrew, as was common for letters between scholars at the time. No particular note is taken of this fact. When he first comes to the key phrase, however, he says "in Yiddish," meaning "I am telling you this in plain Yiddish, in which there can be no misunderstanding." The letter is significant because here in private (alas!) communication he was able to shed all the Hebrew circumlocutions ("the whole world is full of His glory," etc.) and say exactly what he meant: *Als iz Got* (alles ist Gott).

The fact that this document comes from within the *ḤaBaD*/Lubavitch school is no accident. Among the many disciples of the Maggid, it was Shneur Zalman of Liadi (1745–1813), the great systematizer of Hasidic thought and the founder of *ḤaBaD*, who maintained the greatest consistency in promulgating this aspect of his master's teaching. The second portion of his *Tanya*, even now the daily read spiritual guidebook of *ḤaBaD Hasidim*, is a brief tract on mystical cosmology. It works chiefly around the notion of *ẓimẓum* and the contemplation of God's oneness, forming a contemplative exercise to accompany the recitation of the *shema*ʿ. It is structured, however, as an exposition of a biblical verse, one that has a long history in the realm of Jewish mystical speculations: "Know this day and set it upon your heart that the Lord is God in heaven above and on the earth beneath; there is none else." (Deut 4:39) In the course of Shneur Zalman's reading it becomes quite clear that the concluding phrase is rather to be taken as: "There is nothing else," for nothing but God may be truly said to exist:

Now behold, after these truths, that anyone who carefully considers the matter [will realize] that every created and existing thing should really be considered as nought when compared with the power of the maker and the breath of His mouth in the creature, always giving it being and bringing it forth from nothingness. All these things appear to us to be extant and real only because we cannot conceive or see with the eyes of the flesh the power of God in His creatures or the breath of His mouth in them. But if permission were given the eye to see and conceive the life and spirit flowing by the word of God into every creature, the physical aspect of creatures and their substance would not be seen by us at all. They are completely unreal in the light of the life-flow and spirit within them. Without this spiritual essence they would be as nothing, quite as they were before the six days of creation. And the breath/spirit flowing into them out of the mouth of God alone takes them constantly out of nothingness and non-being, causing existence. Therefore it is said: "There is nothing without Him" [Is 45:6]—literally.[15]

Shneur Zalman's disciple Aaron of Starroselje, another important systematizer of Hasidic thought, emphasized a strand in the Maggid's thought that distinguished "God's point of view" from the limited perspective of man. From God's point of view, taught Aaron, there has been no *zimzum*, there is nothing outside of God, and the phenomenal world may not be said to exist. It is only from man's viewpoint this world has existence. Of course it is from within our own perspective that we must conduct our daily, and even our religious, lives. More on that below.

It was not only in the Maggid's school that the new experience of Hasidism was giving birth to surprising ways of religious speaking. A younger contemporary of Shneur Zalman, and one often thought to be his very antithesis as a type of Hasidic thinker, was arriving through somewhat different formulations at many of the same ideas. Rabbi Nahman of Bratslav (1772–1810) was the great-grandson of the Ba'al Shem-Tov and the founder of a unique sect within the Hasidic community, one for which he still stands as first and only master.[16] Nahman was a theologian of paradox, one who filled his traditional-sounding homilies with contradictions so intense that they seemed to force conventional theology, even Kabbalism, to a breaking point. Note first how he subverts the meaning of an old adage, originally meant to show how impossible it was for man to truly know his maker:

Eternal life belongs only to God, who lives forever. But he who is included in his root in God also has eternal life. Since he is included in the One and is One with God, he lives eternally just as God does. . . . The basis of this inclusion within God is knowing Him, as the sage says: "If I knew Him, I would be Him." The core of a person is his mind; where the mind is, there is the whole person. One who knows and attains to a divine understanding is really there. The greater his knowing, the more fully he is included in his root in God.[17]

Frequently Nahman's teaching involves a dialectical movement through stage after stage of religious discovery, doubt or challenge, and new integration within an expanded faith. In one of the homilies in which he speaks of this ascent, he describes its highest point in the following way:

When one finally is included within *'eyn sof*, his Torah is the Torah of God Himself and his prayer is the prayer of God Himself. There is a Torah of God, to which our sages have referred as follows: "I was first to fulfill it"; "The Holy One, blessed be He, clothes the naked, visits the sick" etc.; "How do we know that the Holy One, blessed be He, puts on *tefillin?*" There is also a prayer of God, of which the sages say: "How do we know that the Holy One, blessed be He, prays? From the verse: 'I shall grant them joy in My house of prayer'" (Is 56:7).
We thus find that there exist a Torah of God and a prayer of God. When a person merits to be included within *'eyn sof*, his Torah and his prayers are those of God Himself.[18]

The Talmudic sages had told these tales in the course of humanizing God; the biblical God is transformed by them into a picture of the ideal rabbinic Jew, studying Torah, performing the commandments, and even saying his prayers. Little might they have thought that a mystic of a millennium and a half later would use their descriptions as an avenue of identification with God in a wholly different manner, claiming through his prayer and study to so ascend through the rungs of being that his own study and prayer be those of God. There is almost no distance that need be traversed between this position and the much more shocking version of the same formulation reported in Nahman's name by his faithful (and usually rather conservative) disciple:

I heard from Rabbi Nathan: . . . our master said . . . that you have to reach such a state of self-negation that you come to God's Torah and prayer and are able to say: "May it be my will!"[19]

Prayer here has reached its apex and transformation: so intently has the worshiper said "May it be *Thy* will" that his own will is finally utterly negated, and he may fully identify with the will of God. Behold where all this pious talk of humility and self-abnegation has finally led! Here Hasidism, indeed Judaism, comes as close as it ever has to violating that ultimate taboo of western religion, that of the devotee proclaiming "I am God."

At the psychological-devotional root of this entire complex of ideas stands the experience of the negation or transcendence of self, and the discovery, in the wake of that experience, that it is only God who remains. One would expect that this apex of mystical transformation would be greeted with great if trembling exultation. Indeed, that is the case in certain of the Hasidic accounts. There are some that see this as the source of prophecy as well, including indications that ecstatic prayer, following such an experience, is overtaken by a state of divine possession, one in which "the *shekhinah* speaks through his mouth." At the same time, we can find in any number of Hasidic renditions of this mystical moment a great hesitation, a hesitation that seems to treat negation of self as more a danger than a blessing. We have heard the Maggid say that *zimzum*, of the sort he proposes, must take place, else "our existence would be negated." But is not the negation of our existence precisely the goal of the religious life he so avidly preaches? Why not, to use a metaphor commonly found in these sources, stare directly into the sun and be blinded by its light? Nahman too warns us that we must maintain an awareness of the void whence God has departed, lest "the space not be empty and all would be *'eyn sof* (endless God)."[20] But what could be better, from the point of view of an unequivocal mysticism? Here Hasidism totters at the brink and returns, refreshed and renewed, but on the road to that compromise that would make it synonymous with ultra-orthodoxy only a few generations later. It is upon this return and compromise that we must now seek to focus our attention.

It is possible in viewing any period in the history of Kabbala to see the imperfect grafting of a mystical branch on the non-mystical tree of biblical/rabbinic Judaism. Insist as the mystic may that his views represent the true intent of the earlier sources, and weave as he may a seemingly convincing thread of argument through an impressive array of such quotations, the necessary transformations of earlier meanings can always be found. Whether it is "nothingness" that has reappeared as "the Nothing" or creation that has taken on the new garb of emanation, the mystic in Judaism is ever a daring reinterpreter of the original sources. At the same time, most of the mystics were deeply committed to maintaining the normative in the daily life-patterns of rabbinic Judaism. Hasidism has in common with the Kabbalistic writings of the thirteenth century (including the *Zohar*) a need to *defend* what each saw as the authentic rabbinic tradition, the one against the inroads of medieval rationalism and the other against an array of enemies, including heretical mysticism, petrified Talmudism, and, after the turn of the nineteenth century, the advent of modernity. Reinterpretation was thus to function in part to underscore the value of the normative, to strengthen it by a deepening of its meaning. Given the nature of Judaism, the norm at issue was the *halakhah* or the life of the commandments.

The old Kabbala had devoted a great part of its energies to just that: the literature of *sodot ha-mizwot* or esoteric rationales for the commandments occupies a major part of Kabbalistic writings. Hasidism however turned aside from this literary *genre* (with a few noteworthy exceptions) and in fact devoted rather little of its intellectual attention to the commandments themselves, despite its full commitment to a life-pattern that was entirely within the traditional rabbinic mold. It rather tended, as Rivkah Schatz-Uffenheimer has noted, to focus its attention on the two areas of contemplative prayer and the worship of God through the uplifting of corporeal things, while avoiding the rather major question of interpreting the commandments.[21] The fact is that the commandments constituted a problematic *datum* for the radically spiritualized value system that Hasidism was proposing. It ultimately was for this reason, we shall suggest, that Hasidism saw itself forced to retreat from its own mystical insights.

The old Kabbala had preached a carefully graded ascent to God through the many rungs of being. In the course of such a journey, an uplifting of the commandments through successive grades of spiritualization could prove an appropriate accompaniment to the mystical voyager. In each "world" or rung the same deed might gain a new level of symbolic meaning, providing at once a richness of texture and that constancy which the mystic so frequently seems to need. Hasidism, however, has little patience for the grades and rungs of ascent. If the *Hasid* seeks to rush up to God all at once in a sudden burst of ecstatic fire, would not the commandments seem to hold him back? For one who sought to see through the illusion of material existence, must there not have been a certain impatience with a religious life that kept him so very bound to earth? The commandments, after all, require the body; pure spirit cannot don the *tefillin*, wave the *lulav*, or eat the *matzah*. Their proper performance, moreover, requires a wealth of knowledge and awareness of bodily things, constant reminders of the limits of mortal existence in both space and time.

We see this tension in Hasidism through a rather frequent need by Hasidic authors to justify corporeal existence, indeed to justify God's creation of the material world altogether. Usually the justification is portrayed in the garb of the age-old contest of men and angels. Now man is proven God's best-beloved creature because he, unlike the hosts of heaven, can make spirit out of mere matter; the fact that he can uplift the sparks of God's light from among the *qelipot* of darkness represents not only his vindication but the greatest triumph of creation itself. The Maggid was also apparently responsible for an apt if rather grotesque image, according to which the King turns aside from the exquisite music of the angelic choirs in order to listen to the prayers of mortal man, his talking parrot. But the preference for a life of pure spirit is not the only challenge that Hasidism had to meet in its defense of rabbinism. The other side of the coin, as it were, was equally problematic. The Ba'al Shem's followers had insisted that divinity is to be found throughout all of creation, that "the power of the doer in the deed" could be attested everywhere. Why, then, we may ask, in the cow and not the pig? How can one distinguish holy from profane, permitted from forbidden, pure from taboo—distinctions which lie at the very essence of *halakhah*—if all is holy? We see Levi Yizhak of Berdichev, a leading proponent and popularizer of the Maggid's teachings, struggling with this question:

We should understand the nature of the snare by which the serpent seduced Eve to transgress God's commandment. The snake argued as follows: Were not heaven and earth created by the word of God? Is it not well known that all the worlds and everything in them were brought into being by the divine utterances ("Let there be . . .") and word? Is not the very root of their existence and life-essence drawn from the utterance of God, the source of all life, whose words continue to live? If this is so, how is it possible that the Tree of Knowledge, also the creation of God's word, could be harmful and cause death? Was not it too created from the source in the Life of Life?

Therefore, said the serpent, even though God did say "You shall not eat," etc., what place does this statement have? Was the Tree not created by the word of God? . . . If this is so, surely it gives life and not death. Even though God said "You shall not eat," why not obey His first saying, that which created the tree, rather than this one?[22]

Of course Levi Yizhak will find an answer to the "snake," invoking the raising up of sparks, the need to separate and purify, and so forth. But the questions here placed in the mouth of the serpent are not accidental. Some challenger, either in Levi Yizhak's circle or within his own self, was demanding an answer.

The dangers to the commandments from this embrace of God in all creation are also seen in the tendency of early Hasidism to want to *expand* the notion of commandment, allowing it to embrace the full range of human activities. The author of *Me'or 'Eynayim* occasionally lets slip such a phrase as "eating, drinking, and the rest of the commandments," and it does not seem from the context that *kashrut* restrictions are what he has in mind. The Maggid himself shared in this tendency toward a limitless expansion of the rubric of *mizwah:*

The sages said: "God wanted to lend merit to Israel; therefore He multiplied Torah and commandments for them." This means as follows: The commandments themselves are six hundred and thirteen. But when a person fulfills: "Know Him in all your ways" [Prov 3:6] he may fulfill many many more times 613, endlessly, for all his deeds are for the sake of heaven. He is fulfilling the command of his Creator in every moment . . . that is why they say that He "multiplied" the commandments. This term applies properly to that which is without limit. If there were only six hundred thirteen, why would the sage have called them "multiplied"? Our interpretation resolves this question: For the one who knows God in all his ways there is no end to his commandments. . . .[23]

If the commandments are without limit, however, what place is there for the very specific commandments of the tradition? Why not celebrate the presence in some other and more original way? Here one cannot but sense, as did some of Hasidism's more astute opponents, that religious enthusiasm is on the verge of spilling over into religious anarchism.

The Talmudic sages, in the course of claiming that there was no life of piety outside of the commandments, had expended much effort in the projection of rabbinic *halakhah* back onto the heroes of the Bible, much as we have seen them ascribe it to the Lord himself. In this the patriarchs were a particular problem, having lived before the Torah was given and thus seemingly having been unaware of the divine commandments. Not so, concludes the dominant rabbinic voice on the subject: Abraham observed every one of the commandments, even down to restrictions promulgated by the rabbis themselves. The echo of anti-Pauline polemic is not hard to trace in this Talmudic dictum. Now in Hasidism we find the rabbis challenged (by reinterpretation, of course!) on this uniquely touchy of subjects. The demurral is heard through several voices in the Maggid's school. The rabbis do not mean that Abraham knew all the laws and commandments, but rather that through his love of God, his single act at the 'aqedah, or whatever, he did all that we do as we follow God's commands. Once again Levi Yizhak expresses the challenge with particular clarity:

There are two ways to serve God: one is a service by means of total dedication, and the other is the service through the commandments and good deeds. The difference between them is this: one who serves through dedication alone, without commandments and deeds, is truly in the Nought, while the one who serves by means of the commandments is serving Him through some existing thing. The commandments are in existence. Therefore, the one who serves in dedication and is wholly within the Nought cannot cause divine blessing to flow down upon himself: "he" does not exist, but is fully attached to God. The one who serves through deeds, however, is still attached to being, and thus he can bring blessing forth.

Now within the service of God through commandments and actions there may still be both of these aspects of non-being and being. In doing that which is pleasing to the Creator alone, one may be said to be in a state of Nought, while he who does that commandment in order to bring blessing down upon himself is yet attached to being. In fulfilling the Creator's will one is intending to reach the Nought, while that selfsame commandment also binds you to existence, since the commandments partake of existence, and you draw forth blessing. Thus there are people who sustain themselves through their deeds.

Our sages tell us (Yoma 28b) that our father Abraham observed the entire Torah, even the details of how to prepare Sabbath food on a festival, before the Torah was given. We have tried to understand how he came to know the Torah. By separating himself from the corporeal and looking into his own 248 limbs, each of which corresponds to one of the 248 commandments and receives its life from that source, he was able to know them all. Each of the limbs receives its life from a particular commandment, and without it that limb could not be: thus he saw that the head is sustained by *tefillin* and all the rest; he knew the entire Torah before it was given.

It was for this same reason, however, that Abraham was not able to serve God through the commandments before he entered the Land of Israel. Outside the land he was not able to fulfill those commandments which apply only to one living in the land itself; thus various limbs in the system of correspondences would have been lacking. . . . Therefore, as long as Abraham was outside the land, he served God through total dedication alone: he cast himself into the fiery furnace and underwent various other great trials, all before he entered the land. When he entered the land, however, he was able to fulfill all the commandments and thus be a complete being, one possessing all his limbs. At that point he turned to the commandments as his way of service. In the Land of Israel he no longer needed to be dedicated unto death, for he had the commandments. As for the binding of Isaac: there too he was fulfilling an explicit command of God.

As long as Abraham was outside the land, he was serving God from the place of Nought, and could not bring blessing upon himself. In the Land of Israel, when he turned to the commandments and was thus attached to being, he could bring blessing forth. Therefore Scripture says: "Go thee from thy land" [Gen 12:1] and RaSHI commented: "For your own benefit and good"—go to the land for your own good, for there you will serve God through the commandments and bring forth the flow of blessing, while outside the land you serve Him through dedication and cling to the Nought, thus arousing no blessing. . . .

*Now he who serves God through dedication alone sees Him with
his very eye, while he who serves God through commandments and
actions sees Him through a glass, since his means of service is an
existing thing.* This is the meaning of: "After these things, the word
of God came to Abram in a vision saying" (Gen 15:1)—he saw God
through a glass. And God said to him: "Fear not"—do not be afraid
because you are serving Me by means of commandments and not
through dedication alone; "your reward is very great"—by serving in
this way you will bring forth blessing.

So when the sages said that Abraham fulfilled all the commandments, they were referring to that period when he lived in the land—
but outside the land he served through dedication. In our case, however, even though we are outside the land, we are able to serve by
means of the commandments—for the Torah has already been given.[24]

A number of motifs come together in this most surprising
teaching. The correspondence between the commandments and
the limbs of the body is frequently discussed in both later Kabbalistic and Hasidic works; the notion that Abraham learned
Torah from within is an interesting mystical adaptation of the rational Abraham known in medieval philosophical writings. But
by far most significant here is Levi Yizhak's recognition that
there is another way of service, and one that, from a purely mystical point of view, might even be preferable to the life of the
commandments. The reader is even further tantalized by the notion that it is the purely spiritual service that is appropriate to
life outside the land, in fact the locus in which Hasidim found
themselves. The rather lame postscript to the effect that the situation changes once the Torah has been given is hardly very convincing.

The projection backward may also be related to a projection
forward; there is a good deal of discussion in these same circles
about the rabbinic belief that the commandments will be unnec-
essary after the final redemption. Both Scholem and Schatz-
Uffenheimer have pointed to such statements as evidence of the
deep-seated ambivalence toward the commandments that is to
be found throughout this literature.

In the case of Nahman, ever the most daring and paradoxical
of the lot, it was not only remote past and anticipated future
without the *mizwot* that could be romanticized. While on the return from his famous journey to the Holy Land in 1799 he was

captured by pirates and had some rather realistic fears of being sold into bondage. The worst of such fears for a pious *Hasid*, so it would seem, would be the inability to live as a Jew. Nahman, however, managed to overcome these terrors:

He had reached the understanding of how to serve God even if he were, God forbid, not able to observe the commandments. He had attained the service of the patriarchs who had served God before the Torah was given, fulfilling all the *mizwot* even though they did not observe them in their ordinary sense. Just as Jacob fulfilled the commandment of *tefillin* by stripping the sticks and so forth, so did he come to understand how he would fulfill all the *mizwot* in this way if forced to do so in the place where he might be sold, God forbid.[25]

This confidence that such a purely spiritual Judaism was attainable in this world might have been comforting to the young *rebbe* at the moment, but it would do little to assuage his greater fears or the fears of those around him as to Hasidism's ultimate commitment to life within the rabbinic order. Surely for Nahman, who already saw the start of western "Enlightenment" among the Jews of Russia, it was the very opposite pole that needed strengthening. No wonder that he, and especially his disciple Nathan, pulled back from such dangerous formulations. No wonder that *HaBaD*, the very heart of acosmic radicalism as it emerged from the Maggid's teachings, placed the very physical fulfillment of the sacred act at the core of its religious teaching. The mystical enthusiasm of the Baʻal Shem and the Maggid had brought them to the edge of the transcendence of religion, a transcendence which, as some saw well, was also its destruction.

NOTES

1. *Ben Porat Yosef* 55a.
2. *Toledot Yaʻaqov Yosef* 7a.
3. *Zawaʼat RIVaSH* (Cracow, 1896) 3b.
4. *Ibid.*, 14b; *Liqquṭim Yeqarim* 17d.
5. This insight is originally that of Gershom Scholem. Cf. *Major Trends in Jewish Mysticism* (New York, 1954), pp. 341ff. Here is as good a place as any to say that this essay, like all contemporary study in the field of Jewish mysticism, is much indebted to the work of Scholem and his students in Jerusalem. With regard to Hasidism the latter include particularly Joseph Weiss and Rivka Schatz-Uffenheimer. Several of the sources quoted in this

article have been previously discussed, in one context or another, by these scholars.

6. *Me'or 'Eynayim* (Jerusalem, 1966) 16d–17a. A major portion of this work, the homilies on Genesis, has been translated into English by the present writer and is soon to appear in the Classics of Western Spirituality series of the Paulist Press. It is hoped that there the reader who is unfamiliar with Hebrew will be able for the first time to read one of the central homiletical works of Hasidism in English translation.

7. *Ibid.*

8. The Hebrew reader should see the elegant summation of this idea, along with several other key concepts of Hasidism, in Hillel Zeitlin's *Be-Pardes ha-Ḥasidut weha-Qabbalah* (Tel Aviv, 1960).

9. A brief and highly readable summary of this discussion is to be found in Louis Jacobs' *Seeker of Unity* (New York, 1966), chapter 3.

10. *Maggid Devaraw le-Ya'aqov*, opening.

11. *Or Torah, wa-yeze'* (Jerusalem, 1968) 24d.

12. *Liqqutim Yeqarim* (Jerusalem, 1974) 161.

13. *Op. cit.*, 54.

14. The letter has been translated by Louis Jacobs and published as an appendix to the work mentioned in note 9.

15. *Tanya*, second section, chapter 3.

16. On Nahman see my *Tormented Master: A Life of Rabbi Nahman of Bratslav* (New York: Schocken Books, 1981).

17. *Liqqutey MoHaRaN* 21:11; cf. *Tormented Master*, p. 336 n. 59.

18. *Liqqutey MoHaRaN* 22:10.

19. *Avaneha Barzel*, p. 44; see my discussion in *op. cit.*, p. 320.

20. *Liqqutey MoHaRaN* 64:1–3.

21. *Ha-Ḥasidut ke-Mistiqah* (Jerusalem, 1968), pp. 54 f.

22. *Qedushat Levi, bereshit* (Jerusalem, 1958) 7b.

23. *Or Torah* 147a.

24. *Qedushat Levi, Lekh lekha*, 15b–d. (Emphasis mine.)

25. *Shivḥey ha-RaN* II:2. The reference to Jacob is from Gen 30:37.

GERHARD BÖWERING

The Islamic Case:
A Sufi Vision of Existence

Our consultations on world religions began with Peter Berger's analysis of the contemporary situation of religion. He described this situation as one in which the dominant monotheistic traditions of the West are being confronted by fairly massive manifestations of nonmonotheistic religiosity, some of these erupting within the traditional institutions, some appearing from outside. He also stated that the dominant response to these developments, indifference and defensiveness, are misguided, and that the proper response is to face the contemporary contestation as a challenge on the level of truth claims. This would include a willingness to change, radically if need be, on the part of those religions that were founded on the core of the biblical experience.

As a working hypothesis Peter Berger suggested that the religious history of mankind has turned about the two poles of Jerusalem and Benares, the western pole representing the *confrontation* with God who manifests Himself as an overpowering reality external to man (in thunderous speech of Mount Sinai, on the road to Damascus, in the night of Qadr), and the eastern pole representing the *interiority* of the encounter with the Absolute who is the divine ground of the universe (climactically expressed in the watchwords of Upanishadic Hindusim and the noble truths of Buddhism). He noted, however, that the bifurcation between East and West should not be exaggerated. The parallels cutting across the boundaries of this typology define a shaded zone of interface between these two types of religion. This zone is much larger than is commonly assumed in the antipodal typology of religion.[1]

As we look at the case of Islam,[2] we realize that the world cast in the mold of the Muslim religious experience has driven a wedge between the worlds of these two poles, pushing the center of Christianity westward and cutting inroads into South and East Asia. In the perspective of this somewhat simplistic religious topography, does the central position of Islam between East and West also signify a central position of Islam in the religious typology? Is there a way in which Islam, the creed of an emphatically transcendent and omnipotent God, may be understood at the same time as the theater of a widely immanent and divine Reality? The case of Sufism,[3] Islamic mysticism, it is my contention, appears to argue in favor of this assumption.

A person studying the Islamic religious tradition soon realizes that beneath the solid layer of Islam's strict monotheistic dogma and monolithic law there is a vivid underground of rich religious experience, full of tensions and alive with revolt. Behind the heavy curtain of the nostalgic dream about the majesty that was Islam in ages past there are the distant flashes of active unrest lighting up the vision of a new Islam in times to come. Or, to use another image, behind the solid walls of strict and rigid doctrine reverberates a distant thunder of intellectual uproar, proclaiming the revolution toward a new Islamic age.

Tustarī's Commentary on the Qur'ān

As a case in point, I would like to introduce an Islamic mystic living in the ninth century, who may be regarded as a symptom (not necessarily as a universal representative) of this religious underground that has been at work in Islam throughout the centuries. The Ṣūfī Sahl at-Tustarī,[4] a Persian by birth who wrote in Arabic, was born at Tustar in Iran and died at Baṣra in

'Irāq. He led a life of austere practice, traveled to Egypt and Mecca, and was exiled from his hometown because of his ideas. In Ṣūfī legend he is remembered as a man with an outstanding gift for visions and clairvoyance. In the Ṣūfī tradition Tustarī is credited with inheriting certain currents of Hellenistic wisdom, and transmitting them to the Islamic environment by integrating them into the nascent Ṣūfī philosophy.

The most valuable source among the extant works of Tustarī, which includes the core of his teaching, is a commentary on the Qur'ān that has Tustarī as the principal author and a group of his companions and disciples as the actual compilers. This commentary, *Tafsīr al-Qur'ān* (in short, *Tafsīr*),[5] constitutes the most reliable compendium of the Tustarī tradition and was compiled in its final form between the years 888 and 910. It has been appraised as "the earliest product" of Ṣūfī exegesis of the Qur'ān,[6] as "the oldest surviving Ṣūfī commentary on the Qur'ān," and as "the forerunner of an extensive and important literature."[7]

The *Tafsīr* represents a continuous commentary on a selection of almost one thousand Qur'ānic verses or phrases. Despite its rigid framework as a running commentary, it fails to form a unified and neatly structured text but, as a whole, conveys the image of patchwork and disjointedness. This collection of a disorderly sequence of jottings, held together by the quotations of Qur'ānic verses, can be understood as being composed of three main structural levels: Tustarī's predominantly mystical interpretation of the Qur'ān; a variety of his aphorisms and sayings concerning Ṣūfī topics; and later additions and glosses inserted into the text. The text of the work is based on six Arabic manuscripts[8] which include many variant readings of a minor order and derive from an identical archetype that is 250 years later than the original and about 300 years earlier than the oldest textual witnesses. Despite this problematic transmission of the text, and despite the absence of any reference to the *Tafsīr* in the medieval bibliographies, this Ṣūfī commentary on the Qur'ān emerges as the principal, substantially authentic, and oldest extant work of the Tustarī tradition. In a separate study I have examined in detail the technical evidence for this evaluation of the text.[9]

Tustarī's Method of Qur'ānic Interpretation

Most of the recordings of Tustarī's Qur'ānic interpretation in the *Tafsīr* appear in the form of phrases, sentences or at best brief passages, which were jotted down by Tustarī's disciples and represent the substance of his instructions in a condensed form. These stenographic recordings represent the result of an aural way of communication which involves the listening to Qur'ān recitals, the actual encounter of the Ṣūfī listener with the Qur'ānic word, and the response to the tenor of a Qur'ānic verse expressed in the Ṣūfī utterance and its accompanying phenomena. The reception of Qur'ān recitals and the reaction to their impact upon the Ṣūfī's mind involve primarily the auditive energies of the Ṣūfī and result in Ṣūfī speech, sometimes manifested in ecstatic utterance. This auditive and oral process is transposed onto the plane of written record in the *Tafsīr*, where a succinct statement is jotted down next to a Qur'ānic phrase. Thus, the eye which reads a piece of text of Tustarī's *Tafsīr* has to grasp words suggested to a Ṣūfī while listening to Qur'ān recitals and words uttered in his mystically inspired speech.

This process of inspiration of the Qur'ānic word, rather than meditation on the Qur'ānic text, is also reflected in the very texture of Tustarī's *Tafsīr*. There the theme of an item of commentary is usually introduced by a Qur'ānic keynote (a word or a phrase of a particular verse that strikes the mind of the commentator) and is taken up as the focal point of the interpretation. Such keynotes can be historical references, points of religious law, eschatological events, theological terms, philological puzzles, foreign or rare words, legendary figures, and obscure points. A number of keynotes are taken up by the commentary as isolated units, independent from their Qur'ānic context. Other keynotes imply the location of the contextual environment in the mind of the commentator who, experienced in Qur'ān recital, realizes the repercussions of a Qur'ānic passage within its wider context. Almost all Qur'ānic keynotes of Tustarī's *Tafsīr*, however, carry characteristics within themselves that awaken associations in the mind of a Muslim and Ṣūfī.

These associations establish the essential link between the Qur'ānic keynote and the commentary. Called forth by Qur'ānic keynotes (among them certain privileged keynotes in particular), they grow out of the matrix of Tustarī's world of mystical ideas (his experience about himself, God, and the world) and find their expression in a way that can be as allusive as it is concrete, and as general as it is particular. In this process a level of synthesis is achieved which makes it impossible to discern where "exegesis" ends and "eisegesis" begins. The basic method of Tustarī's interpretation of the Qur'ān may thus be described as resembling an encounter event. The encounter between the Qur'ānic keynotes and the matrix of Tustarī's world of mystical ideas leads to an event of association which finds its verbal expression and written recording in the commentary. It is obvious that this method of Qur'ānic interpretation does not follow the frequent pattern in Islamic hermeneutics of employing Qur'ānic verses as proof texts for the justification of ideas, but uses the Qur'ānic recitals as the impulse prompting the mystical inspiration.

Tustarī's method of eliciting mystical insight from the Qur'ānic word is reflected explicitly in his definition of a fourfold Qur'ānic sense, which seems to recall the distinction between scriptural senses made by the patristic tradition in Christianity (*sensus literalis* and *sensus spiritualis*, including the allegorical, tropological-moral, and anagogical senses). Tustarī says: "Each verse of the Qur'ān has four senses, a literal (*ẓāhir*) and a hidden (*bāṭin*) sense, a limit (*ḥadd*) and a point of transcendency (*maṭlaʿ*). The literal sense is the recitation of the verse and the hidden sense its understanding. The limit defines what is declared lawful and unlawful by the verse and the point of transcendency is the command of the heart over the meaning intended by it as understood from God's vantage point. The knowledge of the literal sense is that of common man (*ʿāmm*), the understanding of its hidden sense and the meaning intended by it is for the select (*ḥāṣṣ*)."[10]

Tustarī seems to be aware that his fourfold Qur'ānic sense is actually reduced to two levels of meaning, which combine the literal and moral meaning as opposed to the combined allegorical and anagogical meaning. He equates the *bāṭin* and *maṭlaʿ* levels, making them both the domain of mystic man (*ḥāṣṣ*), whereas he grants common man (*ʿāmm*) access to the combined

literal and moral meaning. This method of Qur'ānic interpretation apparently follows the precedent set by Ǧa'far aṣ-Ṣādiq
(d. 765), who is also on record with a statement concerning a
four-point pattern of Qur'ānic exegesis, but actually, in his commentary on the Qur'ān, applies only two ways of interpretation,
a literal (ẓāhir) and an allegorical (bāṭin) way, stressing the
metaphorical meaning of Qur'ānic verses.[11]

The Framework of Tustarī's Ideas

The exegetical analysis of the Tafsīr shows the basic framework of Tustarī's mystical ideas, which is an articulation of the
genuinely mystical core of his religious experience, namely that
moment in which he penetrates to the certain and immediate
awareness of God's presence within his inmost being. This basic
framework may be understood as a paradigm of transexistential
events converging in Ṣūfī experience, and can be visualized in
the form of a horseshoe or a parabola approaching its zero point
from infinity and returning from it to infinity (or even as a
boomerang traveling to the target and returning to the point of
its release).

Passing from the picture to the paradigm of Tustarī's ideas,
one might say, in a nutshell, that God is envisioned by Tustarī in
His complete oneness and in His crucial manifestations as the
transcendent mystery and immanent secret of man's existence.
God is the absolute and ultimate Reality whom man encounters
at any moment of his life and in whom he experiences the source
and end of his existence. On the one hand God, in His omniscience and omnipotence, remains utterly inaccessible and distant, a transcendent mystery (ġaib) that cannot be penetrated.
In His omnipresence and providence, on the other hand, He
becomes intimately close and accessible to man, an immanent
secret (sirr) that penetrates his inmost being.

The one God of the Qur'ān, though inaccessible in absolute
mystery, manifests Himself in two fundamental events antecedent and subsequent to the phenomenal existence of man in the
world of phenomenal (temporal and spatial) creation. The two
events, the pre-existential Day of Covenant and the postexistential Day of Resurrection, delineate the origin and end of Ṣūfī
experience. By virtue of the reactualization of his pre-existential

past and the anticipation of his postexistential future, man is able to draw these two antipodal events into his phenomenal existence at the climax of mystic experience, and to penetrate the actual realization of God's immediate and certain presence within his inmost being. The Qur'ānic prophets and Muslim mystics, God's messengers and friends, represent the prototypes of this experience. The experience itself occurs on the plane of the total, living reality of man, the obedient and believing creature, in whom the God-centered inclination of the heart has overcome the self-assertive tendency of the human self.

Though not always consistent in the mosaic of its terminology and largely derived from the scattered references of a disjointed commentary on the Qur'ān, Tustari's range of mystical ideas achieves the coherence of a vision that integrates the primordial past and the ultimate destiny of mystic man in the actual experience of his soul. This coherent vision hinges on many subtle points elicited from the flexible roots of the Arabic language, blends seemingly disparate Qur'ānic verses in a synthetic mold, and frequently arranges Qur'ānic characters and images in pairs of type and countertype. Inextricably intertwined with the Qur'ānic vocabulary, the vision is bound to lose some of its depth when it is uprooted from its Qur'ānic context and reconstructed in systematic fashion.[12]

Pre-existence

God, the transcendent mystery and immanent secret of man's existence, is totally one in Tustari's view. This oneness, metaphorically expressed by the symbol of light (*nūr*), is all-exclusive and all-inclusive. On the one hand, it radically excludes all partnership in divine reality, all association with created, thisworldly beings, and any form of man's conscious assertion of his own self or subconscious attachment to his own being. On the other hand it totally includes the pre-existence of man as the articulation of divine light in form of light particles, comprises the phenomenal existence of man under the impact of the divine decree, and encompasses the postexistence of man in the permanence of man's communion with the Transcendent.

On the pre-existential Day of Covenant (*yaum al-mīṭāq*) the human race, in the state of light particles, professed God's oneness (*tauḥīd*), and man tacitly negated the affirmation of his own self (*nafs*). Man's profession of God's oneness, expressed in his confession of God's lordship, affirms man's conscious accept-ance of himself as servant (*'abd*) of his lord (*rabb*). At the height of his mystical experience in the world of phenomenal ex-istence, man reactualizes his primordial profession of God as lord (*sirr ar-rubūbiyyah*) through the mystical recollection (*dikr*) of his heart.

The primordial events are depicted by Tustarī's mystical im-agery as three themes centered around the Day of Covenant. The first theme is developed by the symbolism of light. God, both in His inaccessibility and His manifestation, is concep-tualized as light which issues forth in its radiance and articulates itself as the primordial light of Muḥammad (*nūr Muḥammad*). This emanation of divine light constitutes Muḥammad in his light-nature (a translucent shaft of light) as primal man, who at the same time is the mystic and prophetic archetype of religious man. Muḥammad's primordial adoration of God throughout an immemorial eon of time represents the original idea and the per-petual image of man, the believing and obedient creature fash-ioned in divine light in the world of pre-existence.

The second theme, subsequent to the event of the manifes-tation of Muḥammad's light-nature, depicts the human race, Adam's seeds (*durriyyah*), in the world of pre-existence as a con-glomeration of light particles which spiritually emanate from their prophetical ancestors in order to testify to God's oneness and lordship in the covenant event. Summoned by God to testify through their prophetical ancestors, in whom they are embryoni-cally enshrined as seeds, they intuitively perceive God's testi-mony about Himself and bear witness to Him as the one God and only Lord. The offer of the divine testimony by God and its acceptance by the human race constitute God's covenant with mankind, which at the same time endows individual creatures with the spiritual capacities of the human soul, the intellect and heart.

The third theme is the spiritual constitution of the heart of Muḥammad (*qalb Muḥammad*) as the source of divine revela-tion and mystical union for the believing and obedient creature. The total, living reality of Muḥammad, formed in divine light, is conceived as condensed in its inmost core, his heart. During the eon of primordial adoration of God in pre-existence, Muḥammad's heart absorbed the divine realities and thus carries them within itself like a treasure mine. From this mine, like a quarry, the Qur'ān is broken; from this mine, like a wellspring, the knowledge and love of God are drawn. From Muḥammad's heart, which enshrines the divine reality of light, breaks forth the flood of light which illuminates the hearts of men. God in His inaccessibility has become accessible in the heart of Muḥammad, where He is made manifest through His divine attributes, symbolized by the image of light.[13]

Postexistence

On the postexistential Day of Resurrection (*yaum al-qiyāmah*) man is reintegrated into the lasting presence of the Transcendent Reality (*ḥaqq*). He is granted the encounter with God, the existence in His permanence, and the visual perception of God. Man freed in his heart from the struggle with his own self regains his primordial perfection and perceives himself as an intimate (*walī*) who is absorbed by the Transcendent. At the peak of his mystical experience in the world of phenomenal existence man anticipates his ultimate destiny of the vision of God in His theophany (*tağallī*) through the certitude (*yaqīn*) of his heart.

On the Day of Resurrection, God remains Absolute Mystery and Transcendent Reality, but manifests Himself in His theophany to all those who have reached the permanence of His vision. On the Day of Covenant man experienced God through the mediation of the prophetical prototypes, but now on the Day of Resurrection he is drawn closer to communion with the divine Reality in his own right. He no longer is a pure particle of a prophet's corporate personality, but now lives in the divine permanence as a friend of God. The experience of God's presence has become experience of His intimacy, the profession of the divine lordship has turned into the permanent vision of the divine Reality, and the primordial covenant has been fulfilled in perpetual theophany.

Two themes of Tustari's mystical interpretation of the Qur'ān portray God in His events on the Day of Resurrection. The first theme is developed by the image of the permanent vision and

encounter of the Transcendent Reality (*haqq*). Tustarī emphasizes that God, who stands uniquely in His divine essence and its
attributes, is attained by prophetic and mystic man. On the Day
of Resurrection, when mankind will be summoned to account for
their actions in the world of creation, men found righteous in the
reckoning will be admitted to the eternal life of beatific vision in
encounter with God. Thus in his ultimate destiny man experiences God in beatific vision as the Real, the transcendent
principle and final ground of being. Whereas God in His events
on the Day of Covenant is predominantly perceived and professed as Lord (*rabb*), He is permanently perceived and encountered as Transcendent Reality (*haqq*) in His events on the
Day of Resurrection.

The second theme introduces Tustarī's mystical understanding
of the theophany (*tağallī*) of the Transcendent Reality, the truly
beatific event in the world to come, when God manifests Himself
to His friends, the blessed in paradise. This theophany represents the gist of man's encounter and vision of God, and is the
delight of his life in the permanence of the Transcendent. It
signifies the revelation of unveiling (*tağallī al-mukāšafah*) manifesting God in His hidden totality, namely in His essence and
attributes, and implies the revelation of the divine decree
(*tağallī ḥukm ad-dāt*), established from eternity in primordial
times and now unveiled to fill the eyes of the blessed with
gladness. The theophany, as the perpetual self-manifestation of
the divine Reality, thus transfigures man through its irradiation,
transforms him through its illumination, and brings his life of ultimate destiny and final glory to fulfillment.[14]

The World of Creation

In Tustarī's mystical perspective the course of man's life in this
world is suspended between the Day of Covenant and the Day
of Resurrection as a series of instants in which man stands under
the impact of God's decree (*ḥukm*) as unequivocally ordained by
His command and interdiction. The life of man in this world
thus turns out to be the theater of an inner struggle between the
forces of his heart and his self. In his efforts to realize God
(*Allāh*) as his exclusive Lord and ultimate Reality, man faces a
situation of trial, into which he is called by the command and in-

terdiction of the divine decree as well as by the antagonistic forces of his soul.

On his course from pre-existential infinity (*ibtidā'*) to postexistential infinity (*intihā'*) man passes through his phenomenal existence, marked by the moment of his creation and the instant of his death. In his phenomenal existence man experiences God (*Allāh*) as Creator and Revealer. Both His act of creation and His act of revelation have their privileged peak in the creation of Adam, the father of mankind, and in the revelation to Muḥammad, the Arabian prophet. But both acts are also perceived as an ongoing process. This process is not a continuous flow of being but a series of instantaneous events of the divine decree, established in primordial ages, consummated in eschatological times, and articulated in discrete succession in the world of creation.

In the world of creation man stands under the impact of the divine decree, which unfolds as it were as the indefinite reiteration of the divine *kun* (the creative command) and the divine *qul* (the revelatory command). Man, in his passage through phenomenal existence, thus falls under the reiterated intervention of divine providence made explicit in God's command and interdiction, which is accompanied by divine guidance made explicit in God's help and protection. Tustarī solves the problem of the actions of man in the presence of the divine decree by a series of notional pairs which center on the concurrence of the divine agency with man's activity. In presenting his view, Tustarī employs a dual pattern giving equal stress to the positive and negative aspect of his ideas.

God not only creates what is good, He also creates what is evil. Both good and evil are realities of God's decree, not ontological modes of being, because God lays down what is good through His command, and He sets down what is evil through His interdiction. Man, on his part, has no autonomous, independent capacity of action. Yet, in fact, he performs works of obedience in conformity to the divine command and commits works of disobedience contrary to the divine interdiction, whereas God recompenses his good deeds with eternal reward and keeps eternal punishment in store for his evil deeds. In view of man's incapacity for autonomous action and the actual possibility of his conforming to the divine decree, on the one hand, and God's unimpeachable justice and omnipotence, on the other, Tustarī proposes a pair of notions, divine help (ma'ūnah) and divine protection ('iṣmah), in order to resolve the apparent antinomy created by the negation of man's autonomy and the simultaneous affirmation of God's omnipotence.

God's command is accompanied by an act of divine help whereas His interdiction is accompanied by an act of divine protection. Through His ma'ūnah the divine agency concurs with man's activity in producing works of obedience, namely works of conformity to the divine command. Through His 'iṣmah the divine agency concurs with the human agency in preventing the occurrence of works of disobedience, namely works of opposition to the divine interdiction. When man performs a good deed, he is granted divine assistance and is bound to an act of thanksgiving. In case he commits an evil deed, man is forsaken by God and is bidden to return to Him by an act of repentance.

Through the perpetration of evil man is no longer in harmony with the divine command and interdiction, and automatically, as it were, falls outside the scope of divine succor and custody, because man abandons the divine forethought, God's providence, and follows the planning of his own self. Whether man conforms to or opposes the divine command and interdiction, in each case the action comes from God although it is executed through man and by man. The divine agency puts every action into effect; man's activity only contributes to its execution, while God possesses the divine foreknowledge of the actual action. There is no strict concurrence of the divine agency with the human agency (as in the concurrence of the principal and instrumental causes), but the divine agency is the true cause of human action, whereas man's activity represents the occasion at which the divine agency causes the effect. Tustarī, in resolving the central problem of Muslim theology concerning the interrelation between God's omnipotence and man's responsibility for his actions, sets God's command and interdiction parallel to God's help and protection, and thus has divine grace work simultaneously with the divine decree.[15]

The Secret of the Soul

It has become obvious that God, both inaccessible and manifest in the symbolism of light, is viewed by Tustarī in three basic facets of His manifestation: as Lord (*rabb*) of the covenant in primordial times, as God (*Allāh*) of creation and revelation in the phenomenal world, and as the Transcendent Reality (*ḥaqq*) of the theophany in the world to come. In his phenomenal existence, mystic man, reactualizing his pre-existence and anticipating his postexistence, penetrates to his inmost being where he grasps his Lord as the secret of the soul (*sirr an-nafs*) and perceives the Transcendent as the certitude (*yaqīn*) of his ultimate destiny. Mystic man, on the course from pre-existential to post-existential infinity, penetrates at the peak of his experience to the immediate and certain grasp of infinity, enshrined in his heart as a remembrance of primal being and as a yearning for life to come.

The conception of the secret of the soul defines *nafs*, the human soul, in its positive aspect as the divine spark of light enshrined in man and as the core of human consciousness where man penetrates to the inner nucleus of his self in the presence of God. This conception of the *nafs* stands in sharp contrast to the negative aspect of the *nafs*, the Ṣūfī principle of man's spontaneous self-assertion, namely the seat of his "a-theistic" self-centeredness, egoistic tendencies, and evil inclinations.[16]

Tustarī's theme of the secret of the soul views the soul of man as having been created by God as the locus of intimate colloquy between God and man. The concentrated introspection of man, however, grasps this colloquy as man's listening to God's soliloquy by virtue of the secret of his soul, through which he realizes God's lordship within himself. This self-realization of man is understood by Tustarī as a reactualization of the primordial perfection, possessed by man on the Day of Covenant in pre-existence, when mankind, in the form of particles of light, professed God's lordship and oneness. The reactualization of man's primordial state in God's presence represents the peak of mystical recollection and involves four component features: the creation of the soul as the locus of intimate colloquy between God and man; the revelation of the secret of the soul as God's self-revelatory soliloquy, manifesting Him as Lord; the full realization of this secret of the soul (to be kept secret by mystic man) as a reactualization of the primordial covenant, which neutralizes the mission of the prophets; and the implicit transfiguration of the total, living reality of mystic man through the divine presence in his inmost being.

Man's soul, the core of human consciousness, is created by God as the locus of intimate colloquy between Himself and man, and it enshrines the secret of God's self-revelatory soliloquy which manifests Him as the one Lord. In the Qur'ān the prophet Jesus attains to the awareness of the soul of man as a secret treasure, divinely entrusted to man and "deposited" within him, but he does not realize the deepest dimension of its intrinsic nature, since he does not pass beyond the duality of the human "I" and the divine "Thou" on the level of colloquy.[17] Mystic man, however, recognizes in God's soliloquy (ana rabbukum al-a'lā) the re-enacting of the primordial covenant, when he professed God's lordship by bearing witness to God's manifestation (a-lastu bi-rabbikum).[18] On the same Day of the primordial Covenant the prophets were given the mission to remind mankind of their primal profession. This purpose of prophethood, however, would be neutralized if the self-revelatory soliloquy of God, which is hidden as a secret in man's inmost being, were to be divulged in public. It would then upset the divinely provided order of the world and completely invalidate prophethood, knowledge, and the precepts of religion, since, in a nutshell, it comprises the ultimate sum-total of man's existence and mystic experience.

At one point in the Qur'ān, God revealed this inmost secret of man to Pharao, though Pharao was unable to penetrate to the full extent of the reality of the soul's secret which he proclaimed with his tongue. Mystic man, in mystical introspection, reactualizes this secret as the secret of divine lordship enshrined in his inmost being since the Day of Covenant. He realizes it as his self-identity and the font of his existence, since it was communicated to him when he was a particle of light participating in the light-nature of Muḥammad that issued from divine Light Itself. This seems to lead to the inevitable conclusion that, at the peak of his experience, mystic man overtakes the purpose of prophethood and is excused from being reminded of God's lordship, although at the outset of his experience he is essentially indebted to prophethood which provokes his awareness of God's lordship within himself.[19]

The act of recollection of God (*dikr*) represents the principal practice of mystic man which achieves the actual realization of God's presence within his inmost being. As an act of a predominantly cognitive rather than volitional nature, *dikr* reflects man's concentrated and introverted consciousness of the divine presence within his inmost core. As an act of recollection, *dikr* recalls the memory of the divine presence (remembrance of God), and re-enacts the awareness of the divine immanence (commemoration of God) within man. It is not only a reminiscence of the divine agency in man's heart, but also a reminder of the actual presence of God secreted in the soul of man.

The stenographic recordings in the *Tafsīr* concerning Tustarī's view of *dikr* can best be grouped together in the perspective of three themes. First, man's recollection of God rests on the knowledge of his state before God, his Witness, who takes care of him in any instant of his existence. Second, the commemoration of God is the spiritual sustenance of man, just as the celestial celebration of God's commemoration on the part of the angels represents their spiritual mode of being in the presence of God. Third, at the peak of man's mystical awareness, the remembrance of God is experienced as an act of God who brings about the recollection of Himself within the mystic (*ad-dikr bi'l-madkūr*).[20]

Mystical Certitude

In the act of recollection mystic man realizes that the presence of the divine "I," effected within the secret of his soul by God Himself, gratifies his inmost being with the experience of certitude (*yaqīn*), which includes the firm and assured hope of the mystic in the final attainment of his ultimate destiny: permanent subsistence with the Transcendent. Man's deep-felt experience of God's presence within his inmost being totally gathers him within himself and focuses him on the divine reality. When man, upon the examination of his soul, discards concern for all beings other than God and reaches the unshakable faith in God's oneness, then the light of certitude (*nūr al-yaqīn*) is made manifest to him. The presence of the divine light within man does not denote any kind of union between the human and the divine, but is realized by man in his profession of God's oneness and in his obedience to God and His prophet. The light of certitude is a spiritual quality in mystic man which embraces the subtle substance within man's heart. This subtle core is the uncreated quintessence of certitude (*'ain al-yaqīn*) itself. In his spiritual attainment of certitude, mystic man thus grasps infinity within himself without merging with it, since he perceives it in its light, but does not seize it in its inaccessible mystery.

There are three successive degrees of certitude, *mukāšafah* (unveiling), *mu'āyanah* (beholding), and *mušāhadah* (witnessing). The pattern of this tripartition has its root in the primordial adoration of God by the primal being of Muḥammad in the form of light, and is inspired by the prophetic prototypes, the Qur'ānic figures of Moses, Abraham, and Muḥammad, who each prefigure one degree of this tripartition. The pattern derives its inner dynamics from the expectation of man's beatific vision in the world to come, and from the assured anticipation of man's ultimate destiny in the permanence of God. These three degrees are moments of certitude included in the contemplation of the primal Muḥammad. Muḥammad's primordial vision, in turn, is understood in analogy to man's beatific vision in the world to come. Upon the Day of Resurrection, the moments of certitude of mystic man will achieve their perfection in the permanent "unveiling," "beholding," and "witnessing" of the divine Reality. The certitude of mystic experience will be transfigured and overtaken by theophanic revelation. In this world mystic man anticipates his ultimate grasp of infinity in the experience of all three degrees of certitude. He perceives the divine reality within himself as the quintessence enshrined in the light of certitude radiating in his inmost being, as an anticipation of his future destiny in the world to come, and unfolds its moments as actual prefigurations of his ultimate state in the permanence of God.[21]

The Struggle for Infinity in the Soul of Man

In phenomenal existence, the soul of man is the theater of a struggle between two antagonistic tendencies. The God-centered orientation of his heart is continuously challenged and opposed by the self-centered inclination of his lower self, the locus of his egoistic tendencies. Tustari's terminology of soul (*nafs*) and spirit (*rūḥ*) appears to be linked to a popular anthropological imagination. While "soul," related in Arabic to breath, resides in the breath of the throat which passes from the belly through the mouth, "spirit," of the same root as wind, has its home in the breath of the nostrils which passes through the nose from the brain. With regard to respiration, "soul" is linked with the life breath whose cessation signifies death, whereas "spirit" is linked with the breath of the waking state whose cessation means sleep. "Soul" is considered the vital principle that is "carnal" (and connected with the blood), while "spirit" represents the vital principle that is "ethereal" (and connected with the air).

Tustari's terminology of "soul" and "spirit" rests on his analysis of death and sleep, that is derived from the Qur'ānic reference to God's taking of the souls unto Himself.[22] In death God extracts the luminous spirit from the coarse natural self. God dissociates the subtle substance of man's spiritual self which alone is capable of the beatific vision. In sleep too, God takes the souls unto Himself, but deprives man of the coarse natural self, not of the luminous spiritual self. In the absence of the natural self during sleep, the spiritual self provides a subtle breath (*nafas laṭīf*), enabling the body to perform the functions necessary for the continuation of its life.

The two subtle substances, natural self and spiritual self, have their peculiar sphere of life. While the natural self finds its subsistence in food, drink, and sensual pleasures, the spiritual self finds its subsistence in the awareness and recollection of God. The life of the natural self is rooted in the light of the spiritual self which, in turn, is in no need of the natural self for its own existence. The two principles are not essentially and necessarily interlinked, on the contrary, the spirit is founded in its own essence and is independent from the natural self, as is evidenced by the primordial existence of the spirit.

The elements of spirit, intellect, and heart describe three aspects, not three constitutive parts, of the spiritual reality of man which is centered on God ever since the Day of the primordial Covenant. These three elements, defined as a discerning heart (*fiṭnat al-qalb*), a perceptive intellect (*fahm al-ʿaql*), and an in-

tuitive spirit (*ḏihn ar-rūḥ*), not only represent man's primordial
perfection but also his aptitude for the beatific vision of God in
the world to come. While man is pre-existentially endowed with
spirit, intellect, and heart, he receives the principle of his lower
self (*nafs*), the negative psychic force within man, at the moment of creation.[23]

This carnal soul habitually encites to evil (*al-ammārah
bi's-sū'*), impelling man to follow his instinctive nature, as illustrated by the Qur'ānic figures of Adam and Joseph. Having announced His plan of man's creation to the angels, God creates
Adam (i.e., man) as His viceroy on earth and instructs him
about his carnal soul and her nature. Then He bids Adam to
enter paradise and forbids him to eat from the tree. But the
devil, the enemy of man, induces Adam to acquiesce to the
promise of eternal life by whispering into his carnal soul and
making him follow his passion and lust. Adam abandons God's
covenant, in both the intention and the act, since he is not divinely protected against his sin.[24] Joseph, too, was defeated by
his carnal desire for Potiphar's wife but was rescued from putting
his intention into practice because of the succor of divine protection.[25]

The inclination to sin is rooted in man's adverse principle, the
nafs, which is marked by several characteristics: her selfish desire—she craves her own pleasures through her innate tendencies
of passion and lust; her autonomous claim—she lays claim to her
self-assertive capacity of action and follows her own planning in-
dependently from God's guidance; her antagonistic temper—she
instigates man to act in opposition to God's command and interdiction according to her natural disposition of restless activity
and listless passivity; and her enmity of man as Satan's sister—
she heeds to the whisperings of the devil and associates with him
in scheming against man as his worst enemy. The mystic's task
consists in overcoming the incentives and drives of his self-centered tendency which, since the moment of creation, militate
against the impulses and inclinations of his God-oriented force.

The moment of creation, however, does not signify the corrup-
tion of man's "spirituality," nor does the moment of resurrection
denote the destruction of man's "corporality." Man's soul is a
total, living reality and passes through three existential stages. In

pre-existence humans are defined predominantly as beings endowed with intellects (*'uqūl*), existing in their spiritual perfection as particles of light and seeds of Adam. In the world of creation they are marked predominantly by the self-assertive inclination of their carnal souls (*nufūs*), but are capable in their physical nature to realize their spiritual nature by reactualizing their primordial perfection and by anticipating their ultimate destiny. In the world to come they are distinguished predominantly by the total orientation to God on the part of their hearts (*qulūb*), enjoying the physical and spiritual blessings of paradise as saints and friends of God, whose "corporality" has been integrated into the perfection of their "spirituality."

Conclusion

In retrospect, it appears, that Tustarī's God is light, issuing forth in its radiance and articulating itself in the primordial light of Muhammad, the primal man and archetypal mystic. This divine light pervades the whole universe of the this-worldly and otherworldly realities and represents the hidden marrow of their existence. In pre-existence, the divine light communicates itself to the pristine realities through a process of emanation, but in the world of creation it is spiritually absorbed through a process of illumination. God engulfs the creatures through revelation of His divine light, not through emanation of His divine being; man spiritually absorbs the divine light but does not participate in the divine being. The primordial Muhammad represents the crystal which draws the divine light upon itself, absorbs it in its core, the heart of Muhammad, projects it unto mankind in the Qur'ānic scripture, and enlightens the soul of mystic man. Thus, in His inaccessible oneness, God becomes a symbolic presence in mystic man.

God manifests Himself in events antecedent and subsequent to the existence of man in the world of creation. On the Day of Covenant in pre-existence God manifests Himself as the omnipotent Lord to mankind and its prophets, who appear in His presence in their pristine state of particles of light and seeds of Adam. Man's profession of God's lordship, by which he bears witness to God's testimony about Himself, completes the event of the primordial covenant, endows man with the intellect (i.e., his self-consciousness), and spiritually constitutes man as aspirant to his final fulfillment in postexistence. On the Day of Resurrection in postexistence, God is encountered by man as the Transcendent Reality in whose permanence and vision man achieves his ultimate destiny. Man, admitted to paradise, is gratified by the truly beatific event of the divine theophany in the world to come, the irradiation of the divine Reality which reveals God in His hidden totality and in His inscrutable decree.

Man issues as an infinitely small particle of divine light in pre-existential eternity and achieves his final fulfillment when he is engulfed by the divine light in postexistential eternity. In the world of creation mystic man reactualizes his pre-existential past and anticipates his postexistential future within his mystical experience, for he penetrates to the immediate and certain awareness of infinity enshrined in his soul as the secret of the divine "I." The soul of man, however, is the theater of a struggle between two antagonistic tendencies, that of the God-centered orientation of man's heart, his spiritual self, and that of the self-centered inclination of the carnal soul, his natural self. Whereas Tustarī envisions God in the symbolism of light issuing forth in its radiance, he sees man in the symbolism of grain growing to perfection. Man, the pristine particle of light and seed of Adam, is, upon creation, invested with the coarse elements of his physical nature and, through the struggle of his soul, grows out of his husk to ultimate and total perfection which unites his spiritual and natural identity in the harmony of permanent subsistence with God.

Tustarī's range of mystical ideas forms a synthesis marked by the coherence of its vision and a specific terminology. This synthesis rests firmly on his own mystical experience and his Ṣūfi interpretation of the Qur'ān, and is inspired by the cultural matrix of his time which seems to include unspecified trends of neoplatonic philosophy, gnostic speculation, rabbinic wisdom, and patristic theology. The contribution of the *Tafsīr*, the oldest continuous commentary on the Qur'ān compiled in the Ṣūfi milieu, to Islamic intellectual history lies in its testimony to Tustarī's unified mystic world view.

The main ideas of this world view, transmitted in the Tustarī tradition of Ṣūfi literature, had a powerful influence on the works of Sarrāǧ (d. 988), Makkī (d. 996), and Sulamī (d. 1021) in the early Middle Ages and inspired the thought of Muḥammad Ġazzālī (d. 1111), Rūzbihān Baqlī (d. 1209), and Ibn ʿArabī (d. 1240) in the later Middle Ages. Still active in the early modern period of Ṣūfī literature, Tustarī's ideas, in the twentieth century, have attracted the attention of scholars such as Goldziher and Massignon.[26] Some of Tustarī's ideas were violently opposed for centuries by the Ḥanbalī and Mālikī doctors of Islamic religious law,[27] while others were proclaimed in public by Ṣūfīs like Ḥallāǧ (d. 922), ʿAin al-Quḍāt Hamadānī (d. 1131), Yaḥyā Suhrawardī (d. 1191), and Nūrbaḫš (d. 1464), who shared the fate of being put to death in public for the audacity of their mystic claims. It may not be farfetched, therefore, to suggest that the leading ideas of Tustarī's world view appear to have spawned some unrest in the underground of Muslim religious experience and created some tensions in Islamic intellectual history.

One may venture a step further and envisage the possible ramifications of Tustarī's range of mystical ideas on the typology of religion. Obviously, behind Tustarī's symbolism of light, his paradigm of transexistential events, and his polarity of transcendence and immanence, the student of comparative religion may discover the model of a corresponding microcosm and macrocosm, the pattern of cosmologic descent and mystic ascent, and the code of the conjunction of opposites. But this is not the end of the story: in its conception of time and space, Tustarī's world view appears to occupy a middle ground between the eastern and western poles of the religious typology. His paradigm of transexistential events reveals a philosophy of time and history that is parabolic, breaking open the cyclical conception of time predominant in the eastern type and bending to its full shape the linear notion of time common to the western type. Tustarī's cognitive conciliation of transcendence and immanence suggests a philosophy of space, ever expanding from an original point of light to an infinity of irradiation, which fills the notion of static, empty space predominant in the western type and unites the dynamic "plenum" of the eastern space. Tustarī's vision might therefore be understood as a bridge stretching across the great divide running between eastern and western religions.

NOTES

1. For a recent study of the contemporary religious situation, cf. Peter Berger, *The Heretical Imperative* (Garden City, New York, 1979).

2. Some handy introductions to the religious tradition of Islam are H. A. R. Gibb, *Mohammedanism* (Oxford, 1969); F. Rahman, *Islam* (New York, 1968); and A. Guillaume, *Islam* (London, 1969).

3. Comprehensive studies on Sufism are rare. One may consult A. Schimmel, *Mystical Dimensions of Islam* (Chapel Hill, North Carolina, 1975); A. J. Arberry, *Sufism* (London, 1950); and R. A. Nicholson, *The Mystics of Islam* (London, 1914).

4. Cf. G. Böwering, *The Mystical Vision of Existence in Classical Islam* (Berlin and New York, 1980), 43–99; L. Massignon, in *Shorter Encyclopaedia of Islam* (Leiden, 1961), 488 f. Tustarī was born about A.D. 818 and died in A.D. 896.

5. Sahl at-Tustarī, *Tafsīr al-Qur'ān al-caẓīm* (Cairo, 1911).

6. I. Goldziher, *Richtungen der islamischen Koranauslegung* (Leiden, 1920), 215.

7. A. J. Arberry, *Sufism*, in B. Spuler, *Handbuch der Orientalistik*, vol. VIII/2 (Religion) (Leiden, 1961), 457 f.

8. Cf. F. Sezgin, *Geschichte des arabischen Schrifttums* (Leiden, 1967), vol. I, 647.

9. Cf. G. Böwering, *op. cit.*, 100–42.

10. Tustarī, *Tafsīr*, 3.

11. P. Nwyia, *Exégèse coranique et langage mystique* (Beirut, 1970), 156–207.

12. For further detail, cf. G. Böwering, *op. cit.*, 145–261.

13. Cf. G. Böwering, *op. cit.*, 145–65.

14. Cf. G. Böwering, *op. cit.*, 165–75.

15. Cf. G. Böwering, *op. cit.*, 175–84.

16. Cf. D. B. MacDonald, "The Development of the Idea of Spirit in Islam," *Acta Orientalia*, 1931, 307–51; E. E. Calverley, in *Shorter Encyclopaedia of Islam* (Leiden, 1961), 433–36; J. Chelhod, *Les structures du sacré chez les Arabes* (Paris, 1964), 147–77.

17. Cf. Qur'ān, 5, 116; Tustarī, *Tafsīr*, 34.

18. Cf. Qur'ān, 79, 24, and 7, 172; Tustarī, *Tafsīr*, 41.

19. Cf. G. Böwering, *op. cit.*, 185–200.

20. Cf. G. Böwering, *op. cit.*, 201–07.

21. Cf. G. Böwering, *op. cit.*, 207–16.

22. Cf. Qur'ān, 39, 42; Tustarī, *Tafsīr*, 80 f.

23. Cf. G. Böwering, *op. cit.*, 241–53.

24. Cf. Qur'ān, 2, 30; Tustarī, *Tafsīr*, 10 f.

25. Cf. Qur'ān, 12, 53; Tustarī, *Tafsīr*, 49.

26. Cf. I. Goldziher, "Die dogmatische Partei der Salimijja," *ZDMG* 61

(1907), 73–80; L. Massignon, *Essai sur les origines du lexique technique de la mystique musulmane* (Paris, 1968), 294–300.

27. Cf. Abū Yaʿlā b. al-Farrāʾ, *Al-Muʿtamad fī uṣūl ad-dīn* (Beirut, 1974), 217–22; ʿAbd al-Qādir al-Ġīlānī, *Al-Ġunyah li-ṭālibī ṭarīq al-ḥaqq* (Cairo 1322/1904), II, 106 f.; Abū Isḥāq Ibrāhīm aš-Šāṭibī, *Al-Muwāfaqāt fī uṣūl al-aḥkām* (Cairo 1341/1922), III, 238–43.

Part II

The Polarity in Hinduism and Buddhism

DIANA ECK

The Dynamics of Indian Symbolism

Introduction

For people of the West, the single most prominent mental image of the religions of the East is the yogi or the Buddha, seated in the lotus posture, eyes half shut in the inwardness of meditation. Focusing inward, the spiritual adept withdraws the senses from the external objects of sense, as a tortoise withdraws its legs and tucks them under its shell.[1] The truth most worth discovering is to be found within.

Yet despite India's reputation for such inward spirituality, nothing strikes the visitor to India more forcefully than the colorful exuberance of Hindu worship. The senses, far from being withdrawn from the external world, are fully engaged in the sensual world. The eyes are directed toward multiarmed, brightly clothed deities. The ears are filled with the sounds of mantras and the clanging of bells. Flowers, leaves, incense, and camphor lamps are offered to the deities. Food and water are presented to them and redistributed as consecrated "blessings" to the worshipers.

India is well known for diversity and contrast. However, this

particular contrast between the silent inwardness of the yogi and
the noisy clamor of the temple deserves special attention, for it
runs through the entire tradition, from ancient times to the
present.

The sages of the Upaniṣads sought the knowledge of the
ātman, the "soul" which was elusive of description and which
was to be discovered within. The ātman was not different from
the one Brahman, which could only be described negatively, by
saying, "Not this . . . Not this. . . ." Sometimes the goal was
spoken of as if it were "out there," although it was clearly an interior goal they sought. For example, it was called the "far
shore"—indistinct, indescribable, but most certainly there, on the
far side of the flood. One could reach it, they said, only by "casting off" (sannyāsa) from this shore of birth, growth, and death,
of name and form. "Casting off" would surely lead to freedom,
mokṣa. In this tradition of spirituality the truly religious person
is "free" of concern for the world, society, and kinship. That person is also "free" of concern for what the traditions of the West
call "God." It is this tradition of radical inwardness which has
dominated the western understanding of the traditions of India,
including Peter Berger's notion that in these traditions the Divine does not confront one from the outside, but is to be sought
within. Curiously, this tradition of radical "inwardness," by refusing to identify or compare this Divine with any name or form
of this earth, bears superficial resemblance to the traditions of
radical transcendence to be found in the West.

In India, however, the tradition of the "far shore" has always
lived in close company with the traditions of "this shore," which
are firmly rooted in this world and its concerns—birth and death,
fertility and longevity, health and disease. It is on this shore, in
the web of interconnections between people, that dharma is the
sustaining principle of order and ethics. And it is on this shore
that the religious imagination has flourished, with its legendary
330 million gods and the countless stories of their deeds and
their dealings with people. The sources of this tradition are, in
great part, in the indigenous traditions of India which have been
characterized as the "Life Cult," in that their concerns were with
the vitality of life, not its transcendence.[2]

This paper concerns the Hindu world of symbol and image

generated by the "Life Cult." As we shall see, there are significant similarities between the "plenum" of India and the plenum which Michael Fishbane has described in his discussion of the "Mothers of Israel." In brief, it is the sense of living "cosmic continuum." As Fishbane puts it, "The world is not merely the garment of the gods, it is also their very body and substance —in all the circuits of their vigor and force."[3]

Perhaps the most significant difference between the plenum of the ancient Near East and that of India is in the historical fate of this religious sensibility. In the West, the radical sense of nature as "incarnation" or "embodiment" was suppressed with the rise of the religion of YHWH. The monotheistic consciousness of the incomparable One "out there" triumphed in the traditions of the prophets, although, as Fishbane hints, the Christian movement might be seen as a return to the ancient notion that the Divine is embodied *in* the world, and is not only the *totaliter aliter*. In India, however, the "Life Cult" of "this shore" has remained the predominant religious tradition, continually growing and changing from its ancient beginnings into the many strands of the Hindu tradition. The partisans of the "far shore" never won out. While the yogis rested in a tranquillity in which Brahman had no name or characteristic, the men and women of the village spoke a thousand names of the Divine and ascribed to that Divine a hundred perfect qualities. Whether preoccupied with this shore or the far shore, they came to see themselves as part of the same tradition.

This paper is a preliminary investigation of the nature of the religious images and symbols which the Hindu tradition has produced so abundantly. It explores the originary symbols which have served to shape the Indian world view. They are the organic symbols of this shore—the golden embryo, the body of the primal Person, the lotus, and the cosmic tree. The world they create and into which they usher those who are imaginatively engaged in them is an organic, living whole.

While exploring the nature of this living whole, I also want to make some suggestions about the dynamics of Indian symbolism. Living symbols are active. They do not "stand for" but rather they operate, they move the mind of the religious participant into what Ricoeur calls the "surplus of meaning."[4] In the Indian tradition (and here I would include the Buddhist, although I speak primarily from Hindu materials), the movement of symbols corresponds to the dynamics of the organic and biological world. Two such dynamics are immediately evident. First, the simple seed or embryo grows and expands to produce a complex plant or person, which, in turn, condenses its complexity into another simple seed or embryo. The movement is of expansion and condensation, *pravṛtti* and *nivṛtti*, which is visible throughout Indian symbolism. Second, the sap of the plant and the veins of the body move the essence of vitality from one part to another. The movement of the sap, rather than expanding to become the whole, extends to link part to part along subtle, intricate, and sometimes esoteric lines. Both examples, the seed (*bīja*) and the sap (*rasa*), suggest that the ways in which symbols move in the organically imaged world of India is perhaps different from the dynamics of symbolism in the West.

Organic Ontology

From the standpoint of the history of religions, it is clear that one of the most ancient and persistent strands of the Hindu tradition is the popular cultic life which focuses upon waters and pools, trees and groves, with their attendant *nāgas, yakṣas,* and *genii loci.* Moticandra speaks of it generally as the *yakṣa dharma.* From his work on Kāśī, that of Charlotte Vaudeville on the Mathurā area, and that of Anncharlott Eschmann on Purī, it is evident that this *yakṣa dharma* is the most ancient tradition of the most prominent of *tīrthas,* the sacred "fords" of pilgrimage.[5] Much scholarly work has been done on these cults, such as that of J. Ph. Vogel on the *nāgas* and that of Odette Viennot on the cult of trees.[6] It was Ananda Coomaraswamy in his work on *Yakṣas* who called this ancient tradition the "Life Cult" and assembled vast evidence from the early visual "texts" of art and iconography to show the ways in which these life forces and powers of abundance shaped a living cosmos of aquatic *makaras* and *nāgas,* lotuses and trees, brimming water pots and human figures lithely depicted in the "Plant Style" of art.[7] The realms of Life Cult were health, longevity, fertility, and productivity, and not immortality or salvation. To the extent that wisdom traditions, such as the Buddhist, assimilated the symbology of the

Life Cult, they too took on the this-worldly generative meanings conveyed by that symbology.

The early Vedic and Sanskrit traditions also contain a powerful symbolic and sacramental vision of nature and a sense of its living wholeness. It is not my purpose here to distinguish the Vedic and the indigenous Life Cult elements, but rather to see the ways in which the Indian "consensus" on the unity and the organic life of nature came to generate the structure of Indian symbolism.

The ontology of the Hindu tradition, insofar as it is a worldly tradition, is organic. Betty Heimann has called it a "biological world view" in her suggestive essay on India's biology.[8] By an "organic ontology" I mean that being is, by its very nature, living, growing, and divine. Creation, *sṛṣṭi*, is not an act of fashioning by a creator, but literally a "pouring forth" from the creator, as a spider emits a web from the stuff of its own body, or as a plant emerges from the contents of the seed, or as a whole person is shaped from the very cells of the embryo. *Samsāra,* which is this world, is not a created order, but an ongoing process, a flow, a growth. And *prakṛti,* nature or matter, the substance of the whole universe, is virtually synonymous with *śakti,* the energy and enabling power which generates everything.

The basic images for the dynamic system of meanings and relations which is this cosmos are biological images: the body and the vascular plant. Both are fundamental and complex, and both become originary or primary symbols which provide the semantic context for other symbols. The many ways in which the body functions as a system of meanings are well known and have been explored by a wide variety of scholars such as Mary Douglas, Stella Kramrisch, and Brenda Beck.[9] The system of meanings created by the plant paradigm has been the work of such scholars as Betty Heimann, Odette Viennot, F. D. K. Bosch, and Ananda Coomaraswamy.[10] The body and the plant are different images, but in many ways they merge into one another as symbolic systems of the whole.

The merging of body and plant is not surprising, since the sense of the life continuum of all "creatures" (*prajāḥ*)—"from Brahmā to a blade of grass"—is prominent in the tradition. As we shall see, the creator god, Brahmā, is born, alternatively, from an embryo or from a lotus pod. Another instance of the merger of life forms is in the yogi's slowing and simplification of life processes to approximate the metabolism of the plant.[11] It is occasionally said that sap rather than blood flows in the veins of the true yogi. Although it is well known that plants have the capacity for movement, they move very slowly and are therefore known in the Hindu systems of classification as the "stable ones," the *sthāviras*, to distinguish them from their cousins the *jaṅgamas*, or "movers." It is not only the relative stability of the plant which makes it a model for the yogi, but also the fact that the plant is much more of a closed system, without the obvious vulnerabilities which the entrances and exits of the human body occasion.

In Indian art as well, the vegetative, the animal, and the human are intertwined and sometimes transposed. The aquatic animal called the *makara*, "crocodile," spews forth the lotus plant from its mouth and, indeed, becomes part of the plant system itself in much of Indian decorative art.[12] The inhabited vines of Bhārhut, Sāñcī, and Amarāvatī show the life of vegetation circling and inscribing the scenes of human and animal life.[13] These vegetative motifs are part of what is often called "decorative" art, but it is clear that in Indian art this "decoration" shapes the world into which human icons come only much later in history. The merging of human and vegetative form is also seen in the bas-relief medallions of Bhārhut and Amarāvatī which show thick streams of vegetation emerging from the mouths of human or *yakṣa* figures.[14] The *yakṣīs* of Bhārhut and Mathurā are often entwined in trees. So powerful is this visual style that in the birth scene of the Buddha rendered at Amarāvatī, the Queen Mayā is depicted as a *yakṣī*.[15]

As the Indian depiction of the human body develops in the classical sculpture of the fourth to eighth centuries, the body no longer "inhabits" the circling vegetation of the vines; rather, the vegetation inhabits the limbs of the body. Characteristic of the Plant Style of Indian art is the body which has incorporated the grace of stems and vines into its very limbs. Stella Kramrisch calls this development in Indian art the "transubstantiation" of the body.[16] "The principle of the vegetative movement persists, while the vegetation in which it had been beheld originally withdraws. It immigrates into the human body and makes it its vessel."[17] She goes on to say that the movement and plasticity of vegetation is seen as the clearest expression of the inner vitality which courses through the whole of life, both without and within. "The ceaseless movement originally seen and felt in the outer world, and mainly in vegetation, became felt also as belonging to the substance of the inner life. This experience is visualised by showing the human body entirely made up of that movement."[18]

That the inner life of the human being bears close analogy to the unseen but indomitable source of life in the vegetative realm is a notion at least as ancient as the Upaniṣads. The sage Uddālaka likens the *ātman* to the inside of a tiny fig seed. It appears to be nothing, but from that apparent "nothing" the mighty fig tree grows.[19] The sage Yājñavalkya also articulated the analogy of the human and vegetative in asking after the "root" of life:

> As a tree of the forest,
> Just so, surely, is man.
> His hairs are leaves,
> His skin the outer bark.
>
> From his skin blood,
> Sap from the bark flows forth.
> From him when pierced there comes forth
> A stream, as from the tree when struck.
>
> His pieces of flesh are under-layers of wood.
> The fibre is muscle-like, strong.
> The bones are the wood within.
> The marrow is made resembling pith.
>
> A tree, when it is felled, grows up
> From the root, more new again;
> A mortal, when cut down by death—
> From what root does he grow up?[20]

The "root" which always produces life from the ashes of death is what generates all the life of this shore. The twentieth-century poet Rabindranāth Tagore, who celebrated the vitality of this

shore and spurned the very idea of "renunciation," wrote in his
Nobel Prize-winning *Gitāñjali:*

That same stream of life that runs through my veins night and day
runs through the world and dances in rhythmic measures.

It is the same life that shoots in joy through the dust of the earth in
numberless blades of grass and breaks into tumultuous waves of
leaves and flowers.[21]

The Symbolic Dynamics of Bija and Rasa

The primary organic symbols which govern the dynamics of
Indian symbolism are seen most clearly in cosmogonic myths.
Cosmogonies are, of course, legion in the Indian tradition, but I
will take up two cosmogonic themes which collect and systema-
tize a whole range of symbolism and shape the nature of Indian
thought. The first is the Golden Embryo, Hiranyagarbha, from
which the whole of creation emerges and which, in its seed state,
contains the all within. When the embryo or the egg breaks
open, the creator god emerges, pillaring apart heaven and earth.
The top of the shell becomes heaven, the bottom, earth. The
creator—be it Indra, Prajāpati, or Brahmā—spans the midspace
between heaven and earth, like a tree. The second theme is the
dismemberment of the primal person, *puruṣa,* in which the universe becomes the completed sacrifice, shaped part by part from
the body of the *puruṣa.* Each part of the universe corresponds
directly to a part of the cosmic giant: the sun to his eye, the
moon to his mind, the sky to his head, the atmosphere to his
navel, the earth to his feet. Both cosmogonies—the incubation of
the embryo and the dismemberment of the body—have their origin in the Rig Veda, and both continue to live in the Hindu tradition in one transformation after another. In some later accounts, such as that in the opening chapter of the *Laws of Manu*
and that in *Bhāgavata Purāṇa* II 5-6, the two are linked together
as sequential myths, the first speaking of the origin of life itself
from the vast formless potential, and the second continuing with
the creation of all the particulars of the universe.

The symbolic dynamics which emerge from these cosmogonies
are what I call in shorthand for our purposes here *bija* and *rasa,*
the dynamics of the seed and the sap. Symbols are never static or

isolated, but always active and transitive, moving us into some system of meanings. Seed symbols are characterized by the intensification and condensation of the whole in the part, and the amplification of the part to the whole. Their growth is like the growth of the simple embryo or seed into the abundant complexity of the systemic whole. Seed amplifies to tree, and tree condenses to seed. The dynamics of the system are of *pravṛtti*, "rising," and *nivṛtti*, "returning," expansion and condensation.

Seed symbols are those high-density symbols in which the whole is gathered together. The examples of such symbols in the Indian world are many and well known. The *bija mantra*, for example, is a "seed prayer," in which the entire wisdom of the Vedas is said to be contained in a single word. Similarly, a *maṇḍala* or a *yantra* contains the entire universe in single sacred circle or geometric diagram. The ancient Vedic fire altar may be seen as an archetype for such symbols, for in bringing together the bricks for its construction, the whole of the scattered *puruṣa*, distributed in the parts of creation, is brought together again in a single ritual arena. The Hindu temple is structurally patterned on the fire altar as a divine image of the whole universe. The temple has its seed center in the *garbhagṛha*, the "womb chamber" of the inner sanctum, where, in fact, a small casket called the "seed" of the temple is implanted during construction. From the dark center, the temple expands outward, blossoming in the variety and exuberance of the exterior, which is often covered with the prolixity of life in sculptural relief. A city such as Kāśī or Benares is also this type of symbol, for as a sacred "cosmopolis" it gathers the entire universe into its boundaries. The quadrants of space and the divisions of time are present there, as are all the mountains, rivers, cities, and gods of India. Just as a plant may develop outward in successive sheaths of leaves, the innermost being very subtle and the outermost being thicker and tougher, so it is with the sheaths of a person, the innermost being sheer bliss and the outermost being the material body. And so it is with the city of Kāśī, which is said to have five successive zones, increasing in subtlety and power as one approaches the center.

Perhaps the most vivid exemplars of this condensive seed symbolism are the gods themselves. Each of the great gods in its

icons of multiple heads or limbs, in its emblems, and in its deeds
and appearances is amplified to cosmic significance. In the Bhagavad Gītā there is Arjuna's vision of the cosmic Kṛṣṇa, of
infinite form, with faces in every direction, with the sun and the
moon as his eyes. In addition, there are the painted images of
Viṣṇu in which all the worlds and all the gods are circling within
his sixteen-armed body. There are the many mythic occasions on
which Brahmā enters into the body of Viṣṇu to look around and
discovers the whole world inside. In the mythology of the goddess, there is the amplification of the Devī to include the powers
of all the gods, and there is the marvelous episode in which
Brahmā, Viṣṇu, and Śiva visit the Devī on the Island of Jewels
and see her as having a thousand eyes, a thousand hands, a thousand feet; in her toenails they see the entire universe reflected.
In Śiva mythology, there are the various occasions on which all
the mountains and rivers, planets and gods, all the elements and
all the sounds gather to form Śiva's chariot or his wedding dais.
Śiva's symbol, the *liṅga*, also comprises both Śiva and Śakti,
puruṣa and *prakṛti*, divine spirit and divine matter. Any one of
these great gods is the "seed" of the whole universe, the origin
from which it all may grow.

While *bīja* symbols are dense and concentric, *rasa* symbols are
extensive and linear. They are connected to their referents by a
common "essence": *rasa*. The word *rasa* has a wide range of
meanings: the sap or juice of trees; any juice or nectar; the essence of taste of something; and, by extension, the taste or flavor
of beauty, since in the Indian view the aesthetic experience is
one of "tasting" the essence of art. Here *rasa* is sap or essence.
The universe is imaged as a web or as an intricate fabric,
"woven, warp and woof."[22] In its extension of meaning, the *rasa*
symbol moves from link to link along a particular strand or a particular thread. (1) The strand might be the correspondence between a particular part of the earth and a particular part of the
cosmic whole. For example, from the veins of the primordial egg
came the rivers of the earth; from its fluid, the oceans of the
earth. (2) The strand might connect the heavens above with
the earth and its various kingdoms of life below. For example, the
divine liquid, Soma, enclosed within the vault of heaven, is the
stream of the River Ganges which fell from heaven to earth and

flows along the earth, and it is the milk of mother cows, and it is the stream called *pingala* which flows as one of the major veins in the human body, and it is the sap of plants. From the veins of the plants to the ocean of heaven there is a common essence, in this case *soma*, which flows along. (3) The strands along which meaning extends might also be the *gunas*, literally the "threads" or "strands" which run through the entire cosmos and link everything which is of common essence. There are three *gunas: sattva* (the good or pure), *rajas* (the passionate or active), and *tamas* (the dark or sluggish), and the three are the weaving threads of all that is. The connection of the upper-caste Brahman, with the head of the cosmic *purusa*, with the cultivation of wisdom, with certain kinds of foods, with certain colors of clothing—all this is extended along the strand of *sattva guna*. (4) Finally, the strand along which symbolic meaning moves might connect one level of interpretation to another. A single phenomenon might be understood from the worldly (*adhibhūta*) perspective, or the ritual (*adhiyajña*) perspective, or the heavenly (*adhidaiva*) perspective, or the interior (*adhyātma*) perspective. Benares or Kāśī, for example, is a city from the worldly perspective, a sacrificial arena from the ritual perspective, a heavenly city propped up above the world on Śiva's trident from the heavenly perspective, and the place of *ātman* where the nose and eyebrows meet from the interior perspective.

The common feature of all these *rasa* symbols is the extension of meaning along the lines of "essence" or "sap." Like the xylem and phloem running up and down the stem, extending through the intricate pattern of branches and leaves, this kind of symbolism extends its threads of meaning up and down and from stem to branch. The religious movement of Tantra, which informs so much of the Indian symbolic universe, means, literally, "extending" and is built upon this type of symbolic dynamics.

Many of the great symbols of the Hindu tradition participate in both dynamics. Viṣṇu, for example, swells from a tiny dwarf to become a cosmic giant (*bīja*) and then strides through the triple universe with three giant steps to claim it for himself (*rasa*). The *linga* which gathers the whole in the part (*bīja*) splits the three worlds in a fiery column of light (*rasa*). And the temple, with its dense universe of signification (*bīja*) also rises upward through the various *bhūmis* or "levels" of the universe, through the "foothills" of its massive spire, called a *śikhara* or "peak" to its culmination in the *āmalaka*, the sun symbol of heaven. Of course, a great plant or tree participates in both *bīja* and *rasa* movement too, unfolding from its seed while extending its roots downward into the soil and its branches upward into the sky.

What are some of the particular images of creation and generation which have produced this sense of a living universe in which symbols always seem to move the mind into the fullness of life and death on this shore?

The Garbha: Embryo and Womb

In the famous, but obscure, hymn of creation, Rig Veda X.129, "that one" (*tad ekam*), which existed and breathed in the beginning on the motionless deep and in windless space, came to life by the brooding heat of its own creative force (*tapas*). Something came into being, some form amid the formless. The mere outline of the embryo image is there.

The creation motif which comes to be called the Hiranyagarbha, the Golden Embryo, is seen more clearly in the hymn to Prajāpati in Rig Veda X.121 (verses 1 and 7):

> In the beginning the Golden Embryo
> [Stirred and] evolved:
> Once born he was the one Lord of [every] being;
> This heaven and earth did he sustain. . . .
> What god shall we revere with the oblation?

> When the mighty waters moved, conceived the All
> As an embryo, giving birth to fire,
> Then did he evolve, the One life force [*asu*] of the gods. . . .
> What god shall we revere with the oblation?[23]

Rig Veda X.82 speaks of the primal *garbha*, firmed up upon the waters, offered upon the "navel of the unborn" where all the gods were gathered together. Such an image of the genesis of form in the waters is projected repeatedly in the Vedic literature. In the Atharva Veda IV.2.8 it is said:

> In the beginning, generating offspring, the
> Waters brought an embryo into being; And even
> as it sprang to life, it had a covering of gold.[24]

In the Śatapatha Brāhmaṇa this primary symbol begins to generate a mythology: The waters labor in *tapas* with the desire to create. They generate an egg (*aṇḍa*). It incubates for a year, hatches, and produces the creator Prajāpati, who, in turn, creates the earth, the sky, and heaven with his speech, then day and night, the gods and *asuras*, with his upward and downward breaths.[25]

The extension of correspondences from the contents of the egg to the earth is widely explored in the Brāhmaṇas and Upaniṣads. The Chāndogya Upaniṣad contains a succinct statement of such strands of connection:

> In the beginning this world was merely non-being.
> It was existent. It developed. It turned into an
> egg [*aṇḍa*]. It lay for the period of a year. It
> was split asunder. One of the two eggshell parts
> became silver, one gold.

> That which was of silver is this earth.
> That which was of gold is the sky.
> What was the outer membrane is the mountains.
> What was the inner membrane is cloud and mist.
> What were the veins are the rivers.
> What was the fluid within is the ocean.[26]

The Body

The body, like the embryo or egg, serves as a primary image of genesis and creation. The world, it is said, with its diversity and organic unity, is like the human body. The most famous myth of bodily creation is the dismemberment of the primal *puruṣa* in Rig Veda X.90. There, the *puruṣa* as the oblation is offered by the gods in sacrifice. From his various parts the Vedas are born. Horses, cattle, goats, and sheep are born. The social order is generated: from his head, the *brāhmaṇa*; from his arms, the *kṣatriya*; from his thighs, the *vaiśya*; and from his feet, the *śūdra*. From his mind, the moon was born; from his eye, the sun; from his mouth, Indra and Agni; from his breath, the wind. In essence, the universe we know and inhabit is formed from and adds up to the very body of *puruṣa*.

In the creation account which introduces the *Laws of Manu*, Brahmā, the creator, is born from the egg. He is the one who splits the shell in two to make heaven and earth, and from his body he emits everything: the mind, the senses, the gross and subtle elements which are the objects of sense, the gods, the social order, men and women, and the ten sages who, in turn, create the other particulars of the world.[27]

The Aitareya Upaniṣad makes clear the functional similarity of the egg and the *puruṣa* in creation, for here the *ātman* gathers together the primeval waters and shapes the *puruṣa*, upon whom he broods, "like an egg [*aṇḍa*]":

And from that *puruṣa*, brooded upon like an egg,
A mouth broke open. From the mouth came speech; from speech, fire.
Nostrils broke open. From the nostrils came breath; from breath,
     the wind.
Eyes broke open. From the eyes came sight; from sight, the Sun.
Ears broke open. From the ears came hearing; from hearing, the
     quarters of heaven.
Skin broke forth. From skin came hairs; from the hairs, plants
     and trees.
A heart broke forth. From the heart came mind; from mind, the
     moon.
A navel broke forth. From the navel came the out-breath; from the
     out-breath, death.
A penis broke forth. From the penis came semen; and from the
     semen, the waters.[28]

In later Purāṇic mythology, the Hiraṇyagarbha, the Golden Embryo containing the full potential and diversity of life, appears in bodily form as Viṣṇu, floating on the vast waters, having withdrawn the whole of the universe into his body for the period of universal dissolution called the *pralaya*. In the *Matsya Purāṇa* one finds the story of the sage Mārkaṇḍeya who, during this time, wanders through the condensed cosmos of the interior, visiting all the mountains, rivers, and *tīrthas* contained therein, until one day he falls out of the mouth of the sleeping Viṣṇu and into the vast sea. He finds, to his horror, that he has, literally, fallen out of the world! And he is relieved to be snatched up and swallowed again by Viṣṇu.[29] When the new creation is about to begin, the lotus springs from the "navel of the unborn." Its stem rises; its bud is closed, containing, like the egg, the full potential of creation. When it opens, there sits Brahmā, who proceeds to fashion the particulars of the universe in one way or another.[30]

The Lotus

In imagining the emergence of form on the surface of the formless "deep," Hindus have seen the Golden Embryo or the body of the sleeping god Viṣṇu. How natural also to see the lotus in this role as cosmic progenitor of form, for the lotus is the plant which rises from the deep, with its root in the unseen waters below, to float and flower on the surface of the water. Anyone who has seen the lotus in flower on a pond can well see how readily this natural form would serve the Hindu imagination we are here describing. The lotus came to be seen as the quintessence of living form on the waters of potential. Thus, in the above mythic episode of creation, it is not surprising to see Brahmā emerging, not from the egg, but from the blossoming lotus bud.

The lotus becomes the plant *par excellence* in Indian symbolism. While it is an extremely unusual plant, it lends itself to symbolic interpretation. Its "root," *mūla,* is in the mud below the waters. The plant has no dominant stem; rather the root grows laterally through the mud, producing "nodes," *parvans,* at regular intervals. Each node sends up a stem to the surface of the water, where the leaves and flowers of the lotus appear. Thus all the blossoms are linked to a common lateral root, although there is no common stem.[31] The seemingly free-floating flower has a root in the mysterious deep. The seemingly perfect lotus flower is, indeed, rooted in the mud below. And the seemingly independent flowers on the pond's surface are linked directly to a common root. All of these features of the lotus stimulated the mythic imagination.

The nodes of the lotus, as F. D. K. Bosch has brilliantly demonstrated, were imaginatively identified with the open jaws of the aquatic animal, the *makara*; and the lotus, like the *makara,* became a visual symbol of all the life that is produced from water.[32] The blossom of the lotus, fully expanded, is the universe itself: its petals the various continents, its collection of sporophylls Mount Meru in the center of the world. Not only does Brahmā come into existence on the firm base of the lotus, but the yogi sits on such a base, his posture being that of the lotus, his root or *mūla* located at the bottom of his spine, and his centers of power, called *cakras*, imagined to be a series of lotuses ascending with increasing numbers of petals to the *brahmarandhra*, at the top of the head. The firm base of the lotus, the first form of creation, is also that upon which the Buddha sits or stands in his artistic renderings throughout Asia. And, of course, the lotus, in symbolizing the nourishing source of the plenum of the universe, is also seen as the interior source of human life. In Upaniṣadic imagery, for example, the *ātman* is sometimes referred to as the "lotus within the heart."[33]

The Tree

The tree, like the egg, the body, and the lotus, also functions as a primary image of the universe as an organic system of meanings. Whereas the lotus system is mysterious, subaquatic, its perfect blossoms linked only by a common root, the tree system is visibly unified by a common trunk. It is a vivid paradigm for the whole universe: its huge canopy of branches above, its unseen but vast system of roots below, and its trunk linking and separating these two complex networks. A tree has the remarkable ability to grow both up and down at the same time. Its food- and water-bearing vascular system circulates life energies up and down through an intricate network of channels, both below in the earth and above in the sky.

The notion of the world tree is not at all uncommon in Vedic and early Sanskrit literature. Rig Veda X.31.7 (and, similarly X.81.4) asks:

> What was the wood, and what the tree of which
> they fashioned heaven and earth?[34]

The Taittirīya Brāhmaṇa (II.8.9.6) responds:

> The wood was Brahman, Brahman the tree
> Of which they fashioned Heaven and Earth;
> It is my deliberate word, ye knowledgeable men,
> That there stands Brahman, world-supporting.[35]

The *skambha*, the pillar, the support, which propped apart the earth and heavens, may be *puruṣa* or Prājapati or the great Tree of Brahman.

Firmly did Skambha hold in place heaven and earth—both these,
Firmly did Skambha hold in place the far-flung atmosphere,
Firmly did Skambha hold in place the six wide-spread directions:
Into this whole world hath Skambha entered in.[36]

The symbol of the world tree with its two great branch systems, above and below, is expanded in the Upaniṣads and the Gītā, where one finds the notion of the heavenly tree: an inverted tree, with its roots above in heaven and its branches here below.[37] Bosch, Coomaraswamy, and Emeneau have all written extensively on the subject of the inverted tree.[38] It is suggested that the tree may refer to the banyan, the *nyagrodha*, which sends great aerial roots down from its branches. However, the tree is explicitly referred to in literature as an *aśvattha*, the sacred fig tree, not a *nyagrodha*. The explanation has been offered that the *aśvattha* is a species of fig which begins life as an epiphyte on another tree and grows downward, weaving a virtual basket of branches around the trunk of its host. I will not attempt to recapitulate the extensive discussion of the inverted tree here. What is most significant in this context is the perception and image of a tree which grows downward as well as upward, carrying the flow of life in both directions. While rooted in the earth, the "root" of this system of meanings is also "above," in Brahman.

In *The Golden Germ,* F. D. K. Bosch uses the image of the two interlocking trees, one growing up and one growing down, to construct what he sees to be a "basic form" of Indian visual symbolism.[39] The tree links the world below, nourished by the waters, to the world above, nourished by the sun. The lotus-style tree grows from the root below the waters, the *padmamūla,* transporting upward the liquid energy of *soma.* The fig tree grows from the root above in the heavens, called the *brahmamūla,* transporting downward the fiery energy of *agni,* whose source is the sun. These two "roots" in the earth and in heaven, and the stem or trunk that joins them, and the multiple branches they produce, constitute the "basic form," each part of which is symbolized in a variety of ways, according to the principle of "substitution." One thing may substitute for another, with which it shares a common "essence," or *rasa.* For example, the *padmamūla,* the rounded lotus rhizome, may be replaced in Indian

visual imagery by a *pūrnakumbha*, a "brimming water jug," or
by a *yakṣa*, a fat, often squatting, figure associated with the plenitude of vegetation. The *padmamūla*, the *pūrnakumbha*, and the
yakṣa all may share the rounded form of fecundity from which
prolific vegetation emerges. The stem of the basic form, growing
upward from the *padmamūla*, may be replaced by a standing
figure such as a god, a pillar (*skambha*) or sacrificial post
(*yūpa*), or the human spinal column. The *brahmamūla*, the
"root" which draws nourishment from above, may be replaced
by the sun, the sun shade or umbrella, or the inverted water jug,
which pours its contents downward. In the Hindu temple, to
give an example, the *padmamūla* is the seed casket which is
planted deep in the sanctum of the temple. The stem is the
śikhara or spire which rises, layer on layer, over the sanctum.
While the *śikhara* is likened to a mountain rising from earth to
heaven, it is also seen as the stem of the planted seed, or even as
the pillar which props apart heaven and earth. The *brahmamūla*
is the *āmalaka* or cogged ring stone at the very top of the *śikhara*.
It is the sun, it is the sky lotus, it is the heavens.

The elaborate documentation of details in Bosch's presentation
of the "basic form" is impressive. His "texts," of course, are the
extensive art-historical texts of South and Southeast Asia in
which one can see the replacement and substitution of parts. For
our purposes here, however, it is the organic world view
suggested by the two-tree image that is significant. The meaning
of the two trees is quite simply that there are two "roots" of life:
in the watery depths below the earth and in the light-filled
heavens above. The interchange of life from above and life from
below constitutes an intricate organic system, and a system
which is self-contained.

The question of the "fruits" of the tree is an interesting one.
On the one hand, the world tree is the *kalpataru*, the "wishing
tree" which grants abundant blessings and is often depicted as
laden with a multitude of marvelous fruits. *Vṛkṣa pūja*—the
wrapping of trees with colored threads, daubing them with
sindūr, and watering them with the waterpot—is still a common
and very visible phenomenon, and is associated with the realms
of life growth, and health which the tree embodies. At the same

time, "fruits" are the fruits of *karma*, as the Bhagavad Gītā puts it:

> Below and upward extend its branches,
> Nourished by the Strands, with the objects of sense as sprouts;
> Below also are stretched forth its roots,
> Resulting in actions, in the world of men.[40]

In the Bhagavad Gītā, it is suggested that this tree should be pulled out at its roots, cut down "with the stout axe of detachment."[41]

The world tree, writes Coomaraswamy, is the "procession of incessant life." It is precisely for this reason that, from the point of view of some, it should be felled, cut at the root. But for most, the tree remains a vehicle for imaging the abundance of life in its many lush branches and delicious fruits, as well as the transcendence from earth to heaven and the divine descents from heaven to earth. It is in the world of the living tree that Indian symbolism moves.

It is described in the Mahābhārata:

> Sprung from the Unmanifested [*avyakta*], arising from it as only support, its trunk is *buddhi*, its inward cavities the channels of the senses, the great elements its branches, the objects of the senses its leaves, its fair flowers good and evil [*dharmādharmau*], pleasure and pain the consequent fruits. This eternal Brahma-tree [*brahma-vṛiksha*] is the source of life for all beings. This is the Brahma wood, and of this Brahma-tree That (Brahman) is.[42]

The Symbolism of the Plenum

Let us return again to the dynamics of symbolism suggested by these organic symbols, myths, and images, and to a few concluding speculations about the nature of symbols in the Indian view.

First, the world shaped by these originary symbols is one which is a systemic whole. Whether it is the egg or the seed, the body or the tree, the system is intact, complete. Nothing is left out; nothing is lost. The whole is a vast ecological system in which the process of creation, growth, flourishing, dying, and decaying describes the fundamental nature of the world, everything included, even the gods. Within the systemic whole, everything is alive. Even those things we do not think of as "living" participate in the life of the whole. Creation is not an establishment, but an evolution, like the growing of a plant. It is an evolution which is bipartite, or bisexual, whether its twofold dynamics be called breath and water, *puruṣa* and *prakṛti*, sky and earth, *agni* and *soma, śiva* and *śakti*, male and female, or the two roots of the *brahmamūla* and the *padmamūla*.

Of this organic universe, Betty Heimann writes, "Nothing stands isolated. Everything has its repercussions in a wider sphere of time and space beyond its immediate present."[43] These "repercussions" or connotations mean that everything situated within the systemic web of meaning is a symbol. In Eliade's terms the symbol reveals the continuity between the human or the earthly, and the cosmic. He writes, "Religious symbols are capable of revealing a modality of the real or a structure of the World that is not evident on the level of immediate experience."[44] Symbols "break open" the interlocking meanings of the cosmos. They "reveal a multitude of structurally coherent meanings."[45] In India, the coherence of meanings revealed by symbols is like the coherence of the body or of a living plant.

What is the "fundamental structure" of the world which symbols break open? In Eliade's terms it is the Sacred, or the real. The human creation of meaning is grounded in that "ontic thirst" for the real, which for Eliade is identical with the Sacred. This is not the place to enter into a discussion of the term "Sacred," but the understanding of the term which Eliade presents is inherited, in part, from Otto, whom he explicitly cites at the outset of *The Sacred and the Profane. Das Heilige,* the Holy, presents itself in experience as the numinous, the Wholly Other. Tillich as well stands upon the ground of Otto, and in writing about symbol he speaks of its capacity to point beyond itself to the Other, to open up transcendent dimensions of reality.[46]

It has long been recognized that the dichotomy between "sacred" and "profane" is somewhat problematic in the Indian context. It is a tempting and even an apt dichotomy, because there are continual distinctions of this sort made in Hindu thought and practice. However, it is at the same time very misleading because the relevant Hindu distinctions—pure and impure; auspicious and inauspicious—overlap only partially with what is meant by sacred and profane. Without entering further into a discussion of what terms such as "sacred" or "holy" might mean in the Indian context, I think it is clear that the referent of symbols within the organic ontology of India is *not* the Holy, the Wholly Other, in the sense in which Otto and those influenced by him use this term. The referent of symbols is, rather, the Whole, or a particular lifeline in the network of the Whole. The primary symbols of this tradition which give cohesion to the multitude of secondary symbols and provide the context for their meaning and movement are organic symbols. They do not lead one beyond the life of the whole, but into it: into its very kernel, down to its very roots, out to its farthest branches, and along its intricate veins. If, as Eliade writes, "The first possible definition of the sacred is that it is the opposite of the profane,"[47] how are we to use this vocabulary profitably with regard to the Indian context we have here described? If "sacred," "holy," or "Wholly Other" does not quite fit in the sense in which Otto uses it, "profane" fits even less.

The distinction mentioned at the outset, however, between the indescribable "far shore" and "this shore" of the plenum, is a useful one in understanding the context of Indian symbolism. The primary or originary symbols of the plenum are organic and the entire world they create is "this shore." From the waters under the earth to the highest heavens of the gods—all the life that rises and falls, grows and decays, and circles from birth to birth is the life of "this shore." Indian symbols lead *into* the fullness of this life and not "over" to the "other shore." The language of the supreme Brahman applies equally to both shores. Although Brahman may be "unmanifest" and "indescribable," it is that across which the universe is woven, warp and woof.[48] It is, in the sage Uddālaka's terms, the "finest essence" which inhabits every part of the universe.[49] While one may "describe" Brahman negatively, saying *neti, neti,* "not this, not this,"[50] one must simultaneously say *asti, asti,* "it is this, it is this."

There is no reason to suppose, of course, that western understandings of symbolism should help us to understand the nature and dynamics of Indian symbolism. There is much to be done in order to generate a notion of symbol illuminative of the Indian context. Such a study might begin with "comparable" notions,

such as *pratīka, lakṣaṇa,* or *liṅga,* all of which are sometimes
translated as "symbol," and explore the dimensions of their
meanings. It might include a further analysis of the notions of
pratyakṣa and *parokṣa,* which suggest the visible and the invisi-
ble, the direct and the secret, the phenomenal and the noumenal,
the literal and the metaphorical, along the lines outlined by Coomaraswamy in his essay on *parokṣa.*[51] Such an analysis of symbol
might also take as its starting point the *alaṁkāras,* the "figures of
speech," which are elaborated in works on Indian literature,
bearing in mind that some of the most profitable symbol theory
in the West has emerged in the task of thinking about symbol in
relation to and distinction from allegory and metaphor, for example. Beginning with "figures of speech" and "figures of thought,"
one would inquire about the patterns in which language creates
new meanings in the play of multiple significations.

In the meantime, lacking such a difficult analysis, it seems
to me that Ricoeur in *Interpretation Theory* has something
significant to offer by way of a middle ground between the numinous and the structuralist understandings of symbol. On the
one hand symbols have what he calls a "semantic moment,"
which is accessible to the models of analysis that one might
bring to language.[52] Semantics, the science of the sentence, is
concerned with words, not individually, but in their larger networks of meanings. Similarly with symbols, a structuralist would
be concerned to see and interpret patterns and structures of
meaning. But according to Ricoeur, this "semantic" understanding of symbolism will not alone suffice, for, as he writes,
there is something in a symbol which "resists any linguistic,
semantic, or logical transcription,"[53] which is missed by *logos.*

He cites the symbols produced by the religious imagination as
examples of what he calls the "non-semantic moment" of a symbol. The semantic understanding of a symbol does not "explain"
its capacity to engage the human imagination. (This linking by
which a person is engaged in a pattern of meanings is an important meaning of *religio.*) In thinking about the nonsemantic moment of a symbol, Ricoeur mentions both Otto's notion of the
numinous and Eliade's notion of hierophanies by way of saying
that religious "reality" (whether one calls it "holy" or not) is not
completely culturally constructed in language; it also *presents it-*

self. And it presents itself most powerfully in the various phenomena of nature. He writes that the symbol "hesitates on the dividing line between *bios* and *logos*."[54] Symbols are not, like metaphors, capable of the free invention of the imagination, but are "bound" to the cosmos and its capacity to signify, to reveal meanings, according to its own threads of relationship. Although Ricoeur uses terms such as "sacred universe," he is concerned to see the ways in which the roots of religious symbolism are deeply embedded in *bios,* in the living organism of the cosmos itself. He writes, "Within the sacred universe there are not living creatures here and there, but life is everywhere as a sacrality, which permeates everything and which is seen in the movement of the stars, the return to life of vegetation each year, and the alternation of birth and death. It is in this sense that symbols are bound within the sacred universe: the symbols only come to language to the extent that the elements of the world themselves become transparent."[55]

Ricoeur's sense of the way in which symbols are "bound" to life, to *bios,* is especially suggestive for Indian symbolism. The system of meanings into which Indian symbols lead is *bios*—life and death and life again. They do not lead out of the world toward some transcendent "Other." Whether the symbol generates its pattern of meanings like a seed, expanding to include the whole of the cosmos, or like the sap which runs along intricate esoteric channels, it is into this life, not beyond it, that symbols move and carry the imagination.

NOTES

1. Bhagavad Gītā II.54. See, for example, Franklin Edgerton, tr., *The Bhagavad Gītā* (1944; reprint ed., New York: Harper & Row, 1964).

2. Ananda Coomaraswamy, *Yakṣas* (2 vols., 1928–31, reprint in one volume, New Delhi: Munshiram Manoharlal, 1971), part II, "Water Cosmology," pp. 13–17.

3. Michael Fishbane, "Israel and the 'Mothers,' " in this volume.

4. Paul Ricoeur, *Interpretation Theory: Discourse and the Surplus of Meaning* (Fort Worth, Texas: Texas Christian University Press, 1976).

5. Moticandra, *Kāśī kā Itihāsa* (Bombay: Hindi Granth-Ratnaker Private Limited, 1962), pp. 32–34. Charlotte Vaudeville, "Braj Lost and Found," *Indo-Iranian Journal,* 18 (1976), pp. 195–213. Anncharlott Eschmann in

A. Eschmann, H. Kulke, and G. C. Tripathi, eds., *The Cult of Jagannāth and the Regional Tradition of Orissa* (New Delhi: Manohar Publishers, 1978), chapters IV and V.

6. J. Ph. Vogel, *Indian Serpent Lore* (1926, Varanasi: Prithivi Prithivi Prakashan, 1972). Odette Viennot, *Le Culte de l'arbre dans l'Inde ancienne* (Paris: Presses Universitaires de France, Annales de Musée Guimet, 1954).

7. Coomaraswamy, *Yakṣas*, part II, pp. 13–17.

8. Betty Heimann, *Facets of Indian Thought* (London: George Allen and Unwin Ltd., 1964), chapter III, "India's Biology," pp. 37–48.

9. Mary Douglas, *Natural Symbols* (New York: Random House, Inc., 1970); Stella Kramrisch, *The Hindu Temple* (Calcutta: University of Calcutta, 1946), on the *vastupuruṣamaṇḍala*, the body-cosmos architectural diagram of the Hindu temple; Brenda Beck, "The Symbolic Merger of Body, Space, and Cosmos in Hindu Tamil Nadu," *Contributions to Indian Sociology*, vol. 10, no. 2 (1976), 213–43.

10. Betty Heimann, *Facets of Indian Thought;* Odette Viennot, *Le Culte de l'arbre dans l'Inde ancienne;* F. D. K. Bosch, *The Golden Germ* (Gravenhage: Mouton & Co., 1960); Ananda Coomaraswamy, *Yakṣas*.

11. Mircea Eliade, *Yoga: Immortality and Freedom* (Princeton: Princeton University Press, 1958), pp. 66–67.

12. See Bosch, chapter 1A, "Parvan and Makara," for an analysis of the ways in which the *makara* is transformed into a plant; Coomaraswamy, plate II.38.

13. See Bosch, plates 4 and 5; Coomaraswamy, plate II.12.

14. See Bosch, plate 32; Coomaraswamy, plates II.34 and 35.

15. See Coomaraswamy, plate I.20.

16. Stella Kramrisch, *Indian Sculpture* (Calcutta: Y.M.C.A. Publishing House, 1933), II.3 "Transubstantiation," pp. 54–89.

17. *Ibid.*, p. 55.

18. *Ibid.*, p. 56.

19. Chāndogya Upaniṣad 6.12. See Robert E. Hume, tr., *The Thirteen Principal Upaniṣads*, 2nd rev. ed. (London: Oxford University Press, 1931).

20. Hume, tr., Bṛihadāraṇyaka Upaniṣad 3.9.28.

21. Rabindranāth Tagore, *Collected Poems and Plays* (London: Macmillan & Co. Ltd., 1962), "Gītāñjali," LXIX.

22. Bṛihadāraṇyaka Upaniṣad 3.6 and 8.

23. R. C. Zaehner, tr. and ed., *Hindu Scriptures* (London: J. M. Dent & Sons Ltd., Everyman's Library, 1966).

24. Ralph T. H. Griffith, tr., *Hymns of the Atharvaveda* (1894, reprint ed., Varanasi: Chowkhamba Sanskrit Series, 1968).

25. Śatapatha Brāhmaṇa XI.1.6. See Julius Eggeling, tr., *Śatapatha Brāhmaṇa*, The Sacred Books of the East, vols. XII, XXVI, XLI, XLIII, XLIV (Oxford: The Clarendon Press, 1882–1900).

26. Hume, tr., Chāndogya Upaniṣad 3.19.

27. Mānavadharmaśāstra, chapter I. See Georg Bühler, tr., *The Laws of Manu*, The Sacred Books of the East, vol. XXV (1886, reprint ed., New York: Dover Publications Inc., 1969).

28. Aitareya Upaniṣad 1.4, my trans.

29. *Matsya Purāṇa* 167. The most accessible version of this myth in English is in Heinrich Zimmer, *Myths and Symbols in Indian Art and Civilization* (Princeton: Princeton University Press, 1946), pp. 35–53.

30. See *Matsya Purāṇa* 168–71.

31. See Coomaraswamy, *Yakṣas*, part II, pp. 57–58.

32. Bosch, part IA, "Parvan and Makara," pp. 23–33.

33. Maitri Upaniṣad 6.1–2; Chāndogya Upaniṣad 8.1.1–2.

34. Cited in Bosch, p. 67.

35. *Ibid.*

36. Zaehner, tr., Atharva Veda X.7.35.

37. See Kaṭha Upaniṣad 6.1; Maitri Upaniṣad 6.4; and Bhagavad Gītā 15.1–2.

38. Bosch, *The Golden Germ*, chapter III, "The Two Trees," pp. 65–83; Ananda Coomaraswamy, "The Inverted Tree," in Roger Lipsey, ed., *Coomaraswamy*, vol. I, *Selected Papers: Traditional Art and Symbolism* (Princeton: Princeton University Press, 1977), 376–404; Murray B. Emeneau, "The Strangling Figs in Sanskrit Literature," in *University of California Publications in Classical Philology*, vol. 13 (1949), 364–69.

39. Bosch, pp. 79–81.

40. Edgerton, tr., *The Bhagavad Gītā* 15.2.

41. *Ibid.*, 15.3.

42. Mahābhārata XIV (Anugītā-parvan), 47.12–15. Cited in Bosch, p. 67.

43. Heimann, p. 20.

44. Mircea Eliade, "Methodological Remarks on the Study of Religious Symbolism," in Mircea Eliade and Joseph M. Kitagawa, eds., *The History of Religions, Essays in Methodology* (Chicago: University of Chicago Press, 1959), p. 98.

45. *Ibid.*, p. 99.

46. See, for example, Paul Tillich, "The Meaning and Justification of Religious Symbols," in Sidney Hook, ed., *Religious Experience and Truth: A Symposium* (New York: New York University Press, 1961), pp. 3–11.

47. Mircea Eliade, *The Sacred and the Profane* (New York: Harcourt, Brace & World, 1959), p. 10.

48. Bṛhadāraṇyaka Upaniṣad 3.6 and 3.8.

49. Chāndogya Upaniṣad 6.8–15.

50. Bṛhādaraṇyaka Upaniṣad 4.4.22.

51. Ananda Coomaraswamy, "Parokṣa," in *The Transformation of Nature in Art* (1934, reprinted, New York: Dover Publications, Inc., 1956), pp. 119–38.

52. Ricoeur, *op. cit.*, pp. 54–57.

53. *Ibid.*, p. 57.

54. *Ibid.*, p. 59.

55. *Ibid.*, p. 61.

JOHN B. CARMAN

Hindu Bhakti as a Middle Way

I. Between Confrontation and Interiority

I am interested . . . in exploring the polarity, the tension, between
two centres which are to be found in different degree within all our
spiritual traditions and indeed within each one of us. This is in part a
dialogue between West and East. . . . Martin Buber's *I and Thou*
. . . gave definitive expression to one of the poles in the dialogue. . . . In the beginning is relationship . . . the relationship . . .
of I–Thou . . . there is one Thou . . . the ground of all relationship
who can never become an It. . . . In the beginning and in the end is
relationship, which can never be transcended or absorbed—even in
God. . . . There is the closest possible mystical unity between I and
Thou, but always it is a mysticism of love, which insists upon and re-
spects the *non-identity* of the other. . . . The other centre—is that
which insists on *non-duality, advaita*. . . . The emphasis is on union
rather than communion or the overcoming of separation and individuation. The norm is nothing less than identity, the return or
reabsorption of the ego into the divine. . . .[1]

Thus has John A. T. Robinson recently set forth the initial understanding for his attempt at a Christian dialogue with the Indian
religious perspective. The distinction is one that many recent

western thinkers have made, and it is rather similar with the two
poles that Peter Berger proposed as the basis for our discussion:
confrontation and interiority. Dr. Robinson readily acknowledges
what has been brought out repeatedly in these essays, that there
are many exceptions and many intermediate positions. Perhaps
the stance of Hindu bhakti is but one such "exception" alluded
to by Dr. Robinson when he says, "In one form or another the
absorption or annihilation of the 'I' in the divine Being or ultimate Reality is the *dominant* presupposition of the Hindu and
Buddhist traditions, at any rate in their abstract thought, if not
in their devotional piety."[2] If so, bhakti is a massive exception,
but within bhakti's own traditions of "abstract thought" Śankara
is not, as Dr. Robinson presents him, "the archetypal Hindu philosopher and exegete," but a misguided teacher, a "crypto-
Buddhist." I mention this, not to entertain you with an Indian
example of the sectarian name-calling with which we are all too
familiar in western history, but to emphasize at the outset that
the stance of Hindu bhakti implicitly or explicitly calls into question the very polarity that we have been using as the basis for
our discussion. More precisely, the intellectual as well as the cultic expressions of bhakti see both poles as meaningful in relation
to a common center, the divine-human bond that is bhakti. The
mysticism of love, which Dr. Robinson regards as expressing the
irreducible dualism of I-and-Thou, is generally seen as the one
center encompassing both the duality and non-duality of finite
and infinite Reality.

I have argued elsewhere[3] that the general category of "mysticism" may best be understood, not as the pole of identity or interiority, but as the spiritual effort to recognize and reconcile
both poles in human religious experience. Whether or not my
more general argument is convincing, it seems to me clear that
Hindu bhakti is such a mediating or synthetic approach. Bhakti
taken most literally means "sharing" or "participation" and both
in concept and in practice includes some notion of the all-en-
compassing unity as well as a vivid awareness of a relationship
between two distinct centers of consciousness, between two distinct but very unequal selves, since one is finite and the other is
Infinite. Most forms of bhakti seem to me clearly to fit this char-
acterization, which is not affected by the unanswerable question

of whether bhakti is more or less important in Indian religion than Śankara's Advaita or by the more speculative question of whether bhakti can be intellectually reconciled with Śankara's Advaita or stands unalterably opposed to it. It can also remain unsettled for our present purpose how close bhakti is typologically to various forms of western monotheistic religion, specifically to forms of theistic mysticism.

Since the word bhakti means "sharing," *extreme* emphasis on either "confrontation" or "interiority" would seem to be opposed to bhakti, and bhakti would be opposed to them, for in such extreme positions "sharing" is impossible. Such, indeed, seems to be empirically the case. On the other hand, less extreme emphasis on either of our poles is easily comprehended within the theory and practice of bhakti. Bhakti may thus be viewed as between the poles or encompassing them. It is in any case the path of divine-human relationship, a path with all the emotional power and all the intellectual puzzles that we might expect of a lifelong keeping in consciousness of the vivifying bond between finite beings and infinite Being.

II. *Bhakti's Relation to Advaita: Some Views from the Side of Bhakti*

There are a number of different views, both in the Hindu tradition and in modern scholarship, concerning the relation of devotional piety to the absolute monism or, more literally, "non-twoness" (*a-dvaita*) of Śankara and his followers. The western scholar of a previous generation who dealt most systematically with this question was Rudolf Otto.[4] He has touched on four interpretations of the relation of bhakti to Advaita. One is to see bhakti as the passionate protest of simple faith or theistic piety against the impersonal mysticism of Śankara's Advaita: "a struggle for a real and living God."[5]

A second interprets bhakti as the theistic foundation for the lofty flights of Śankara's higher mysticism, quite comparable to the relation of orthodox Catholic piety to Meister Eckhart's mysticism. Otto considers the theistic foundation of crucial importance for both Śankara and Eckhart, yet it is a stage that may finally be transcended. The "lower knowledge" recognized by Śankara is very close to Rāmānuja's interpretation of Vedānta,

which insists on "the personal conception of Brahman." The
lower knowledge, even though it is surpassed (*aufgehobene*) "is
nevertheless lower *knowledge* . . . to be clearly distinguished
from error in the ordinary sense of the word!"[6] So high an esti-
mate does Śankara have of this lower knowledge of the personal
Brahman that the borderline between the higher and lower
knowledge often entirely disappears.[7] But while there is "a shifting and interpenetrating relationship" between the impersonal
Brahman and the personal Lord, there is a characteristic notion
of *jñana* that is clearly distinct from the different Advaita of the
great bhakti texts. When a Śankara advaitin returns to ordinary
consciousness after the realization of identity with Brahman in
the state of samādhi, "the knowledge remains with him that
Brahman alone is, and that he is himself Brahman, but it is then
only knowledge and not knowledge in experience."[8] He does not
return to bhakti, the worship of the personal Lord. For a real
disciple of Śankara, "Bhakti or states of emotion are not a step
on the ladder to samādhi."

Bhakti, however, *is* such a means to monistic realization for
the bhakti hero of the Vishnu-Purāṇa, Prahlāda, who,

cast into the depths of the ocean by his unbelieving father on account
of his belief in Vishnu, remains firmly true to his faith, directs his
thoughts unperturbed to Vishnu in prayer, and brings Him daily his
offerings of praise. This elevation of his spirit to the Lord, this
upāsanā, passes gradually into mystical experience. . . . In this instance we see that the mystical experience arises from a determined
act of Bhakti (State 1). In State 2, the personal, beloved, trusted
Lord of ordinary theistic religion expands into the mystical All-Being,
which is the One. After He has been "seen" in such a form, the state
of union results; the objects seen consume the seer. He is Me and so I
am He. Object and subject glide into one another and he who experiences is himself the Lord of all being. In the reverse order, this mystical experience afterwards slips back into simple bhakti worship . . .
this personal intercourse is here not something lower or of less value
. . . but is equal in value to the mystical experience. . . . The characteristic of this God is that he can be interchangeably present with
the soul, either as blessed all-absorbing All, *or* as personal lover and
friend of the soul. We have here what we must call a "mysticism of
poise". . . . The religious experience of Śankara is not more "consis-

tent". . . . Prahlāda's religion is thoroughly consistent. It is by its nature "polar," but that is not inconsistent. Such a nature is rather consistent in itself when it acts in a twofold way.[9]

Otto goes on to observe that there are differentiations within
bhakti mysticism itself. The type of Prahlāda "stands nearer to
the quiet, collected Rāmānuja," whereas in Chaitanya's type,

Bhakti becomes "Prema," a fevered, glowing, Krishna-eroticism, colored throughout by love passion; and intoxication enters into the experience. In the heat of love's emotion, which breaks through the limitations of the individual in ecstasy, and seeks union with the beloved,
the state of unity is striven after. With Prahlāda it is clearly different.
On the contrary for him bhakti is the stilling of the soul before God, a
trustful, believing devotion. . . . Neither fiery Eros nor sentimental
Caritas, but complete Faith as Fiducia, a trustful, concentrated believing contemplation leads here to the loss of self, and to becoming
one with Him.[10]

The relation of these third and fourth understandings and expressions of bhakti has been seen somewhat differently by the
Hindu historian of Indian philosophy, S. N. Dasgupta. He sees
devotional mysticism developing from the self-abnegation and
self-surrender to God taught in the *Gītā* through the story of the
faithful devotee Prahlāda in the *Vishnu Purāna* and the elevation
of devotion to the supreme plane in the *Bhāgavata Purāna*, a devotion realized and illustrated in the life of Chaitanya of Bengal
(1486–1534 C.E.). The movement away from yogic suppression of
the senses to the later bhakti inclusion and redirection of sensible feelings in religious experience is indicated already in the
quest of Prahlāda.

This inmost and most deep-seated love for God . . . stirred him to
withdraw his mind from all other things and to enter into such a contemplation of God that he became absorbed in Him, his whole personality lost in an ecstatic trance unity with God. But this did not satisfy Prahlāda. He desired such a devotion to God that the very
thought of Him would bring the same sort of satisfaction that persons
ordinarily have in thinking of sense-objects. He desired not only contemplative union but longed also to taste God's love as one tastes the
pleasures of the senses.[11]

The *Bhāgavata Purāna*, Dasgupta continues, develops still further this emotion-laden devotion. Those following the path of devotion

come to experience such intense happiness that all their limbs and senses become saturated therewith and their minds swim as it were, in a lake of such supreme bliss that even the bliss of ultimate liberation loses its charm. . . . The bhakta who is filled with such a passion does not experience it merely as an undercurrent of joy which waters the depths of his own heart in his own privacy, but as a torrent that overflows the caverns of his senses. Through all his senses he realizes it as if it were a sensuous delight; with his heart and soul he feels it as a spiritual intoxication of joy. Such a person is beside himself with this love of God. He sings, laughs, dances and weeps. He is no longer a person of this world.[12]

Still different interpretations of bhakti's relation to Advaita have been given by two leading scholars of the Śrī Vaishṇava community, which follows the teachings of Śankara's philosophical adversary Rāmānuja. Both treat mysticism as the central category of religious experience, but both reject the advaitin claim to represent pure mysticism or "higher knowledge." They consider the fusion of wisdom, devotion, and service in the theistic interpretation of the Upanishads to constitute the central strand of mysticism. A. Govindāchārya of Mysore holds that the quest of mystics is to discover God dwelling in the heart ("the Heart of all hearts")[13] and believes that "the Vedic notion of the Husband or Bridegroom" furnishes "the keynote to the Indian mystic."[14] Krishna reveals God as the supremely beautiful One, and "mystic experience everywhere points to the realization of the Beautiful, and the summit of Vedāntic thought proclaims this by the term *Ānanda* [joy]."[15]

P. N. Srinivasachari of Madras, in striking contrast to S. N. Dasgupta, begins by excluding many religious phenomena and even whole religious systems that have sometimes been referred to as mystical. Mysticism is *Brahmananubhava,* the experience of Brahman. It is not limited to Hindus, but it is restricted by its definition to the soul's quest for union with God.

It is not a special mystic faculty . . . everyone can directly realize God or Brahman as the Inner Self of all beings. . . . Mysticism is a body of eternal, spiritual or religious truths which were verified by the ancient Indian ṛṣis, Christian mystics and Sufis.[16] . . . The Divine

Spirit which hides within man is made manifest and the soul sees the light realisable beyond sight.[17] . . . Mystic feeling is not an explosion from the subliminal state, as James says, but the overflow of super-conscious love into the heart of man. In moments of spiritual crisis and conversion, pangs of remorse are followed by feelings of redemptive assurance. The emotional center shifts from the mood of tranquil-mindedness or equanimity or *śāntabhāva* to that of God-intoxication or divine drunkenness (*madhurabhāva*)[18]. . . . Bhakti breaks into the spirit, melts it down and becomes an infinite longing for the Infinite. God is infinite and human love expands into the infinite love of God.[19]

For both Govindāchārya and Srinivasachari, as well as for Dasgupta, it is the theistic mysticism of both Christian and Islamic traditions that comes closest to Hindu devotional mysticism. All three of these Hindu interpreters would insist on the unity of the two forms of Hindu devotional mysticism that Rudolf Otto so sharply separates: the devotion of balance and peaceful repose (*śānta*) and the devotion of intense emotion and transmuted erotic feeling (*mādhurya bhāva* and *sṛṇgāra rasa*). The two Śrī Vaishṇava scholars would go a step further, however, in identifying this life of devotion with the correct interpretation of the Upanishads, and Srinivasachari would proceed still further in identifying Śankara's "practical Advaita" with Rāmānuja's devotion-filled understanding of the Vedānta.

III. *Distinction and Unity in Mystical Union: The Teachings of Rāmānuja*

The different Vaishṇava theologians were all steeped in the cycle of stories of Krishna, as well as of the other divine incarnations, not only in reading or recitation, but also in sculpture, drama, and temple liturgy. In view of the varied pictures within this cycle of God's relation to devotees, it is not surprising that these theologians approached both the epistemological and the ontological questions for such devotion in somewhat different ways. The Gosvāmins adapted the older theory of aesthetic categories (*rasas*) to provide a finely nuanced analysis of the range of devotional states but referred to their philosophical position as *acintyebhedābheda*—the relation of God and cosmos understood as an "unconceivable combination of distinction and unity." Vallabha, while heir to a similar tradition of Krishna-Rādhā devotion, emphasized a pure metaphysical unity (*śuddhādvaita*) devoid of any doctrine of illusion but held up an experiential dualism as its goal: the vivid anguish of the Lord's remembrance in separation is preferable to the loss of devotional consciousness in complete union.[20] Madhva and his school are the most emphatic in their affirmation of eternal distinctions between the Lord and all finite beings, as well as among those finite beings.

The community of Rāmānuja was nurtured, not only on the hymns, meditations, and stories in the Sanskrit scriptures, but also on the hymns of the Tamil poet-saints, known as the Āḷvārs. The most philosophically inclined of these, Nammāḷvar, wrote a great theological poem of more than a thousand verses, the Tiruvāymoḷi, which the later Śri Vaishnava tradition calls the Tamil Veda. The complexity of the poet's vision of God is set out in some of the opening verses:

He is not: He is. Thus it is impossible to speak of Him, Who has pierced the earth and the sky and become the inner ruler in all. He is unaffected by defects. He is in all without intermission. He is the abode of bliss. Such a person have I attained. [I.1.3]

All is He—that which is called that, this, and that between [mid-thing]. That man, this man, mid-man, that woman, this woman, mid-woman, what is that, what is this, and what is in between, those, these and things in between, good and bad, past things, present things and future—all is He. [I.1.4]

He is the material cause of all ākāśa [ether], air, fire, water and earth, pervading all this like the soul its body. He is the Shining One in all. The scriptures intimate Him to be the end of Śri [the Goddess Lakshmī], and as having contained all these elements in Himself during the period of deluge [cosmic dissolution]. [I.1.7]

He is the Inner Lord of all; whether said to be existent or non-existent, He is. Possessing both the existent and the non-existent within Him, He pervading all as self is the Total Being. Pervading all He is yet their destroyer and as such He is the eternally permanent Being. [I.1.8][21]

These verses display a monistic version of reality that at times seems close to pantheism and at times seems deliberately paradoxical. It is clearly different from the Advaita of Śankara, yet it includes familiar themes from the Upanishads as well as other

Sanskrit scriptures. Several centuries later Rāmānuja attempted
to spell out a rational synthesis between the Sanskrit and Tamil
Vedas, between the wisdom of ascetic meditation and the wisdom of fervent devotion. His theory was named by his followers
Viśishtādvaita: the nonduality of the Reality that is internally
differentiated. In this view the finite centers of consciousness
(selves) form the body or the mode of the Supreme Self just as
the physical form provides the body for each finite self. This
teaching is synthetic but intentionally nonparadoxical, and the
emphasis on the devotee's servant relationship to the Lord gives
the impression of rational balance that accords with the community's own self-understandings, but neither paradox nor passion is
altogether lacking in Rāmānuja's theistic mysticism.

The first apparent paradox to be resolved is the combination
of supremacy and accessibility in the divine nature. The access
to God's presence that neither lesser gods nor great yogins can
gain by their own powers is freely granted to those who humbly
resort to the Lord and seek refuge with Him. The righteous king
Rāma seems to provide the model for God's action in the universe: His voluntary exile from kingly rule, His heroic conquest
and destruction of Rāvana, the demon king who abducted His
faithful wife Sītā, and above all Rāma's generous forgiveness of
all those enemies who surrender and appeal for His grace. The
devotion of faithful attendants and forgiven enemies to the exemplary monarch provides a model that may seem to approximate the piety Otto calls simple faith and to differentiate it from
mysticism of any variety. Such trusting faith, however, proves
later on in Rāmānuja's tradition to contain its own complexities
and perplexities.[22] There are indeed followers who take the divine incarnation in Rāma as the major model for their devotion,
and there are some other Vaishnava groups in India organized
more exclusively around devotion to Rāma. The community of
Rāmānuja, however, has a much broader heritage and a more
complex system of devotion, one that includes all the divine descents (avatāras) of Vishnu and that is grounded in a theistic interpretation of the Brahman of the Upanishads as the personal
overlord of all lesser cosmic lords, the inner controller of each
finite being and the Supreme Self ensouling the entire cosmos.[23]

The most famous metaphysical doctrine of Rāmānuja is deservedly that of *śarīraśarīribhāva*: the self-body relationship that characterizes both the unity of finite reality with the Infinite Lord and the real distinction between them. With some important qualifications, the relation of the Supreme Self to finite selves is like that of the finite selves to their material bodies, and this relation has three characteristics: the indwelling self—whether divine or finite—is the body's ontological support (*ādhāra*), its controller (*niyantā*), and its owner (*śeshī*).[24]

What has not been so widely recognized outside of the Śrī Vaishnava tradition is that for Rāmānuja the goal of bhakti is the realization in intense feeling of what is metaphysically always true in the divine-human relationship. Each of the three characteristics of this fundamental fact needs to be personally experienced by the serious devotee. First, all finite beings are sustained by the Divine Support, but the bhakta desperately yearns for the felt presence of the Lord in order to maintain his very existence or, more paradigmatically, *her* very existence, for the soul is more "she" than "he" in relation to the Supreme Lord. Second, all creatures are under the divine control, but the devotee seeks to remain perpetually conscious that his (her) actions are not his (her) own doing: "they are not mine but Thine." It is the Lord Himself, as the Inner Controller (*Antaryāmī*), who is the active agent in the life of the devotee. Third, it is true that the whole world is the Lord's property and every creature is totally at His disposal, but the devotee is not satisfied with that metaphysical fact, and he (she) yearns to perform some service for the Lord, not as a means of attaining the goal of *moksha,* release from the imperfections of physical existence conditioned by inherited karma, but as the highest privilege to which finite beings can aspire: eternal service to the Lord and the Lord's servants. This service is personal service, at times conceived in the most personal and intimate terms as the wife's service to her husband. At the point of the devotee's union with the Lord, such intimate belonging to the Lord is metaphysically continuous with that most basic and commonplace belonging to the Lord shared in by every blade of grass.

The doctrine of grace is closely linked to the royal metaphor, but that very social metaphor itself seems to me in the traditional Indian context to contain a significant ambiguity. In much of his writing Rāmānuja follows a strong Hindu tradition for which the law of karma is basic; bhakti then becomes a higher karma, and the "good deed" of devotion, the humble service done to please the Divine Lord, is suitably rewarded by the Lord's grace or favor. Even more fundamental to Rāmānuja's own thought, however, is the concept of belonging noted above. The love of the universal Owner and Master for His creatures both precedes and stretches far beyond the insignificant service rendered by His subjects. Service is now seen as the consequence of grace instead of its cause. Both groups of Rāmānuja's followers stress the theme of divine grace, but the ambiguity in his teaching may have contributed to a widening gap in interpretation that helped split the community, the southern school stressing "grace without cause"; the northern, "grace with a pretext": i.e., a modicum of human effort to satisfy the requirements of divine justice.[25]

IV. *The Paradox of Grace and Devotion: The Ignoring or Reversing of Cosmic Hierarchy*

Such ambiguity in the fusing of two previous traditions linking divine grace and human effort does not seem to me paradoxical. There is a point in Rāmānuja's interpretation of the divine-human relation, however, where this generally balanced and rational teaching does approach paradox. It is alluded to at several points in his commentary on the *Bhagavad Gītā*, where it is not difficult to see behind the friend-to-friend and teacher-to-disciple relationship of two warriors, the mischievous and amorous play of a much younger Krishna in the fields and forests surrounding a cowherd village.

This theme is first touched on in a phrase at the end of Rāmānuja's Introduction: *āśrita-vātsalya-vivaśah*: overwhelmed with protecting and forgiving love (*vātsalya* originally denotes the eager and urgent affection that impels a cow to lick clean its newborn calf) for his dependents, i.e., those who have come for refuge. The Supreme Personal Spirit, Overlord of all lesser lords, Who has become mortal for the world's sake, Who here on a world stage is about to teach the yoga of devotion to Arjuna, is said to be "overwhelmed with love for His dependents." Rāmānuja understands the Krishna who teaches in the *Gītā* to be the Supreme Lord, Who presides over the exchange of gifts between human beings and lesser gods and Who recommends that His followers also participate in such exchange, not for personal gain, but for the holding together of the world (*lokasaṃgraha*). This God is entirely self-sufficient. He does not need the sacrificial offerings, for His every wish is satisfied and His will is ever accomplished. And yet this majestic Krishna, speaking as divine Teacher, when referring to those few who cannot sustain their souls without constant remembrance and extreme affection for Him, goes on to speak of His answering response: "unable to bear the separation."

The mutual dependence between God and His favorite devotee is put quite emphatically in the comment on *Gītā* 7.18. This immediately follows verse 17, which expresses the mutual affection between God and the single-minded devotee. In his commentary Rāmānuja refers to Prahlāda, "preeminent among the wise" and roughly quotes a verse about him from the *Vishṇu Purāṇa* (I.17.39):

"But he with his mind absorbed in Krishna, while being bitten by great serpents, did not know his body, feeling only the rapture of remembering Him."—in the same way he too is dear to Me.

The comment on verse 18 includes the following:

"I consider that the wise person [jñanī] is My very self [*ātmā*]." This means that the support for My existence is under his control. Why so? Because the wise person finds it impossible without Me to sustain His self. He take Me alone as his superlative goal. Therefore without him, I cannot sustain My self. Thus he is indeed My self.

Rāmānuja affirms the monistic thrust of this verse, but he interprets it in a somewhat surprising way, considering the *Gītā's* emphasis on God's independence or aseity, and the necessity for finite beings to acknowledge their total dependence on Him. For here Krishna, clearly speaking as God, declares His need for the love of His cherished devotees, a need so great that He cannot live without that love. Rāmānuja stands in a tradition of wise saints who know their total dependence on God, yet who precisely in their own moments of greatest need for God's presence know the corresponding need of God for their support and affirm

this paradoxical mutuality between Creator and creature, King
and subject, a mutuality so complete that the Lord can say, "He
is My self."

In his comment on *Gītā* 9.29, which affirms God's equal regard
for all beings but special relation to His devotees, Rāmānuja
seems to take a step beyond the mutual indwelling affirmed by
the text. He paraphrases Lord Krishna:

> But those who worship Me with such worship as their sole aim, with
> intense love because they cannot sustain themselves [their souls]
> without worshipping Me, whether they are born in high caste or low,
> dwell within My very self in unembarrassed content as if [*iva*] their
> qualities were equal to Mine. "I, too am in them" means: I treat them
> as if [*iva*] they were my superiors.

Here Rāmānuja asserts not only that God treats His devotees of
different castes quite equally—denying the worldly hierarchy—
but that He treats them all as superior to Himself, thus shock-
ingly reversing the cosmic or ontological hierarchy. It is true that
as a rational theologian he must add the qualifying "as if" (*iva*),
but more than a hint of paradox and mystery remains.[26]

In terms of Indian culture this paradoxical reversal may be understood as the hyperbole of the generous host, but the social
analogues for such temporary reversal of values between high
and low can only partially help to make intelligible the incomprehensible fact of this mystical experience: the union of Infinite
and finite. For Rāmānuja this union never means an identity beyond all distinction, but it does mean an incredible mutuality,
with some hints of mysterious intimacy.

In the Tamil devotional poetry of the Āḷvārs centuries before,
the whole range of devotional relationships to Vishṇu in His various incarnations is sensitively explored, sometimes with great
philosophical subtlety but without the rational theologian's need
to avoid inconsistency or seeming contradiction. The daring of
the human partner in the divine-human encounter is perhaps at
its greatest in the lover's quarrel, a motif of still earlier Tamil literature that enlivens the erotic mode in this devotional mediation, on divine-human love.

Some centuries after Rāmānuja the love of Krishna and Rādhā
is masterfully expressed by Jayadeva in the *Gitāgovinda*.[27] The

final triumph of Rādhā over Krishna in this context of love again expresses the paradoxical reversal of values in this kind of devotion. What is unthinkable is experienced as a reality of devotional experience. It is true that there are divine and human analogues that make this relationship more intelligible within Hindu culture. In the tāntric tradition the Goddess may stand alone without need of male consort or may provide the vital energy to an otherwise lifeless male deity. By a few Rādhā has been regarded as such a feminine and finally triumphant divine power (*śakti*). On the other hand Rādhā may well be understood as the paradigmatic human devotee, vastly inferior to her divine love in ontological status, but holding her own and finally triumphing over him within their mutual love. The human analogue is not confined to India (*She Stoops to Conquer*),[28] yet the expression of womanly triumph may seem even more surprising in a culture that appears to denigrate women so systematically in the social hierarchy. I would suggest that the "triumph" of Rādhā has various levels of meaning, of which the female enthrallment of the physically stronger male is not the most important one. It is the fervent love of Rādhā and the tireless devotion of Andāl (in her own Tamil poem as well as in the stories about her in the Ālvārs' hagiography) that win Krishna's heart, not simply or mainly their feminine beauty. There is an evident power in such love that is linked at a deep level of feeling with the power to bear and nurture children and, more broadly, to fill a home with well-being. All this is summed up in the crucial concept of the auspicious, of which married women are not only the sign but the clearly experienced embodiment. At least in South India, it is not simply sexual union but marriage, the ceremony establishing which is the epitome of auspiciousness, that stands for the most intimate relation between God and the devotional soul, as well as often expressing the central relation between the masculine and feminine persons in divinity. The Hindu wife is expected to be the devotee as well as the servant of her husband, whom she is to treat as a god, but at the same time she is completely necessary to her husband's ritual as well as physical fulfillment. It is woman with such ambivalent roles and with such ambiguous sacred and even ontological status who is considered in Hindu theistic mysticism to be the most appropriate human partner of the Supreme Lord, conceived as the highest male person (*purushottama* or *paramapurusha*). Both the humblest and the most exalted role of the devotee can thus reflect the same human reality in Hindu society and culture, whether the emphasis is on "beloved mistress" or "faithful wife."

It is true that Hindu devotional poetry sometimes moves back and forth between a state of relationship and a state of distinctionless identity, but except where there is strong influence from Śankara's Advaita or some comparably monistic position, the state of identity is not conceived as "higher," and often the state of relationship is explicitly preferred, sometimes in conscious opposition to the Brahmanical establishment. Yet the problem of the bhakti poet or theologian only begins with the affirmation of fundamental divine-human relationship. How can the union of the Infinite with the finite even be conceived? In personal terms, how can my relationship, as insignificant and sin-enmeshed creature, with the Source and Ruler of all being even be imagined, let alone intensely experienced? To describe this as the problem, however, is to adopt too modern and too academic a perspective. For the Hindu theist the relationship is a fact, or at least a potential fact. The problem, if we may call it that, is what it is for all mystics, how the believed truth may be personally experienced or realized.

The previous sketch has dealt with a few of the Vaishṇava devotional movements. The same general points could be illustrated from Śaiva devotion, with some shift in the emphasis. Śaivites have generally been much more tolerant of paradox; some have found in the unpredictable playfulness of Lord Śiva or the rule-shattering intervention of the Goddess the most intense experience of transcendence. It is also true that much Śaiva bhakti, like some North Indian Vaishṇava bhakti and the *nirguṇa* bhakti of the Sants, tends to a goal that appears more advaitin: a distinctionless unity in which the finite self disappears. Yet the concern with the divine-human relationships along the way are common to most forms of bhakti, as well as the wonder that such an impossible link between Infinite and finite, universe and single individuals, auspicious God and powerless man can indeed be a personally experienced reality. For most Hindu bhaktas it is axiomatic that the Supreme Lord in some sense includes all, even is all, but there is also the fervent aspiration that the Lord Who is even more than the all and the devotee who is so much less than the all may find union in love.

V. *The Open Secret and the Hidden Surprise*

No story about Rāmānuja is better known among his modern followers in South India than his shouting the secret of salvation from a temple tower, after his teacher had finally disclosed the secret to him on condition that he keep it to himself. His teacher berated him and angrily asked, "Didn't you know that the penalty for such conduct is to go to hell?" Rāmānuja cheerfully replied, "Certainly I knew, but I alone shall suffer, while all those who heard me now share your secret and will be saved!" The teacher was so moved by Rāmānuja's compassion that he embraced him and acknowledged him the leader of the community, with the divine title of "Our Lord."[29]

Modern versions of the story may stress too much Rāmānuja's democratic spirit, but certainly the story brings out a central feature of most bhakti traditions: the individual relationship of a single teacher to a single chosen disciple so characteristic of Hindu yoga has been greatly broadened into a community of many teachers and many more disciples. What is more, most members of this community are not in the conventional sense ascetics. They practice their spiritual discipline in the midst of their family life, which is to say, in the midst of normal human society. The community has its entrance requirements, but in principle they are those of single-minded devotion, not of caste, and the secret transmission of arcane interpretations has been broadened to pass on the benefit of such secret knowledge to a larger community.

In some of the other bhakti movements even sharper contrasts are drawn between the secretive tradition of a few elite masters of yoga or Vedānta and the much more broadly based communities of devotees, sustained by the freely offered grace of God. Many of the bhakti movements seem to stand with one foot in the sphere of renunciation and contemplative discipline but the other foot in the relatively popular and this-worldly sphere of temple worship. There seems often only a limited place for the hidden wisdom of yoga, which sometimes is disavowed altogether, as impossibly difficult for the very limited powers of beings in this degenerate age, too much relying on the powers of spiritual virtues and too little on the gracious love of God.

In the community of Rāmānuja, the term *rahasya* (secret) is still very much in use, referring to the interpretation of the three most significant ritual formulas invoked by members of the group. In the generations after Rāmānuja more and more of these interpretations were written down. A new genre developed: commentaries on the *rahasyas*.[30] What is striking about these "secrets," however, is that they are primarily concerned with the doctrine of grace. It was such a secret of grace that Rāmānuja is said to have disclosed.

The doctrine of grace contains a hidden surprise, a reversal of ordinary human conceptions of human action. For Rāmānuja it is most clearly disclosed in Lord Krishna's paradoxical words near the end of the *Bhagavad Gītā* (18.66):

> Abandoning all dharmas,
> Take refuge in Me alone.
> I shall rescue thee from all sins;
> Do not grieve.

For a somewhat ritualistic and moralistic community that interprets Lord Krishna's role to include the restoration of dharma, this verse might seem hard to take. But the community accepts it gratefully and lives by its assurance. Rāmānuja's notes two interpretations in his comment on the verse. The second is more conventional: "all dharmas" refer to the expiatory ceremonies, and this verse excuses devotees from a futile effort to cleanse themselves from an infinite burden of sins. The first interpretation is more radical, for "all dharmas" include not only social and ritual duties but also the paths of action leading to salvation, including the path of bhakti. Rāmānuja does not advocate that the faithful cease walking these paths, but that they recognize that it is God who is acting through them and thus affecting their salvation. His followers go even further. The discipline of bhakti is no longer to be relied upon. The simple act of surrender, long recognized as the starting point of devotion, is now held to be itself sufficient. Indeed, one school even maintains that the act of surrender as a human act does not bring salvation. It is only an acknowledgment that God Himself, at the prompting of His compassionate Divine consort, has wrought salvation of this human community. In any case, God is the means (*upāya*) as well as the goal (*upeya*) of the devotional life. The all-supporting, all-controlling, all-enveloping God is present in one's religious path at the beginning and the middle as well as the end.[31]

This may well look from the outside like one more instance of "cheap grace," and this impression may even be heightened by frequent references in the Hindu tradition to bhakti as the easy way to salvation, appropriate to the weakened intellects and defective wills of all of us enmeshed in the present evil age. Surely nothing could be more simple than abject surrender. In the Śrī Vaishṇava community this was more than an outsider's question, for the split between two parts of the community was due in part to dispute about the relation between human responsibility and divine grace.

If one looks at the behavior expected of those who have thus surrendered to God, however, we quickly discern that "surrender" (*prapatti* or *śaraṇāgati*) is not such an easy way, for the *prapanna* is supposed to perform his daily and special rituals for the welfare of the world without using the power in the ritual or one's special privilege as one beloved by the Lord. Those living in the midst of Indian culture know that the beseeching of a helpless supplicant has its own kind of psychological power. The one who has made the great surrender to God must resist the temptation to use either ritual dexterity or psychological coercion to win some small and immediate benefit from God or even such a not so small benefit as the life of loved ones stricken by disease.

> He who when alone in a deep jungle on a dark night
> With wild animals all around
> With lightning flashing and thunder crashing
> Does *not* call on the name of the Lord
> He is the truly surrendered one![32]

The secret of God's amazing compassion and utter accessibility creates a new community through its disclosure, yet somehow it remains secret, hidden in the mystery of God's love. On the human side of that mystery the easy way of abject depend-

ence becomes the hard way of utter reliance and constant devotion, living without any human support, without even the props
of morality or religion, relying solely on God's mysterious grace
and surprising love.

Other devotional movements in India made different uses and
different reinterpretations of the symbolism of yoga and of ascetic renunciation, as well as of the temple ritual, in some cases
making sharp criticism of mystical as well as popular piety, most
notably the Vīra Śaivas in South India and the Sants in the
North. The community of Rāmānuja did not become to such a
degree a popular or socially radical movement, and has appeared
in recent times to many outsiders a bastion of religious and social conservatism, dominated by rank-conscious Brahmins.

It is true that the import of the "secrets" is primarily a reinterpretation of the motivation for engaging in both ascetic and
popular religious practice, rather than the establishment of a
new ritual or a new social order. In this respect the theistic mysticism of Śrī Vaishṇavas resembles large parts of western mystical movements. Yet the radical impulse is there, and the modern
democratic interpretation of Rāmānuja contains an important
truth. Every so often the secret passed on by Brahmins and ascetics passes beyond the temple gate to the main street of Indian
society outside. Yet those who know the secret best know that it
remains concealed. This is true liturgically: one's personal guru
must whisper the sacred words into one's ear in the moment of
solemn initiation. It is also true theologically: only God can disclose and make real the divine presence in both shrine and mar-
ketplace, make real a sustaining power that enables one to stop
clinging to all other supports, both "religious" and "secular," enables one to pray for the well-being of the world but nothing for
oneself, except the privilege of eternal service to the One of incomparable power and matchless beauty.

VI. *Concluding Reflections*

A few years ago I visited the sacred hills above the town of
Tirupati, where the great temple of Śrī Venkateśvara is found,
perhaps the most popular pilgrimage site in South India. I was
startled when two boys called out to me in Telugu, "Have you
seen God?" They were asking whether we had been inside the

temple to look upon the famous image of Śrī Venkateśvara, conceived as a permanent incarnation in material form of Lord
Vishṇu. I had to explain that we were not allowed inside the
temple "to see God" because we were not Hindus, and I am sure
that my answer left them perplexed, if not incredulous. Why else
would anyone ascend the sacred mountain, if not to catch a
blessed glimpse of the Supreme Lord?

Their question took me aback because of the word they used:
devaḍu, the Telugu equivalent of the Sanskrit *deva* (cognate
with Latin *deus*). In some parts of India the ancient Vedic term
would not be used to refer to the supreme Deity or "high God"
because it denotes one of the many lower deities. Here, however,
the term can denote the Supreme Lord, the one God. What startled me was that this was the same word for God I had known
since childhood, the word used by the Telugu Christians among
whom I had lived. I should not have been surprised, for I knew
the large extent to which the Christian community in India has
borrowed from Hindu bhakti traditions in creating its own theological vocabulary. Western scholars' speculation about early
Hindu borrowings from Christianity is the obverse of the un-
doubted Christian borrowings from bhakti.

Perhaps it is this impressive range of similarities, more than
any single point in common, that leads us to recognize bhakti as a
major challenge to a simple bifurcation of "higher" religious experience into theism and mysticism. That should, however, take
us back to ask whether the joining of theism and mysticism in
pre-modern Christian experience, Protestant as well as Catholic,
Orthodox, and Eastern, is not a major deterrent to any one-sided
understanding of mysticism. This should be all the more evident
since similar forms of theistic mysticism are strongly represented
in the Jewish and Islamic traditions. The middle way of Hindu
bhakti is much better known in the monotheistic traditions of the
West than the low appreciation of mysticism by modern Protestant scholars would lead us to suspect.

Yet there are profound differences between Hindu bhakti and
the western monotheistic religions, and one of them underlies
those boys' innocent question. I was taken aback because the
Telugu Christian name for God was applied to the consecrated
image of Vishṇu in the temple, an image venerated not only as a

real presence of the universal Divine Lord, but also as a distinct
incarnation of that Lord. The name of God seemed to be applied
to an "idol."

Whether the Vaishnava "image incarnation" (arcāvatāra)
should be viewed as comparable to the "idols" against which the
Hebrew prophets inveighed is a complicated question, both
phenomenologically and theologically. Leaving that question
aside, we encounter another related issue. The end of the prologue to the Gospel of John, "No one has ever seen God"
(1:18a), seemed to clash sharply with the Hindu boys'
confidence that God was incarnate in the temple and could be
seen by every pilgrim. Hindu theistic mysticism might thus seem
to be only the intensification of a commonplace truth for every
Hindu, whereas Christian theistic mysticism appears to be the
mysterious approach to that which is beyond the reach, or even
the comprehension, of the ordinary believer in Christ. The second half of the sentence in John both diminishes and clarifies the
difference: "the only Son, who is in the bosom of the Father, he
has made him known" (1:18b). What follows in the Gospel of
John further narrows the gap between seeing and the acceptance
of revelation, yet the theme returns near the end of this gospel.
After the doubting Thomas has been told to touch the resur-
rected Jesus and has exclaimed, "My Lord and my God!" Jesus
responds, "Have you believed because you have seen me?
Blessed are those who have not seen and yet believe"
(20:28–29).

There is certainly an important difference. The Christian believes without seeing his absent Lord while the Hindu can see
the Lord incarnate in the image, both in the temple and in the
home shrine. Yet both the Christian and the Hindu place great
emphasis on remembering the visible presence of the Lord in the
past and on anticipating a spiritual seeing beyond the temporal
plane. Moreover, for the Hindu devotee, the physical vision of
the image, though a real darśana, a seeing of God, is incomplete.
Remembrance is necessary to deepen physical sight into spiritual
insight, and the deeper the insight, the keener the awareness of
the absence of the Lord and the more vivid the anticipation of
more complete union. The relation of distinction and unity is an
epistemological as well as an ontological problem for the bhakta.

Indeed, if the devotee sees the Lord, the theoretical question of their metaphysical relation is eclipsed by the joy of the divine Presence. The devotees' problem is that the omnipresent Lord of the universe, who has graciously entrusted Himself to His worshipers in His countless image incarnations, is nevertheless painfully absent from His devotees' longing sight. During this earthly existence, with only tantalizing glimpses of the Lord's presence, they must persist in their remembering and believe in the goal of their yearning.

The paradoxical dialectic of presence and absence is present in many forms of bhakti, but nowhere is it so elaborated as in the dramatic representations of the cowherd Krishna. At one extreme anyone present at the drama enjoys the "real presence" of Lord Krishna; at the other extreme the divine Rādhā herself experiences the excruciating absence of Lord Krishna. Even when the lovers are united there is the remembrance and anticipation of their separation, while conversely the remembrance and anticipation of their union make bearable the time of separation. In some incomprehensible fashion the extremes meet in the drama—for the players and for the audience. The sharing in the drama brings the divine Presence into ordinary human lives; memory and anticipation are nearly fused in the dramatic vision in spite of (or is it because of?) the absence of the Lord so keenly felt by His most intimate companions.[33]

Once again we move in our phenomenological comparison, this time finding similarity in the midst of difference. This procedure differs from Otto's in that we keep going back and forth; our summing up of the similarities and differences, and of their relative importance, remains provisional.

There is one more point to note that bears on our general notion of bhakti as a middle way. It stands not only between our modern western categories of theism and mysticism, but also between the more venerable western categories of monotheism and polytheism. Bhakti may be expressed in worship of many divine figures in India and also of revered human figures, but it is bhakti only if the figure to which one relates in devotion is linked to or expressive of the *supreme* Divine Reality. In practice this means a great plurality of immediate objects of veneration or worship, sometimes clearly arranged in a hierarchy, sometimes a matter of apparently free personal choice, as in the notion of the "favorite deity" (*iṣṭadevatā*). At the theoretical level this is clearly monotheistic, even when there is God and Goddess and sometimes Divine Son within the Godhead. Even on the level of practice, where one sometimes imitates court practice in gaining the favor of a lower official to lead one to a minister, and thence to the queen and the king, the monotheistic structure is not lost sight of, and there is a clear difference from frankly polytheistic worship, which is certainly also widespread. What does differ from most western religious notions, however, is that the goal of worship may be more important than the form of divinity addressed. Much devotional worship incorporates apparently polytheistic ritual. Not only does it relate it to a single divine center but it elevates it to the level of the ultimate religious concern, final salvation, which means in the bhakti tradition release from worldly bondage but, even more important, eternal communion with the Lord. The middle way of bhakti is one that sometimes seems to comprehend all possible forms of temple ritual and meditation practice, but it divides as well as unifies. The true bhakta may have to make difficult choices, may have to cultivate a hidden devotion unnoticed by the world, or may have publicly to be a fool for God.

I come now to the limit of phenomenological analysis, the theological limit behind the school boys' question. It is true that I was not allowed to see that particular divine image, but it is also true that I have been generously helped by Śrī Vaiṣṇavas to understand the Deity there enshrined. Because, however, the particular word for God with a capital G was in this case the same for Telugu-speaking Vaiṣṇavas and Telugu-speaking Protestant Christians, I am faced directly with a theological question. It is not enough for me to answer, "No, we Protestant Christians believe that we cannot see God in this life. We 'live by faith and not by sight.'" That would be too facile in its implied negative judgment on the Hindu bhakta's "vision of God." It would also be too provincial in its disregard of the Christian tradition's treasury of saints and martyrs, who within this earthly life not only have set their eyes firmly toward the Heavenly City, but also have been granted some glimpse of the glory to come.

This question lies beyond the scope of this essay, but not beyond the bounds of our legitimate concerns as academic students of religion. It is a question that obviously needs translation, but not evasion, as we try to move to a different level of interreligious discussion. When we arrive on some sacred mountain, armed with notebook and camera, we are accustomed to ask the questions. It is well to remember that others may ask us a question, too: "Have you seen God?"

NOTES

1. John A. T. Robinson, *Truth Is Two-Eyed* (Philadelphia: Westminster Press, 1980), p. 8.
2. *Ibid.*, p. 11.
3. In my article "Conceiving Hindu Bhakti as Theistic Mysticism," which is to appear as a chapter of the forthcoming book edited by Steven Katz, *Mysticism and Religious Tradition* (New York: Oxford University Press, 1981). I appreciate the permission to use in this article, approaching the same subject in a somewhat different context, several sections from that article.
4. Rudolf Otto, *Mysticism East and West: A Comparative Analysis of the Nature of Mysticism* (New York: The Macmillan Company, 1932). This is a translation by Bertha L. Bracey and Richenda C. Payne of *West-Östliche Mystik: Vergleich und Unterscheidung zur Wesensdeutung* (Gotha: Leopold Klotz Verlag, 1926).

Rudolf Otto, *India's Religion of Grace and Christianity Compared and Contrasted* (London: Student Christian Movement Press, 1930). This is a translation by Frank Hugh Foster of *Die Gnadenreligion Indiens und das Christentum: Vergleich und Unterscheidung* (München: C. H. Beck'sche Verlagsbuchhandlung, c. 1930).

5. *India's Religion of Grace*, p. 25; *Kampf* might be translated "battle" rather than "struggle."
6. *Mysticism East and West*, p. 153.
7. *Ibid.*, p. 154.
8. *Ibid.*, pp. 158–60.
9. *Ibid.*, pp. 160–61. "Mysticism of poise" is a translation of *balanzierende Mystik* (German text, p. 226). To convey Otto's thought in English, I should prefer "balance" to "poise," or more freely, would translate "mysticism of balanced polarity" or "bi-valent mysticism."
10. *Ibid.*, pp. 161–62.
11. S. N. Dasgupta, *Hindu Mysticism* (New York: Frederick Ungar Publishing Co., 1927), pp. 121–22.
12. *Ibid.*, pp. 125–26.
13. A. Govindāchārya, *A Metaphysique of Mysticism* (Vedically Viewed) (Mysore: published by the author, 1923), p. 1.
14. *Ibid.*, p. 3.

15. *Ibid.*, p. 7.
16. P. N. Srinivasachari, *Mystics and Mysticism* (Madras: Sri Krishna Library, 1951), p. 44.
17. *Ibid.*, pp. 47–48.
18. *Ibid.*, pp. 50–51.
19. *Ibid.*, pp. 194–96.
20. See Norvin Hein, *The Miracle Plays of Mathurā* (New Haven and London: Yale University Press, 1972).

A work on the contemporary religious drama is now being prepared by Srivatsa Goswami and John Stratton Hawley. Cf. also Dr. Hawley's unpublished Ph.D. dissertation at Harvard, *The Butter Thief* (November 1977), and the unpublished Harvard Ph.D. dissertation of Donna Marie Wulff, *Drama as a Mode of Religious Realization: The Vidagdhamādhava of Rūpa Gosvāmin* (December 1977).

21. K. C. Varadachari, *Āḷvārs of South India* (Bombay: Bharatiya Vidya Bhavan, 1970), pp. 178–79.

A. K. Ramanujan is currently preparing a verse translation of some selections from Nammāḷvar's hymns, which is to be published by Princeton University Press under the title *Hymns for the Drowning* (Āḷvār means literally "one who is immersed or drowned").

22. See the comprehensive and well-informed introduction to the post-Rāmānuja's literature of this tradition in Sanskritized Tamil by K. K. A. Venkatechari, *Srīvaiṣṇava Manipravāḷa* (Bombay: Anananthacharya Research Institute, 1978. This was his doctoral dissertation for the University of Utrecht, defended October 24, 1975).

Directly relevant to this topic is the unpublished Ph.D. dissertation for the University of Bombay by Vasudha Rajagopalan Narayanan entitled *The Srī-Vaiṣṇava understanding of bhakti and prapatti* (from the āḷvārs to Vedānta Desika), March 1978.

One succinct treatment of the subject is given in Sabapathy Kulandran, *Grace: A Comparative Study of the Doctrine in Christianity and Hinduism* (London: Luttenworth Press, 1964), pp. 170–77.

Cf. also Ch. 17, "Rāmānuja's Relation to His Successors: The Problem of the Gadyas" in John Braisted Carman, *The Theology of Rāmānuja: An Essay in Interreligious Understanding* (New Haven and London: Yale University Press, 1974).

23. Carman, *op. cit.*, pp. 65–81, 257–58.
24. *Ibid.*, pp. 124–33.
25. Compare Carman, *op. cit.*, pp. 176–79, 212–37.
26. M. R. Sampatkumaran, tr., *The Gītābhashya of Rāmānuja* (Madras: The Rangacharya Memorial Trust, 1969), pp. 210–11, 270. Cf. Carman, *op. cit.*, pp. 190–98.
27. A critical edition, scholarly introduction, and exciting verse translation has recently been done by Barbara Stoler Miller in *Love Song of the*

Dark Lord: Jayadeva's Gītāgovinda (New York: Columbia University Press, 1977).

28. The title of a play by Oliver Goldsmith (1728–74). Cf. also the verse of Alexander Pope (1699–1744):

> She who ne'er answers till a husband cools,
> Or, if she rules him, never shows she rules;
> Charms by accepting, by submitting sways,
> Yet has her humour most, when she obeys.

(*Moral Essays*, Epistle ii, To Mrs. M. Blount I, 261.) Included in *The Oxford Dictionary of Quotations*, Second Edition, Revised, 1966, p. 384.

29. Carman, *op. cit.*, pp. 39–41, drawing on the earliest prose hagiography of Rāmānuja and his predecessors by Pinbaḷahiya Perumāḷ Jīyar, *Arayirappaḍi Guruparamparāprabhāvam* (Trichi: S. Krishnasvāmī Ayyaṅgar, 1968), pp. 176–77.

30. Venkatachari, *op. cit.*, Chapter III, "Manipravāḷa Rahasyagranthas and Independent Works," pp. 95–166.

31. Cf. Carman, *op. cit.*, pp. 212–17.

32. Paddar, entry 417 in *Vārttāmālai* (Saraswati Vandāram, 1887), p. 172. This is an abbreviation of the translation of the verse by D. Dennis Hudson in his Ph.D. dissertation, *The Life and Times of H. A. Krishna Pillai* (1827–1900). (Claremont Graduate School, 1970), p. 91.

33. See note 20 above. Cf. also James N. Redington's Ph.D. dissertation, *The Meaning of Kṛṣṇa's Dance of Love According to Vallabhācārya* (University of Wisconsin, 1975).

ROBERT THURMAN

Confrontation and Interior Realization in Indo-Tibetan Buddhist Traditions

I was pleased with the conclusion of Ewert Cousins' essay that Francis's experience, while "confrontational" in character, moved toward the interior enough to require categorization in the middle somewhere, perhaps in a slot "identity-in-difference," which relates to the *bhedābheda* type in Vedānta. This leads neatly into my thinking, where the razor plane dividing the two controlling categories, "confrontation" and "interiorization," flips ninety degrees, presenting us with an immeasurable plain named "middle ground," with a signpost with arrows left and right saying "confrontation" and "interiorization"—"DISTANCES UNKNOWN!"

After all, the experiential categories "confrontation" and "interiority" and use derive quite clearly from the ontological categories "dualism" and "monism," although numerous commentators have beclouded the issue by injecting such unlikely polarities as "theism-mysticism," or "theism-monism," as if there were not numerous theistic mystics and monists, and nontheistic

dualists, both "eastern" and "western." Dualism in its extreme
form radically separates the ultimate from the relative, arguing
for an absolute lack of connection between the two, the absolute
"transcendentality" of the ultimate. Examples of such dualism
abound in Judeo-Christo-Islamic traditions in the arguments of
individuals who insist on the total "otherness" of God—His
namelessness, unsymbolizability, transcendentality, and incom-
prehensibility. Another example is Kant's epistemological dualism. Another is pristine philosophical Taoism, where the
Nameless is utterly beyond all relative effort. Still others are
rigorously dualistic Saṃkhya, late Vaiśeṣika with the full-blown
category of *abhāvatva,* and extreme Abhidharmic forms of
Hīnayāna Buddhism, which most insistently reified the "uncreated," the "totally extinct," the "blessed cessation" of what
they called "remainderless Nirvana." Examples of "monism" include the world views of animistic tribes, the many forms of
pantheism that have arisen as "heresies" throughout the history
of "western religions," the Advaita of Hinduism in its original
forms, ancient Indian Cārvāka, modern western materialism,
with its "Holy Grail" of the unified field theory, certain forms of
the Vijñānavāda or "Consciousness-Only" school of Mahāyāna
Buddhism, as well as some of the popular forms of the Lotus
Sutra schools (Tien Tai and Tendai) in East Asia.

The self-evident fact in all this, from our experiential or exper-
imental point of view, is that these two hypothetical extreme
ontologies have only existed in the minds of intellectuals. An absolute dualism by definition precludes all contact between the
two realities so divided, invalidating any pretended action of one
on the other. If God is *totally* transcendent, there can be no creation, no Word, no incarnation, etc. and no idea of "God" would
have anything at all to do with it. The "transcendent ego" would
belong to no one, the Tao would never get involved in the ten
thousand things, and Nirvana could never be attained. Similarly,
an absolute monism dictates the utmost incredulity regarding
bifurcated consciousness, so obviously illusory as not to warrant
a second thought. The most logical solution to any subjective dis-
comfort with any aspect of the pluralistic illusion would be sui-
cide, and the general seeking of comfort, an utterly utilitarian
hedonism, would be the only sensible way of spending one's
time.

Therefore, since by definition absolute dualism and absolute monism both preclude the possibility of any sort of experience of anything Real, it follows that all spiritual experience lies somewhere between sheer confrontation and total union, each one representing a unique combination of elements of both. It further follows then that intellectual interpretations of these experiences must describe them in binary language as tending toward one or the other, in the effort to turn the mind in a specific direction. And finally it becomes likely that any psychology of such experiences should refer to the two extremes of subjective cognition as aesthetic modes to be cultivated as a practitioner's stage requires.

FIGURE 1

world view	experience	exclamation
monism	interiority (i)	"I am That"
nondualism	neither i nor c	silence
	both i and c	
dualism	confrontation (c)	"He (It) is Other"

My thesis in this paper is that "Buddhism" does not predominantly lead from or to the "interiority" mode of spiritual experience nor does it lie at the other pole, but rather aims in its most advanced reaches of spiritual discipline at the nondual integration and preservation of opposites that is called "Buddhahood." Further, I argue that "western," or "theistic," religions cannot be accurately located at any supposed "confrontational" pole, as rigorous understanding of "dualism" would absolutely preclude any sort of confrontation (since the Ultimate would be by definition utterly beyond, utterly transcendent of any cognitive contact whatsoever). However, in spite of the heuristic nature of these concepts, they are useful as directional coordinates in studying specific experiences and doctrines in the comparative religious enterprise. Indeed, in such an enterprise, we should not pretend to start all over from scratch, as it were, but should consult previous attempts from within the various traditions to develop a scientific understanding and systematization for the purpose of self-discipline. It is a type of modernity chauvinism to assume that we are the first to take a self-conscious interest in the typology of spiritual experience. And the wealth of data from the philosophic writings of historical figures in the world religious traditions speaks strongly against such an assumption.

My plan is to introduce some of the basic concepts key to our discussion of this issue, follow how the traditional philosophers have dealt with them analytically, turn to some encounters between an individual and Buddhahood in the literature, and conclude with a sketch of some of the contemplative methodologies of the Tantras, the scientific disciplines dedicated to the development of exalted visionary states in the individual practitioner.

I

A major reason why the "East" has been considered so radically different from the "West" from the point of view of its ideal spiritual experiences is that in both Hinduism and Buddhism the goal is for the individual to *become* himself a Buddha, to *become* himself Brahman, whereas in the West it is a terrifying sacrilege for one to proclaim himself God, to claim to have become God, or even to have become "One" with "Him." Often the Christian and Sufi mystics were crucified or otherwise tormented for just this heresy. In Advaitavedānta, where the monistic totality of *nirguṇabrahman-paramātman* is powerfully emphasized and the world is dismissed as mere illusion, there is a radical opposition to the notion of an alienated creature utterly removed from his Creator. On the other hand, in more qualified forms of Hinduism and in all forms of Buddhist nondualism, the degree of sameness between devotee and deity is always less than total, or else is a kind of completeness wherein some form of pluralistic individualism is preserved. And in western religions, God becomes involved with his creation in a variety of ways; He breathes into mankind, He manifests his Laws to the prophets, He grants them visions, and even speaks through them, and through the mystery of grace, He takes them up close to Himself in paradise, although even in heaven a hierarchic separation seems to be maintained.

Buddhism solves this dilemma with its key strategy known as the "two-reality theory" (*satyadvayavāda*), which is central to all forms of Buddhist thought, though with a great variety in interpretation. It is basically an acknowledgment that there are two realities, an absolute and a relative, an ultimate and a conventional, a sacred and a profane, etc. These are conventional polar opposites, although in the Mahāyāna they are ultimately the same. Their precise relationship is described as "actual sameness and conceptual opposition." When this theory is applied to the definition of Buddhahood, this highest achievement is divided into two, a Body of Truth (*dharmakāya*) and a Body of Form (*rūpakāya*). The former is considered the perfection of wisdom and of a Buddha's individual concern, the latter the perfection of compassion and of a Buddha's altruistic concern.

FIGURE 2

| absolute | individual concern | wisdom | Truth Body |
| relative | altruistic concern | compassion | Form Body |

This binary way of considering Buddhahood is invoked in Maitreyanātha's famous response to the question about whether there is only one Buddha or many Buddhas.

There is no oneness of Buddhas, because of different heritages, non-uselessness, completeness, and lack of an original. Nor is there a plurality of Buddhas, because there is no differentiation in the uncontaminated realm.[1]

Vasubandhu explains in his commentary:

It is unacceptable to say there is but a single Buddha. Why? "Different heritages" refers to the fact that there is no end of living beings who have the Buddha-heritage. Hence, how can it be claimed that only one among them has become perfectly and completely enlightened, and that all the others will not? If it were so, the other Bodhisattvas' stores of merit and intuition would be useless, not leading to their perfect and complete enlightenment. . . . Further, the fulfillment of the concerns of other beings would be incomplete if there was anyone that the Buddha did not establish in his own Buddhahood; and that would be unreasonable. Also, there cannot be an original Buddha; for, without the stores of merit and intuition, Buddhahood is impossible, and the stores are impossible without the teaching of a previous Buddha. . . . On the other hand, a plurality of Buddhas is also unacceptable, for the Buddhas' Body of Truth is undifferentiated in the uncontaminated realm.[2]

This strategy also seems to resolve the confrontation-realization dichotomy, in that the Buddha-manifestations which the seeker confronts in extraordinary experiences would be Form Bodies of various sorts (their subdivisions will be given below), while the Truth Body cannot be confronted, as it is not an ordinary object, but can only be realized internally via an experience of the transcendence of subject-object dichotomy through the cultivation of transcendent wisdom (*prajñāpāramitā*). The notion of "interior" or "internal" here is of course only metaphorical and hence deceptive, since states of experience in which subject-object boundaries are dissolved admit of no interior-exterior polarity either. Or, to put it another way, the experience of the Truth Body is only via the confrontation of its ever elusive transcendentality to any sort of grasping by conventional, dichotomous cognition. An intense critical insight (*vipaśyana*) is cultivated which constantly penetrates all apparent absolutes, idolatrous symbolizations, or conceptualizations of the transcendent reality, until a "tolerance" (*kṣānti*) of the inconceivability, uncreatedness, universality, and radical transcendentality of the Truth (*Dharma*) develops in a culminatory experience known as the "spacelike-equipoised intuition," the direct realization of emptiness. This insight is advisedly termed a "tolerance" rather than a "cognition," or "consciousness," to indicate precisely that it is not any ordinary sort of subjective awareness, and is not itself seizable as any sort of objectified absolute. Thus, this is "confrontational" in that every appearance dawns in its automatic self-transcendence, and it is known as "appearance dawning as emptiness." The Form Body, at the same time, is realized subjectively as the world of suffering sentient beings appears before one in the manner of an illusion, mirage, or dream, in what is called the "aftermath dreamlike intuition," which is always coefficient with the great compassion that emanates whatever forms are appropriately liberative to whichever of those sentient beings. This is "realizational" in that the absolute emptiness which has been confronted as the final actuality of all things is realized as apparent in the forms of sentient beings who labor under the delusion of suffering and bondage; and it is known as "emptiness dawning as appearance."[3]

FIGURE 3

Truth Body	emptiness	realization	spacelike equipoise
confrontation	tolerance of transcendence		
Form Body	appearance	confrontation	dreamlike intuition
realization of liberative emanation	compassion		

This two-reality strategy is not at all "mystical" or even "mysterious," as we might expect from an "eastern" tradition, but rather quite sensible, a simple acknowledgment of the basically binary nature of language and conceptuality. It is a precise critical explication of the tension in any transcendentalist concept system between the absolutely "other" Absolute, and relative Absolutes that manifest in various ways in the relative sphere. Thus, the namelessness and essential unsymbolizability of the Judeo-Islamic "G-d" is equivalent to the absolute transcendentality and inconceivability of the Body of Truth. The elegance of the two-reality theory is that, by means of the non-duality of Truth and Form Bodies, it prevents anyone from grasping any particular manifestation of any particular Form Body and absolutizing it in an idolatrous fashion as "the One and Only." It recognizes as inherent in the nature of conceptuality that any dichotomously cognizable form is inexorably relative as the Absolute is ever elusive to all conditioned perception and conception. Therefore, just as no one individual, even after attaining Buddhahood, would assume himself to be the one and only Buddha, so it would be considered an arbitrary and idolatrous presumption to entertain certainty about the impossibility of ever attaining Buddhahood, the intrinsic sameness of Buddhahood, or its intrinsic otherness; indeed any concept of Buddhahood whatsoever would be seen as utterly fabricated. However, the conceptual elusiveness of Buddhahood by no means reduces it to a colorless nonreality, as took place in the West, when Kant first unpacked rigorously the ramifications of transcendence. Indeed, to sense the vividness of the reality of Buddhahood in the literature, we might listen again to Maitreyanātha, presenting Buddhahood as the supreme evolutionary goal of all living beings:

After countless hundreds of ordeals, after countless harvests of virtues, and after countless removals of blocks over immeasurable lengths of time, Omniscience is attained, unspoiled by the slightest obscuration; like a casket of jewels thrown open, it is celebrated as Buddhahood.[4]

II

Śākyamuni Buddha taught in India during the midmillennium crisis of dawning urbanism, pluralization, individualism, and rationalism, such as was experienced throughout the Eurasian *oikumene* from Greece to China at approximately that time. He faced a transcendentalist form of this individualism that was radically alienated from the social life of the times and strongly escapist in its yearnings for union with the cosmic whole, the world soul called *brahman* by the individualistic philosophers recorded in the early Upaniṣads. For Buddha to have taught such persons the supreme teaching of nonduality would have been unskillful and tactless, as they would have become either nihilistic or psychotic, disbelieving or overwhelmed by the Profound. Therefore, he taught first the Four Holy Truths, stressing the reality of suffering and of its escape, a dualistic universe of samsara and its opposite, Nirvana, the extinction of suffering.

The dualism taught here is truly one of the most extreme forms of that doctrine ever proposed. Nirvana is absolutely outside of the compounded world. It is uncreated, uncaused, deathless, and beyond all suffering, and yet ultimately ineffable, as no attribute can confidently be predicated of it. Unlike the ineffable of the Upaniṣadic Brahman, it cannot be said that "it is this," but only that Nirvana is absolutely "other than this" samsara, this cycle of evolution through births and deaths. It is therefore an extreme form of dualism, and hence a suitable anchor for the powerful individualism and transcendentalism that was the effective engine of the Buddhist or "śramanic" revolution in fifth-century India.

One may object here that this is no true dualism, since the transcendent here, Nirvana, is merely an annihilation, a nonexistent, an obliteration of individuality and consciousness; how then can it anchor individualism? One of the ways the Buddha defined Nirvana, even in his Hīnayāna or "Individual Vehicle"[5] teachings, was by cosmologically depicting what it is not. He developed a picture of the world by systematizing the various ideas of heavens and realms of trance current in those times. The following presents in a simplified diagram this cosmos.

FIGURE 4[6]

REALM

FORMLESS

"realm" beyond consciousness and unconsciousness (*naivasaṃjñānaivāsaṃjñāyatana*)	

"realm" of nothing whatsoever (*akiṃcanyāyatana*)	

"realm" of infinite consciousness (*vijñānānantyāyatana*)	

"realm" of infinite space (*ākāśānantyāyatana*)

PURE FORM

pure abode of immeasurable impartiality	(18 Brahma heavens) "Akanistha," "visionary," "beautiful," "carefree," "stable," "unconscious," "fruitful," "meritorious," "unclouded"

---

pure abode of immeasurable joy	"supernal beauty" "boundless beauty" "small beauty"

---

pure abode of immeasurable compassion	"clear light" "boundless light" "small light"

---

pure abode of immeasurable love	"great brahma" "chief brahma" "group brahma"

D   heaven of mastery of others'
    fantasies

E   heaven of fantastic delight

---

    heaven of joy (Tushita)

S

    heaven of Yāma

---

    heaven of the Thirty-three

I   (Indra's heaven)

---

    heaven of the four guardian kings

R

---

    titan realm, human realm of four
    continents, beasts, hungry

E   ghosts, numerous hells.

After looking carefully at the incredible variety of spiritual experiences represented on this map of a psychophysical universe, we cannot fail to be struck by the fact that Nirvana is *none* of them: neither any form of paradisal joy, nor any of the boundaryless states of brahmahood derived from the careful cultivation of the aesthetic fields of love and compassion; nor (and this is most noteworthy considering the long-standing "western" misinterpretation of Nirvana as an annihilation) is it any of the formless, immaterial states; neither an experience of infinite space nor an experience of infinite consciousness, *nor an experience of absolute nothingness,* nor even an experience beyond the polarity of consciousness and unconsciousness. A final point here is that, both in the *Mahāparinibbānasutta*[7] and in the biographical accounts of the enlightenment under the bo tree, the Buddha himself does not attain enlightenment from the highest formless realm. On both occasions he displays his contemplative virtuosity by ranging throughout all eight of the realms beyond the universe of desire, from bottom to top and back to the bottom, then again up to the Akaniṣṭha realm of the abode of impartiality, and from there to "Nirvana." This has important Buddho-

logical implications, since the pure "Buddha-lands" so important
in devotional Buddhism are cosmologically located in areas of
the Akaniṣṭha known as *Ghanavyūha,* or "Densely packed
array." But this digresses. The point to be made here is that the
dualism of samsara and Nirvana is very fundamentally transcendentalist, since all these realms and states are included in
the samsara, and Nirvana is yet something other than any of
them. In thus insisting on "Nirvana as the sole worthwhile
peace" (the fourth epitome of the Dharma), the Buddha was
implicitly criticizing any quietistic seeking of obliteration or even
spiritual boundlessness, and demanding of his students the fundamental transformation of the nature of subjective, ego-cen-
tered consciousness that is implied in the discovery of the transcendent in any form in any culture in any time.

Of course, this rigorous otherness of Nirvana did not prevent
numerous adherents of early monastic Buddhism, members of
the eighteen sects of the Individual Vehicle, from reifying Nirvana into something like a formless state, idolatrizing it into a
kind of superheaven into which they are going to escape, and
the Buddha into an emissary of that superheaven, or leader of
the rush away from samsaric misery. This type of naïve reification of the transcendent is what Nāgārjuna critiques in his famous book called *Wisdom,*[8] which in twenty-seven chapters contains the basic verses of the Central Way. The twenty-second
chapter, which we are going to consider at length, represents
Nāgārjuna's own "confrontation" with the Buddha, viewed by
him in his absolute aspect, as is conveyed by the name *Tathāgata* ("One who realizes absolute thusness"), which Nāgārjuna
uses throughout the chapter. Remember that here this is the "absolute" Buddha, the Buddha as a Body of Truth, that is under
Nāgārjuna's critical investigation.

He begins with a fivefold critique of any reified notion of the
Lord, the Transcendent One. "Aggregates" refers to matter, sen-
sations, cognitions, emotions, and consciousnesses, the five
"heaps" that constitute the psychophysical complex, though here
the "pure aggregates" are meant.

1. The Transcendent Lord is not the aggregates, nor is He other
than the aggregates. The aggregates are not in Him, nor He in them.

He does not possess the aggregates. Where then is the Transcendent Lord?

He starts off rejecting a *naïve monism,* a naïve reification of the immanence of the Body of Truth in all things, from the pure aggregates of a Buddha's Form Body down to every atom in the universe, included in the material aggregate of any sentient being. But that is not the main target here. It is rather the *naïve dualism* of the Individual Vehicle spiritualists who consider the transcendent Truth-Body-Buddha an "other" thing (the same thing as Nirvana in a sense, although this is separately rejected in the twenty-fifth chapter of the *Wisdom*). So first Nāgārjuna rejects the reified "otherness" of the Transcendent in general, then goes on to specify and rule out three forms of hypothetical relationship between a reified Transcendent and the world; that He is *in* the world, that the world is *in* Him, or that He *owns* the world. He then asks rhetorically what kind of reified "Transcendent" there could be outside of these possibilities. He does not argue extensively for these theses in this chapter, as he has already refuted intrinsic sameness and difference of "Self" and aggregates in the eighteenth chapter,[9] and he intends that the same problems would accrue to those positions with "Transcendent Lord" in place of "Self." In brief, if the Transcendent and the world were the same, intrinsically or really the same, what would be the use of the different names? And if they were intrinsically or really different, how could any positing of relationship between them be meaningful? Needless to say, relative or conventional sameness and difference are not precluded by this exclusion of absolute sameness and difference. The critique is carried out with great subtlety and exhaustiveness, but we need not follow it in all its detail.

In our context of "confrontation-realization" or "exteriority-interiority," we see that the Transcendent is rejected as either a reified oneness or a reified otherness. The next verse comes around even more closely to our dilemma of internal-external.

2. There is no aggregate-appropriating Buddha through His intrinsic reality. Not having thus intrinsic reality, how can He have any extrinsic reality?

Having refuted any absolute Transcendent Lord as having

self-sufficient, intrinsic reality status, Nāgārjuna pursues the dualist's reificatory habit even when it seems innocently to retreat into a cognitive relativism: "Well, at least the Transcendent has meaning and reality by virtue of His relation with us others." Nāgārjuna continues:

3. It is argued that what exists extrinsically through dependence is "selfless." But how is the "selfless" going to be a Transcendent Lord?

This move of Nāgārjuna is completely surprising when we consider the usual interpretation of the Mādhyamika Central Way as a dialectical relativism. We expect him at least to go along with the "orthodox" Buddhist doctrine of "selflessness," wherein emptiness and relativity are equated, and the Transcendent is presented in a critically impeccable yet religiously devalued way, as some sort of a limiting case concept. In fact there are other contexts in which Nāgārjuna himself speaks in very much that way. However, here he does not accept that the naïve realist could genuinely adopt such a view, since the reificatory habits are too ingrained to accept a purely negational Transcendent. On another even more subtle level, he insists that the relative, Form Body Buddha cannot be some denatured negative idea, but, because of the emptiness of any reified, empty selflessness, there are indeed relatively substantial Transcendent Lords! Maitreyanātha addresses the same point in his famous verse:

In pure emptiness, the Buddhas acquire the Supreme Self of selflessness, realizing the greatness of the self in the discovery of its purity.[10]

Nāgārjuna continues his critique:

4. If there is no intrinsic reality, how can there be extrinsic reality? And what is a Transcendent Lord without either intrinsic or extrinsic reality?

Thus the extreme dualist's hypostatized totally "other" Transcendent, somehow Real yet totally disconnected from all known modes of reality, is reduced to the "misuse of language" category so clearly elucidated by Wittgenstein in modern times. Nāgārjuna now turns to the problems inherent in assertions of manifestations of the Transcendent in the world, in a devastating series of verses we will pass over more quickly:

5. If there could be a Transcendent Lord without appropriating any aggregates, He should then appropriate them at once and live with their appropriation!
6. But there is no such Transcendent Lord not appropriating any aggregates. And who does not exist without their appropriation, how will He ever come to appropriate them?
7. There is nothing unappropriated, nor any appropriation at all, nor anything nonappropriative; however could there be a Transcendent Lord?
8. Not existing when sought in five ways through sameness and otherness, how is "Transcendent Lord" to be designated with reference to any sort of appropriation?

Any idolatrous sort of grasping of any sort of manifestation, including that of the historical Śākyamuni, is hereby criticized.

9. Further, appropriation itself is not found through its intrinsic reality, and, lacking intrinsic reality, how will it have extrinsic reality?

He begins here his nondualism, critiquing reification of the world as he has just critiqued reification of any manifest Transcendent. The dualist, by this time acquiescent in tolerance of inconceivability of the absolute, still perceives the relative world of appropriated and appropriation as self-evidently intrinsically objective, really right there before him. Nāgārjuna challenges this sense of security about the dualistic world, and continues:

10. Thus, appropriation and appropriator are always empty. How then can an empty "Transcendent Lord" be designated with reference to an empty [appropriation]?

Within the dualistic world, the reified notion of an immanent, absolute, yet conventional or designated, Transcendent Lord is rejected, since the naïve realism of the dualist would only attach itself to such a figure and make an idol out of it. The spiritualist follower of the Individual Vehicle is by this time reduced to despair, and is very close to veering off into the reified nothingness embraced by the nihilistic skeptic. Nāgārjuna wants to turn them back from that, so he abandons his shocking dialectic, and gives them some lessons about the language of the dilemma.

11. "All is empty" should not be asserted [dogmatically], nor should "all is not empty," "all is both [empty and not empty]," nor "all is neither [empty nor nonempty]"; each is [sometimes] maintained in the context of convention [al reality].

Absolute reality cannot be captured by any concept, neither by "emptiness" nor by "fullness." No assertions therefore should be advanced dogmatically, as any such assertion would be idolatrous, vitiating the critical transcendentality of the absolute. After all, any conceptualized idea is just as idolatrous as a golden calf, if it pretends to be adequate to a reality in principle beyond any human concept. Nevertheless, "empty" may be taught as a technique for developing the mind's criticality of any attachment to signs, wishes, objects, or ideas. "Nonempty" may be taught to turn the mind away from quietistic absorption in a reified absolute back into the dreamlike profuse richness of the world. "Both empty and nonempty" may be taught to stretch our conceptuality to cultivate a tolerance of plurality, multivocality, and complexity. And "neither empty nor nonempty" may be taught to inculcate the antidogmatic, nonauthoritarian openness to the word-transcending vivid reality of life that is so aptly greeted by the famous "silence of the Saints." These four teachings are not advanced as final solutions, yet are all part of the conceptual pharmacopoeia of remedies for the illness of clutching at life with constructs, and are used to free conventional reality as the space of living. Nāgārjuna expands on this:

12. Here in this peace, where are the four, "eternity," "impermanence," and so on? Here in this peace, where are the four, "finitude," "infinity," and so on?

13. He who is dense in his addiction to notions, discriminating about the Transcendent Lord that "He exists," or that "He does not exist," will also so discriminate about the Transcendent Lord in His Nirvana.

14. Being empty in His intrinsic reality, such thoughts just have no bearing on Him; such as that "Buddha exists beyond cessation," or that "He does not exist (there)."

15. Those who mentally fabricate the Buddha, who is beyond both fabrication and destruction, they all are ruined by their fabrications, and do not behold the Transcendent Lord.

Thus Nāgārjuna demolishes all idolatrous attempts to reify the

Transcendent, to coerce Him, as it were, with our petty concepts, to be just this or that as it suits our religious or intellectual predilections. Of course, as a radical nondualist, he cannot leave us thus critically freed only in regard to the Transcendent:

16. The intrinsic reality of the Transcendent Lord is the intrinsic reality of this life. The Transcendent Lord has no intrinsic reality, and free of intrinsic reality is this life!

Nāgārjuna emphasizes at the end of his critique of the dualist's notion of the Transcendent that is it not only Buddhahood that transcends our conceptualizing, utterly real yet quite beyond any of the fabrications we impose upon it. Life itself is also like this, always something more than we conceive it to be. And this move from the Transcendent to the Immanent, with no lapse into any sort of naïve monism, powerfully brings home the transcendentality of life itself. It always reminds me of that moment in the *Vimalakīrti Scripture*, when Śākyamuni Buddha places his toe on the ground before Śāriputra and the assembly, and the usual world becomes transformed into a pure land of jeweled arrays, whereby the assembly learns not to insist doggedly on concretizing the wretched world of narrow conventional conceptions.[11] Another famous moment in that scripture, which is perhaps emblematic of this whole section, comes in the twelfth chapter when the Buddha asks Vimalakīrti, who has just expressly come to see Him, the Buddha Tathāgata: "Noble son, when you would see the Tathāgata [the Transcendent Lord], how do you view Him?" From the point of view of our main categories of discussion, this is indeed a paradigmatic moment of "confrontation," to which the scripture has been building for many chapters, as the assembly at Vimalakīrti's house has been discussing nonduality in depth, the nature of both absolute and conventional realities, and the extraordinary conventionality of the realms of salvation, of the "inconceivable liberation" made possible by the profound intuition of the equivalence of emptiness and relativity. So here at last the assembly is in the presence of the Lord Buddha, the physical manifestation of the triumph of the Transcendent over mundane suffering and darkness. And Vimalakīrti, with his unparalleled eloquence, is asked, *by the Lord Himself,* how he views the Transcendent Lord.

Thus addressed, the Licchavi Vimalakīrti said to the Buddha, "Lord, when I would see the Tathāgata, I view Him by not seeing any Tathāgata. Why? . . . He is not involved in the three worlds, is free of the three defilements, is associated with the triple liberation, is endowed with the three knowledges, and has truly attained the unattainable. . . . He abides in ultimate reality, yet there is no relationship between it and Him. . . . He is neither here, nor there, nor anywhere else. He is neither this nor that. . . . He cannot be explained as having any meaning whatsoever. . . . He is neither truth nor falsehood; neither escape from the world nor failure to escape from the world; neither cause of involvement in the world nor not a cause of involvement in the world; He is the cessation of all theory and all practice. He is not an object. . . . No verbal teaching can express Him. Such is the body of the Tathāgata and thus should He be seen. Who sees thus, truly sees. Who sees otherwise, sees falsely."[12]

No more clear example could be found of the two-reality theory in operation. A Form Body of Śākyamuni Buddha stands before Vimalakīrti, and asks him how he views a Buddha Transcendent. Vimalakīrti replies in critical language applicable to the Truth Body of the Buddha, which after all is, while ultimately indivisible from any Form Body, conventionally superior to it. It thus becomes clear how he can say that he sees Him by not seeing Him, without resorting to a nihilistic doctrine of the meaninglessness of words. Words after all are meaningful, and reveal many aspects of reality, either ultimate or relative. It is only when they pretend to capture reality, to reduce it to their own constructions, that they become traps, rather than the useful tools they are. So the Buddhist insistence on the ineffability of reality is not at all a "nonrational," "paradoxical" approach hopelessly mysterious to us "rational" "westerners," but rather a precise and rationally derived demarcation of the limits of words. The silence of the saints is not a mysteriously referential pointing beyond, but rather a judicious restraint in knowing where to stop, in knowing where others must see for themselves, where no authority will provide genuine understanding. Pretentious silence, on the other hand, is clearly criticized in the Buddhist Scriptures, as by the goddess in the case of Śāriputra's evasive silence when asked about his own enlightenment: "Do not point to liberation by abandoning speech! Why? The holy liberation is the equality of all things."[13]

III

It is interesting that the sixth stage of Bodhisattvahood, out of ten in the layout of the path, is called "Confrontation" (*abhimukhī*), as it is the stage in which the Bodhisattva first masters the transcendent wisdom (*prajñāpāramitā*) so essential for subsequent Buddhahood. The "confrontation" involved here is that of the individual with ultimate reality, selflessness, emptiness, and so on with its innumerable synonyms. With typical irony, this "confrontation" is actually the transcendence of the subject-object mode which is connoted in our sense of "confrontation" as a subject in confrontation with an object. However, I think we have considered above fairly clearly the nature of this kind of confrontation with ultimate reality. The type of confrontation I am concerned with in this section is confrontation with Form Bodies of Buddhas, and so at the outset it is necessary to unpack the Form Body in greater detail.

The Form Body, fulfillment of a Buddha's great compassion, subdivides into a Body of Beatitude (*saṃbhogakāya*) and a Body of Incarnation (*nirmāṇakāya*). The latter again subdivides into Supreme, Living, and Artistic Incarnation Bodies (*paramajanmaśilpanirmāṇakāya*). A perfect Buddha with the thirty-two signs and the eighty marks, such as Śākyamuni, a Teacher of Men and Gods, is a Supreme Incarnation; ordinary persons, animals, or even trees and bridges, stones and streams, that perform the work of liberating and developing living beings, are Living Incarnations; and works of art that depict these liberative beings or that otherwise free living beings, as well as the artists that create them, constitute the Artistic Incarnation Body. (I am presently working on this latter category, quite neglected in traditional works, as the root of an interesting theory of aesthetics.)

FIGURE 5

Form Body   Beatific Body (Heavenly Akaniṣṭha, visible to tenth
             stage Bodhisattvas only)
             Incarnation Body   Supreme (Śākyamuni, etc.)
                                 Living Incarnations
                                 Artistic Incarnations

Śākyamuni reveals the Beatific Body of the Buddha, Amitābha, to the Queen Vaidehi, as she nears her death in conditions of the greatest misery, in the *Scripture on the Contemplation of Boundless Life:*

At that moment the Lord flashed forth a golden ray from between his eyebrows. It extended to all the innumerable worlds of the ten quarters. On its return the ray rested on the top of Buddha's head and transformed itself into a golden pillar just like Mount Sumeru, wherein the pure and admirable countries of the Buddhas in the ten quarters appeared all at once illuminated.[14]

The Buddha then begins to describe to Vaidehi, granting her the visions as he speaks, the Blissful Sukhāvati, the Western Paradise of Amitābha (Boundless Light), alias Amitāyus (Boundless Life), the Beatific Body par excellence. He has her consider the great solar orb, then a ground of purest sapphire, divided up with cords of gold and strewn with jewel rays. He then gets to the jewel trees:

Every tree is eight hundred leagues high, and all the jewel-trees have flowers and leaves consisting of the seven jewels all perfect . . . from the color of sapphire there issues a golden ray; from the color of crystal, a saffron ray; from the color of agate, a diamond ray; from the color of diamond, a ray of blue pearls. Corals, amber, and other gems are used for illuminating ornaments; nets of excellent pearls are spread over the trees, each tree is covered by seven sets of nets, and between one set and another there are five hundred millions of palaces built of excellent flowers, resembling the palace of the Lord Brahmā. . . . The leaves of the trees . . . measuring twenty-five leagues each way; every leaf has a thousand colors and a hundred different images on it, just like a heavenly garland. There are many excellent flowers which have the color of roseapple gold, and an appearance of firewheels in motion, turning between the leaves in a graceful fashion. . . . There is a magnificent ray which transforms itself into numberless jeweled canopies with banners and flags. Within these jeweled canopies the works of all the Buddhas of the billion-world galactic universe appear illuminated. . . .

He continues with the waters, the flowery throne of Amitābha, and finally the Lord himself:

The body of Buddha Amitāyus is a hundred thousand million times as bright as the color of the rose gold of the Yāma heaven, and the height of that Buddha is six hundred thousand millions of billions of leagues, innumerable as the grains of sand in the Ganges River. The white tuft of hair on his forehead curling to the right is just like five Sumeru mountains. His eyes are like the water of the four great oceans; the blue and the white are quite distinct. All the hair pores of his body issue forth brilliant rays which are also like Sumeru mountains. His halo is like a hundred million billion-world-galactic universes. In that halo are magically emanated Buddhas, to the number of a million billion trillion, innumerable as the sands of the Ganges, and each of these Buddhas is attended by countless bodhisattvas who are also magically incarnated. . . .

Clearly there is a vision of luminous immensity here that looses a flood of light into the imagination, just as the vow of Amitābha-Amitāyus would have it, that when any living being should faithfully turn his mind to Him, after His attaining unexcelled, perfect enlightenment, that being merely thereby should receive the light rays of His grace, and, at death, should be brought on a path of light from whatever realm he previously inhabited into the pure land of Sukhāvati. Unfortunately, this paradise is not a final destination, even in popular Buddhist pure land devotionalism, as the Bodhisattvas Avalokiteśvara and Mahāsthāmaprāpta manifest themselves before the lotus seats of the many beings reborn in that pure land, and teach them the Dharma of emptiness and great compassion for as many eons as it takes, and the eons pass imperceptibly in that pleasant land. The beings then attain their own stages of enlightenment and themselves voluntarily redescend back into the lower realms for the sake of other suffering beings.

There is one final point to be made here, important for our investigation. Just before Śākyamuni introduces Vaidehi to the vision of Amitāyus himself, after revealing to her the flowery throne, he states:

When you have perceived this, you should next perceive Buddha himself. Do you ask how? Every Buddha, Transcendent Lord Tathāgata, is one whose body is the body of the realm of Truth, so that He may enter into the mind of any being. Consequently, when you have perceived the Buddha, it is indeed that mind of yours that possesses those thirty-two signs of perfection and eighty minor marks of excellence. In fine, it is your mind that becomes Buddha, nay, it is your mind that is indeed Buddha. The ocean of true and universal knowledge of all the Buddhas derives its source from one's own mind and thought. . . .

It is indeed striking that in the midst of such an extraordinary set of visionary passages, in a text usually central in mass popular cults both in India and in the Far East, such a psychologically sophisticated point should be made. Amitāyus is *both* utterly real as a cosmic Beatific Body in a heavenly Buddha-land that dwarfs universes by the billions, whence emanate endless streams of clouds of Buddhas to teach in innumerable solar systems in innumerable galaxies; a vision of massive spiritual substance of an immensity that dwarfs and yet embraces this puny human realm; *and* He is also one's own mind. And this macro-micro interfusion is clearly evidenced in what is essentially a popular text (not that all its readers always paid all that much attention to it). This is truly a case of what Vimalakīrti calls the "mystery of the placing of Mount Sumeru in a mustard seed," which is what must be understood to open up to what he calls the "inconceivable liberation" of the Bodhisattvas.[15] But we will return to this in the final section.

There are many other extraordinary examples of confrontational experiences in the great ocean of the Mahāyāna Scriptures, especially in that great compendium known as the *Garland* (*Avataṃsaka*) *Scripture,* wherein the envisioning of Buddha-lands as numerous as the sands of the Ganges contained within *every subatomic particle* is developed to a consummate degree. But space does not allow pursuing these visions here. Rather, I want to shift to twelfth-century Tibet, and the biography and visionary record of the great saint known as Milarepa (1052–1135), to advance some cases of spiritual experience from times more close to our own (and of course intriguingly close to St. Francis).

Milarepa was born of sturdy peasant stock, was disinherited early on with the death of his father, and, after a rough childhood, was forced on the impetus of his mother's outrage to learn the black arts and kill a number of the offending relatives—thirty-five, as the tale is told. He subsequently repents of this evil deed, becomes terrified of ending up in one of the hells so vividly imagined in the Buddhist cosmos, and seeks out a guru of the Holy Dharma. He finds the famous Marpa the Translator, undergoes a number of horrendous ordeals in expiation of his crimes, receives the full philosophic and Tantric (esoteric yoga) teachings, and withdraws into a lifetime of intensive asceticism. He eventually is said to have attained not only sainthood (*arhatship*), i.e., wisdom and sanctity, but also perfect Buddhahood, i.e., mastery of the energies of great compassion as well. He is renowned as the only Tibetan to attain Buddhahood in one life, i.e., not starting as a miraculous incarnation of some sort, but as an ordinary sinner, and yet reaching the utmost evolutionary perfection any living being can attain. He had numerous disciples later in life, the closest of which were known as "Repas," or "Cotton-Clad Ones," by virtue of the fact that they wore only cotton cloth as garment, even in the bitter Himalayan winter, as they were adepts in the yoga of inner heat, known as Dumo. Milarepa himself was also renowned as a poet, as he always taught his students by singing them songs in the popular singsong verse of his day. Thus his teachings are sung to this day in all quarters of Tibetan society. The extraordinary richness of his own visionary experience makes it difficult to pick out any particular experience. I will therefore take some of the experiences of his main disciples Rechungpa and Gampopa, and conclude with the general account of the miraculous events surrounding his death and Nirvana, as cases for our study of Incarnation Body manifestation. For the mature Milarepa is universally conceded to have been a complete Buddha, hence possessor of all three Buddha Bodies. Especially to his own disciples, recipients of his esoteric teachings, or Vajrayāna, he was considered a manifest Lord Buddha. Therefore, in the cases that follow, we must remember that the (to us) apparently human form of Milarepa is a Buddha-Form to the disciples with whom he interacts. Hence, their visions of him are for them visions of the Transcendent Reality in its compassionate manifestations.

The first set of visions was confronted by Rechungpa, one of his chief disciples.[16] The occasion was not exactly auspicious, as Rechungpa had just returned from a trip to India, where he had collected some scriptures and treatises, and he was inflated with an immature pride that made him look down upon his naked ascetic of a Tibetan guru, namely the sometimes comical Milarepa. To cure him of this dangerous pride, Milarepa delays him on the path by showing a vision of an illusory herd of goats, magically multiplying and frolicking in a field, and then proceeds to burn the treasured books, humming merrily the while (reminiscent of Zen shock tactics). When Rechungpa returns, he becomes furious, an extremely dangerous state to be in with regard to one's Buddha-Guru in an esoteric tradition.

". . . I am leaving for another country now." Saying this, Rechungpa became hostile and disdainful to the Jetsun out of his bad faith toward him. Milarepa then said, "My son Rechungpa, you do not have to lose all your faith in me. All this should be blamed on your dalliance. If you want to be amused, I can entertain you. Now watch!"

Instantaneously, this wondrous vision took form: Upon Milarepa's head the translator Marpa appeared clearly as Vajradhara Buddha, sitting upon the sun and moon lotus seat of gems. Encircling him were the Gurus of the Transmission. To the right and left of Milarepa's eyes and ears shone two suns and moons. From his nostrils streamed rays of light of five different colors like silk threads, and from his eyebrows shone a radiant light. His tongue became a small eight-petaled lotus seat with a sun and a moon orb above it, from which sparkled brilliant and extremely fine letters—vowels and consonants—as if written by a single split hair. From his heart rayed forth other beams of light, which then turned into numerous small birds. . . .

Milarepa then sings a song of teaching in which he interprets on the spot these emanations, basically revealing himself as containing the quintessence of all Buddhas, after all the source of the books Rechungpa is so worried about.

> Hearken to me, my son Rechungpa!
> Above my head,
> Upon the sun moon orb of the Lion Throne
> Sits my gracious Guru Marpa,
> Divine embodiment of Buddha Vajradhara.
>
> Round him like a string of jewels
> Are the Gurus of the Lineage.
> If you behold them with faithful eyes
> You will be blessed by the rain of grace,
> And fulfilled will be your wishes.
> Interesting it may be to watch the play of goats,
> But how can it compare to *this* wondrous game?

Rechungpa, listen to me for a moment!
On the tips of my ears
Shine sun and moon, radiant with rainbows.
This reveals the union of wisdom and technique,
This proves my steadfast illumination.
Amazing it may be to watch the play of goats,
But how can it compare to this wondrous game?

Rechungpa, listen to me for a moment!
The five-colored rays from my nostrils,
Streaming like jeweled threads,
Are the essence of sound, a marvel.
This shows my mastery of *prāṇa* (breath)
Through the Vajra-murmuring yoga.
This proves that I have entered
The central channel of my vital force.
Amazing it may be to watch the play of goats,
But how can it compare to this wondrous game?

Rechungpa, listen to me for a moment!
At the midpoint between my eyes
Appears the good sign of the radiant hair tuft;
This shows the essence of pure form,
This proves the blessed radiance of Buddha-compassion!
Amazing it may be to watch the play of goats,
But how can it compare to this wondrous game?

Rechungpa, listen to me for a moment!
A red lotus with eight petals opens in my mouth,
Adorned with a garland of consonants and vowels.
They are the symbols of all Vajra teachings—
That which is without end or limitation.
Beholding them with reverent eyes,
You will realize that all Dharmas are your speech.
Amazing it may be to watch the play of goats,
But how can it compare to this wondrous game?

Rechungpa, listen to me for a moment!
From the center of my heart stream
Glowing beams of light.
This shows the immutability of the Three Bodies,
This shows the unity of emptiness and compassion.
Amazing it may be to watch the play of goats,
But how can it compare to this wondrous game?

Amazing as it may seem, this extraordinary sight has little effect on Rechungpa at first, so knotted up is he in pride and anger. Mila has to show still further wonders, and finally fly off into the sky, before Rechungpa comes to his senses, feels remorse at his obstinacy, and flings himself off a cliff, praying to meet his guru again in another life. Luckily, he is miraculously borne up by Mila on the way down, who is perched in triplicate in a niche on the cliff face!

Mila's other major disciple, the founder of the Kagyu Order, was Gampopa. He has a series of experiences that are interpreted by Mila in an intriguing way, giving us a sense of the yogic science underlying the Indo-Tibetan tradition of the time. Gampopa has received the main teachings and initiations from Mila and has gone on to meditate in solitude, as was the practice of the Repas.[17]

He continued to meditate thus for seven successive days, heat and blissfulness arising effortlessly. Then, he saw the Five Buddhas in the five directions. In commenting on this, Milarepa said, "This experience is like a man pressing his eyes and seeing two moons in front of him . . . only due to your having controlled the five winds. It is neither good nor bad."

After three more months of meditation . . .

One morning at daybreak, he was overcome by a feeling that all the vast billion-world galactic universe was spinning around like a turning wheel. He vomited many times, and fell to the ground in a faint which lasted a long time. . . . Milarepa commented, "This was because the drop in the great bliss wheel in the brain is increasing. It is neither good nor bad. Just continue with your meditation." . . . Again, one evening, he saw the Black Spot Hell. . . . His upper chest became congested, and a strong current of heart-wind arose. . . . Milarepa commented, "This was because your meditation belt is too short and binds your channels too tightly, so loosen it. This experience was caused by a constriction of the upgoing winds. It is neither good nor bad. Keep on with your meditation."

Gampopa continued in such a sequence, seeing the gods of the desire realm and experiencing his own death, then getting fits of uncontrollable shakes and trembles, then seeing internally eclipses of sun and moon, then directly meeting the *yidam* or "tu-

telary" seraphic form of Buddha known as the red Hevajra (a
male-female deity with twelve arms and six heads, etc.), meeting
the terrific Buddha-Form known as Cakrasaṃvara, in the form of
a male-female skeletal couple. Each time, Milarepa gave him
some specific physiological interpretation and some practical instructions and sent him back to meditation. Then,

One night he felt that his body had become as vast as the sky.
From the top of his head to the tips of his toes, his whole body, including all the limbs, was full of sentient beings, most of them drinking milk. Some were drawing milk from the stars and drinking it. He
also heard a roaring noise like that of a great storm, but knew not
from whence it came. . . . The Jetsun explained, "This was because
the evolutionary winds have driven all the drops into the hundreds of
thousands of channels throughout your entire body. Now these evolutionary winds have become transformed into wisdom winds."
Whereupon Milarepa imparted to him the supreme Dumo instruction
and set him to practicing.

Gampopa has several more visions and then completes his attainment with an extraordinary dream of himself in a mage's costume, a remarkable costume quite un-Tibetan in style, and totally out of keeping with his monastic habit, with green boots, a
silken hat with an eagle crest, a white silk robe adorned with
pearls and golden threads, a magic staff encrusted with precious
stones, and so forth. Milarepa interprets this most beautifully,
and then cautions him not to take dreams too seriously, then
sends him off to found the order and purify Tibet.

Before passing on to the concluding sequence of the Milarepa
story, note the alternation in Gampopa's experience between internal experiences of the universe in his body, the gods within
him, the sun and moon setting within him, and confrontational
experiences of the Buddha Hevajra, Cakrasaṃvara, and so forth,
different ones at different stages, each corresponding to specific
stages of growth of his subtle yogic body, as expertly guided by
Mila.

The Jetsun Mila's Nirvana was extremely spectacular, if somewhat operatic, due to the fact that he kept lying down on the
pyre and going inert, and after a while would again jump up and
deliver another last admonition, when the disciples' pettinesses,
bickering over the relics, and so on would provoke his return

from the between state. Even after being cremated, he reappears inside a crystal stupa borne by *dakinis* (a kind of female angel; some are worldly, some "Buddhine") in a six-inch-tall body, and sings another long song of instruction! We do not have space to capture the profusion of all these events, so let us content ourselves with witnessing the cremation itself, which is vividly described:

> ". . . Lama, yidam, and dakinis, three united in one—
> Invoke them!
> Perfect view, contemplation, and practice,
> Three united in one—master them!
> This life, the next, and the between,
> Three united in one—Unify them!
> This is my final instruction and very last will.
> O Rechung, there is nothing more to say.
> My son, devote yourself to this instruction!"[18]

Having thus spoken, Jetsun dissolved himself into the all-embracing emptiness. The funeral pyre was instantly transformed into a celestial mansion, square in shape, having four entrances with ornate porticos. Above it gleamed a rainbow and a canopy of light. The parapet of the roof was surmounted by parasols, banners, and other ornamental offerings. The flame at the base took the form of an eight-petaled lotus blossom, the curling tips of the fire unfolded into the eight lucky emblems and the seven royal insignia. Even the sparks took the form of goddesses bearing many offerings. The chants of worship and the crackling of the dazzling fire sounded like the melodious tones of various musical instruments, such as violins, flutes, and tambourines. The smoke permeated everything with the fragrance of perfume and, in the sky above the funeral pyre, young gods and goddesses poured a stream of nectar from the vases they held, and offered abundant delights for the five senses. The Lamas and the venerable lay people were filled with joy. All . . . saw the funeral pyre in the form of a resplendent celestial mansion, while the corpse itself was seen variously as Hevajra, Chakrasamvara, Guhyasamāja, or Vajravarāhi. Then the *dakinis* sang with one voice . . .

> (After rephrasing the vision in verse)
> . . . Innumerable *dakinis* of enchanting beauty
>   carry away the bone relics from the pyre,
> Astonished that the Master's body is being cremated,
>   even after being rendered formless, without residuum.

> In the expanse of the Lama's Truth Body, gathers the
>   cloud of his Beatific Body through his resolute
>   will and compassion,
> Producing actions of the Incarnation Body
>   like an unceasing rain of flowers,
> He thereby brings the crop of seekers to fruition.
> The Truth Realm, ultimate nature of all things, is
>   empty, unconditioned, and devoid of becoming.
> The emptiness is free of coming to be and passing away.
> Even conditioned arising and dissolution are empty
>   in their intrinsic nature.
> So cast away your doubts and misgivings.

During the following night, Rechungpa dreams that the *dakinis* take away all Mila's relics without remainder, and he laments bitterly when he awakens, invoking his guru to leave them some memorial.

Rechung thus invoked his Master by singing tearfully in a mournful tone. Thereupon the chief *dakini* cast from her hand a sacred object, as large as a hen's egg, which projected a stream of light in five colors and descended toward the cremation cell. All the chief disciples stretched out their hands, each claiming it for himself. Then the object ascended again and was absorbed into the light which the chief *dakini* was holding. The light then split in two, one part becoming a lion throne with a lotus cushion surmounted by moon and sun. A crystal stupa took shape from the other part of the light and came to rest upon the throne. Lights in five colors began to shine forth from the stupa. The stupa was one foot high, and was surrounded by the Thousand and Two Buddhas. Its four terraces were occupied by resplendent yidams of the four classes of Tantra in their natural order. Seated inside its spherical chamber was the form of Milarepa, about six inches in height.

This stupa is then carried away by the *dakinis* to the eastern paradise of Akshobhya, known as Abhirati, and nothing is left behind on the earth, in spite of the disciples' pleas. The sequence continues with quite a few more admonitions and visions and a humorous episode at the end where they find Mila's "buried treasure," which consists of a lump of sugar and a square of cotton cloth, and a raucous little note from the Master that gives them all a good laugh. But the above will suffice to give us something to imagine in the way of confrontational spiritual experiences, this time on the part of a large crowd of the faithful.

IV

I speculated above that any psychology of spiritual experience could be expected to refer to the two extremes of subjective cognition—the sense of total otherness of an object and the sense of total oneness with an object—as aesthetic modes to be cultivated as a practitioner's stage requires. In fact, when we look at the systematic methodology of the cultivation of spiritual experience in Buddhism, known as Tantra, classified variously as Mantrayāna, Tantrayāna, or Vajrayāna, we find that many of the most important distinctions can be elucidated conveniently by applying our controlling concepts. To be specific, we can examine (1) the basic distinction of Tantra from Sutra sections of the Mahāyāna as presenting an "effect vehicle," as opposed to a "cause vehicle"; (2) the stratification of the four sections of the Tantra according to the degree of externality/internality of the practitioner's sense of the Deity; (3) the distinction in Unexcelled Yoga Tantra between "creation stage" and "perfection stage" practices; (4) perhaps most strikingly, the distinction in "creation stage" between "confrontative creation" (Tib. *mdun bskyed*) and "self-creation" (Tib. *bdag bskyed*); and finally (5) the distinction in perfection-stage practice between "symbolic yoga" and "signless yoga." I will not be able to delve too deeply into each of these categories, but will only touch on them briefly to indicate their presence and open avenues for further discussion and research.

(1)

Tantra as the traditionally esoteric spiritual methodology of Mahāyāna Buddhism is not to be considered a separate teaching that in any way contradicts or supersedes ordinary Mahāyāna. Rather it is the elucidation of elements tacitly present in the ordinary path for the sake of gifted and advanced practitioners. The degree of esotericism involved has more to do with prevailing social conditions in an era, i.e., size of educated classes, liberality of political authorities, etc., than it does with anything intrinsically secret. The Tantra vehicle is presented as an "effect vehicle," in that it begins at the effect desired, starts at the goal, as it were, namely Buddhahood. In this sense Ch'an/Zen, Hua Yen, and T'ien/T'ai as well as the more radical forms of Pure Land Buddhism can be classified as Tantric, in that they also employ a strategy of starting at the goal, which technique is actually made explicit by Fa Tsang, among others. In another, more subtle sense, all Buddhism is Tantric in essence, by teaching the doctrine of "selflessness," from the very beginning, but this question takes us too far afield. Suffice it to say for the moment that Tantra begins with the consecration or anointment (*abhiśekha*) of the practitioner at the plane of perfect enlightenment, in a *maṇḍala* or magical, ritual construction of the sacred space of the Pure Land realms in earthly microcosm, in the imaginative, aesthetic reconstruction of the universe as perfect and blissful, and in the divine confidence about himself as perfected in wisdom and compassion, i.e., sensitive and responsive to the needs of all sentient beings in all universes without limit and without termination. This practice is made possible by a preliminary realization of emptiness as the ultimate lack of intrinsic objectivity, substantiality, and identifiability of all aspects of the relative world, but it significantly goes beyond this realization in its program of aesthetic re-creation of the universe as motivated by the compassionate drive that all living beings be free of suffering and possessed of happiness. The new technique is clearly expressed by the following quote from the *Vajrapañjara Tantra*, made famous by the great scholar and mystic, Tsong Khapa (1357–1419) of Tibet:

> If emptiness were the [only] technique,
>   one would never gain Buddhahood.
> An effect is never dissimilar [in kind] from
>   its cause, so emptiness is not the technique.
> The Victors teach emptiness to remove "self-habits,"
>   both from self-view-seekers and from viewless cynics.
> Thus, "mandala and environment" integrate the technique
>   of bliss; through the yoga of Buddha-pride,
>   Buddhahood will not be far away.
> A Teacher has thirty-two good signs and is Lord of
>   the eighty auspicious marks.
> Thus, the Technique is to take on the goal, which
>   is the Teacher's Form itself.[19]

Thus, the Tantra involves the "creative meditation" of aesthetic re-envisioning of the universe, the harnessing of the imagination to the task of creating a pure Buddha-land, a realm such as that of Sukhāvati which is ideal for the most rapid and efficacious maturation of living beings into higher stages of wisdom and compassion, always indivisible. The new component is the transmutation of compassion of the wishful stage into compassion of the effectual stage. That is, compassion is empathetic sensitivity to the sufferings of others and the powerful wish to remove that suffering and take it upon oneself if need be. Finally to be effectual, therefore, it has to develop a technique, an ability actually to carry out that wish. This is represented in the case of the Pure Land teaching by the cosmic teaching capacities of the land itself, presented as evolving out of the vows of Dharmākara Bodhisattva made prior to his becoming the Buddha Amitābha. And the process of the realization is accelerated in the Tantra by the practitioner's imaginative, artistic revisualization of the universe as a Pure Land, in order to generate great bliss (mahāsukha) and emanate it to all sentient beings. It is much as an artist sees hidden beauties in the world and communicates his vision to others through his creations; only here the medium is imagination, which the Buddhist cosmology, of course, considers ultimately physically effective as well. This new technique can be presented schematically as follows:

FIGURE 6

ultimate reality	emptiness yoga	wisdom	Truth Body
	and		
relative reality	cause vehicle	transcendence yoga	
compassion	countless lives	Form Body	
	or		
relative reality	effect vehicle	Deity yoga	compassion
effectual as great bliss	one life	Form Body	

main substitutions

cause	effect
transcendence yoga	Deity yoga
(goal is beyond)	(goal is here within)
compassion	bliss
(receptive from others)	(emanative to others)
long evolution	immediate realization

It is to be stressed here that the new technique can only be employed by those who have cultivated their critical wisdom through emptiness yoga to the point where their sense of the "massive facticity" of the "intrinsically objective" world, either material or spiritual, has been overcome, and where they understand the constructedness of all realms of appearance. This then both enables them to engage in the imaginative reconstruction of an aesthetic universe and protects them from becoming psychotically attached to the newly constructed "pure" universe. So, the esotericness of the technique is merely to not distract those entrenched in various forms of naïve realism from their primary task to develop their insight of critical wisdom.

Finally, we note that the basic Mahāyāna practitioner operates on the basis of the perception of his goal as extremely remote and "other" than himself, although the awareness of the dynamism of the Buddhas' compassion serves to bridge the gulf between himself and Buddhahood, which gulf is of course radically unmitigated in the Hinayana total separation of Nirvana from samsara. When he gets to the point where he will not reify immanence into a naïvely realistic monism, he enters into the sacred space of consecrational anointment, undergoes a radical "paradigm shift," and thenceforward operates on the basis of a cultivated perception of his goal as "within" himself, as realized in body, speech, and mind, in the here and now, although such a practitioner should be at a stage of psychological flexibility where he is capable of shifting paradigms further to cope with different conventional settings. Thus, the new Buddha-land, Buddha-Form, and even Buddha-confidence are simultaneously perceived as utter emptiness, just as are the old impure planet, frail human form, and human humility. This new path is thus conducted within the indivisibility of emptiness and appearance that was previously mentioned.

(2)

Of course, naïve realism is not that easily overcome, and there is a gradual process of critically alleviating its conceptual iron grip over our perceptions. Therefore, there are different classes of Tantras that introduce the creative meditational technique to practitioners who are differently prepared to confront the ultimate reality—at differing distances, so to speak. Thus the four

main sets of Tantras are called, respectively in order of advanced-
ness, Action (*kriya*), Performance (*caryā*), Yoga, and Unexcelled Yoga (*anuttarayoga*) Tantras. For our purposes the criterion of classification is fascinating, in that it is said that the Action
Tantras are taught for those who perceive external reality with
the greatest degree of massive facticity or objectivity, and hence
must look upon the Deity-forms as external to himself. The ultimate reality here is symbolized as a goddess, Transcendent Wisdom (Prajñāpāramitā), the Mother of All Buddhas, and here she
is considered as a consort, the practitioner identifying himself as
the Father, that is, the Buddha as diamond compassion. Thus, in
the Action Tantras, the symbol of the degree of otherness or ex-
ternality is that of a lover's gaze, the longing look of one to the
other without actual touching.

Next, the Performance Tantras are taught for those who are
aware of a balance between external objectivity and internal
constructivity, and hence can see themselves in the other and
vice versa to some degree. The symbol here is that of lovers who
gaze at each other longingly and also laugh joyously together.

The Yoga Tantras are taught primarily for those who are in
the stage of having discovered the staggering power of the mind
in constructing external reality and hence are, in a sense, overly
preoccupied with the "internality" of all things, considering everything as somehow in the mind, who have, in a sense, trans-
ferred naïve realism to an internal mentalistic realm of ideational
forms. These persons see the Deity as within their own mind,
and the symbol of their attitude is that of lovers holding hands.

Fourthly, the Unexcelled Yoga Tantras are taught for what is
called the jewellike practitioner who reifies neither internal nor
external, who has understood the utter emptiness and hence
sheer conventionality of all forms of relative or superficial reality, and who therefore has the imaginative vividness as well as
psychological flexibility to consider the Deity as both external
and internal; who, without aesthetically emasculating the mas-
siveness and vividness of absolute otherness and transcendentality of a Buddha-Body such as the Beatific Body of
Amitābha, ninety million billion trillion leagues in height and so
forth, can contemplate that Amitābha as contained within a tiny
mustard seed on the tip of his nose, or can contemplate the

Sukhāvati universe itself as present within each atom of this Sahā universe, and so forth. The symbol here is that of full sexual embrace, an intimate union of opposites, male and female, wisdom and compassion/technique, absolute and relative, although note that this is the integration of "nonduality" wherein the duality is preserved in blissful contact, and is not the mere opposite of duality, namely unity, where the poles have been lost entirely. Intriguing here is the fact that the progression of Tantra classes does not simply go from external to internal, or other to same, but goes beyond this initial trend represented in the first three, and in the fourth and highest Unexcelled Yoga class returns to a transcendence of both, having, as it were, encompassed in previous experience both the outer and the inner poles. These four classes can be schematized as follows:

FIGURE 7

Action	external	a loving look	
Performance	outer/inner/balance		a joyous laugh
Yoga	internal	lovers holding hands	
Unexcelled Yoga	nondual	lovers' full union	

(3)

Within the Unexcelled Yoga Tantras, there is a division of practice into two stages, known as the Creation Stage (*utpannakrama*) and Perfection Stage (*niṣpannakrama*). This division is extremely complex with many points of subtle controversy within the voluminous literature developed over the fifteen hundred years of the literary tradition, so I am not going to go into it in detail. In the very briefest compass, then, the stages are divided, as their names indicate, according to whether the concern is to construct a reality, either of an external Deity or of the self or of an aesthetic sphere of bliss or beauty, or to move beyond all such constructions in transcendent experiences in which Death, the Between (state between death and rebirth), and Birth (or at least one of the things we mean by "life") are re-experienced and mastered as the Bodies of Truth, Beatitude, and Incarnation, in that order. Of course, there are elements of "creation" or construction in the perfection stage, and elements of transcendent experience in the creation stage; it is very complex.

But the main distinction is as above, and it is in the former stage that both "confrontation" and "internalized realization" categories are involved most strikingly; although, on the other hand, the perfection stage cannot be said not to encompass both categories as well, transposed onto a plane of ultimate subtlety.

(4)

Within the creation stage, the variety of contemplative and/or ritual moments includes centrally two processes, known respectively as "creation of self" and "creation in front." The former is cultivated with a view to simulating experientially the aesthetic outlook of the Deity, how a Buddha looks out upon the world of sentient beings with love and compassion. The latter is cultivated with a view to generating experientially a deep sense of the proximity of the Deity, a sense of His or Her immanence and presence as extender of grace and recipient of devotion. There are some contemplative practices wherein the "creation in front" precedes a sequence of absorption or fusion between self and Deity, and there are some contemplative practices wherein the self-creation precedes a sequence of emanation of Form Bodies of the Deity in order to receive the offerings and worship of sentient beings. So, contrary to what we might expect, i.e., that one or the other might be conceived as a final state, we find that there is an alternation between the two as aesthetic modes of spiritual experience. This is perhaps made possible by the fact that the only final state in the light of the two realities is the transcendent absolute of emptiness, total death transmuted into the Body of Truth, and therefore all fusions and fissions are experienced as part of the play of life, in these exalted stages as the play of the rainbow body of great bliss emerging for the sake of sentient beings out of compassion for them. Here I am going to quote briefly from a visualization text, showing briefly the two sequences. First, the self-creation of a Buddha-Form of the female Buddha, Tārā, the "Savioress":

OM SVABHĀVA-ŚUDDHĀḤ SARVA-DHARMĀḤ SVABHĀVA-ŚUDDHO 'HAM! (A *mantra* evoking the fact that "all things are intrinsically pure, as I am naturally pure!") In the realm of emptiness is an A in my heart, and from that a moon, above which is a green TĀM. It fills my body with its light, cleansing my karmically ripened transience together with my sins and obscurations. I myself become the body of Tārā: her body colored green, having one head and two hands, the right in the gift bestowing gesture and the left holding to her breast the stalk of a blue lotus flower whose petals blossom next to her ear. She sits in the half-crossed posture of royal ease, her right foot extended and her left drawn up; she is adorned with silken garments and ornaments of precious gems. Light radiates forth from the TĀM placed on the moon in my heart and invites the hosts of deities who are the holy noble Tārā's knowledge being.

VAJRASAMĀJAḤ! JĀḤ HŪM BAM HOḤ!

The knowledge being dissolves indivisibly into me, and I am marked on the top of my head with a white OM, on my throat with a red ĀḤ, and on my heart with a blue HŪM.[20]

Thus, one contemplates oneself in the vivid appearance of the female Buddha, green Tārā, one appropriates the divine pride of radiating light and love outward to all sentient beings, one invites the spiritual essence of an externally objective Tārā to come and merge with oneself as her Form Body, and so forth. This sequence can be used in a ritual setting, where one goes on to act in a ritual function, blessing an assembly, etc., as consubstantial with the Deity Tārā. Or it can be used in a contemplative setting, where one proceeds into a sequence of yogic transformations involving experiences of dissolving, transmigrating, being reborn, and so on, all from within the psychologically totally concrete state of *being* the Goddess Tārā herself, going through these experiences out of compassion for sentient beings.

The "creation in front" is mainly for a ritual, not so much a contemplative, application. In the text from which I am quoting here, the confrontative creation follows the self-creation, which precedes as a technique for empowering the succeeding ritual with the sense of confidence and grace derived from imaginative enactment of consubstantiation with Tārā herself, which is of course even more powerful when the practitioner has himself previously cultivated the sequence contemplatively, and thus has actually experienced himself *as* the Goddess, in body, in speech, as well as in mind. The text proceeds:

OM ŚŪNYATĀ-JÑĀNA-VAJRA-SVABHĀVĀTMAKO 'HAM! (mantra evoking that "I am the self whose nature is the diamond of the direct intuition of emptiness!") From the realm of emptiness is PĀM, from which comes a multi-colored lotus; in the center thereof is A, from which comes the orb of a moon; above that is a green TĀṂ, from which comes a lotus flower marked with TĀṂ, which transforms into the holy blessed Tārā, her body green in color, bedecked with various precious ornaments, having one face and two hands, with her right in the gift-bestowing gesture fulfilling the wishes of all beings, with her left holding a full lotus flower, wearing clothes of beautiful silk, adorned on her crest by the Victor Amoghasiddhi, sitting in a posture of royal ease upon a lotus of sun and moon, in the midst of countless Buddhas and Bodhisattvas. Around her on twenty lotus petals, going counter-clockwise from the front: The Tārā swift and heroic, who destroys hindering demons and injuries, her body red in color, holding the red flask that subjugates. The Tārā white as the autumn moon, who defeats diseases and evil spirits, holding the white flask that pacifies. . . . [There are a total of twenty of these other forms of Tārā, each is described and visualized.] On all their foreheads is OṂ, on their throats ĀḤ, on their hearts HŪṂ; from those light radiates forth, whereupon from Potala come the holy noble twenty-one Tārās, surrounded by countless Buddhas, Bodhisattvas, high patron deities, ḍākiṇīs, and protectors of the Dharma. OṂ VAJRA-SAMĀJAḤ!

Note again that there is the dual sequence, first of imaginatively constructing the Deities and second inviting the "intuition-beings" (*jñānasattva*) to emerge from the real external Deities, dwelling on the sacred, heavenly Potala mountain, and merge with the imaginatively constructed icons, whence the duality of internally imagined/externally real is overcome. The text continues with a long series of ritual procedures carried out in the presence of these Deities, "created in front" by an officiant who is already "self-created" as himself consubstantial with the holy Tārā herself! These particular Form Bodies are relatively simple, although the "self-creation" as a female for a male might be complex for the neophyte, and one can imagine how involved it becomes to perform these self-creations in the case of one of the high patron deities who have several heads and many arms and legs, are conjoined with a consort, and so forth. And let me close this section briefly quoting just such a visualization, which can be used either in self- or confrontative creation, from the *Saṃvarodaya Tantra:*

One is the hero Heruka, three-faced, six-armed, and standing on a solar disc in the posture of triumphal dance. One's central face is deep black; one's right face is white like a kunda flower, and one's left face is red and very terrible, adorned with a crest of twisted hair. Treading on Bhairava and Kālarātri, he abides in the great bliss, embracing Vajravairocanī in great joy of desire of compassion. He has attained concentration of mind through the union of vajra and bell, embracing the goddess with the first two arms, holding a garment of elephant skin with the second two arms. He holds in the right hand of his third pair of arms a damaru drum to be sounded according to the nature of all things, and a khatvanga staff and a skull bowl in his third left hand. His crown is decorated with a wreath of skulls and is adorned with a crescent moon. He is marked with a vajra-cross on his head, and has the Lord of the [Buddha-]family on the top of his head. His face is distorted, very terrible, and assuming the aesthetic mood of the erotic. He has a tiger-skin as his garment and wears a necklace of human heads. He is the God having five consorts and he dances in manifestation of all nine of the aesthetic modes. The Goddess embraced by him has two arms, one face, and three eyes. . . . Her body is like the fire of a super-nova. She constantly enjoys the great bliss, clasping him tightly between her thighs. . . .[21]

The description goes on to describe their retinue, palace, the burning ground in which they reside, and so on. The terrific aspect cultivated here, truly seraphic in mood, is especially cultivated in advanced Unexcelled Yoga practices wherein the fear of death and evil in the deepest recesses of egoism is triumphantly overcome in profound spiritual experiences of integration. The creation-stage self-creation of this Buddha-Form, for example, leads into the most advanced transdeath yogas contained in the *Saṃvara Tantras,* giving the practitioner the type of heroic dauntlessness required for the confrontation of the deepest level of psychic content.

Finally, there is, in advanced visualizations of the creation stage, a type of visualization that is hard to classify according to our controlling concepts. This is the macro-microcosmic type of contemplation known as the subtle yoga, wherein, for example, the *mandala* originally contemplatively constructed as the space around one becomes absorbed into the body of the yogi. And the deities therein—five in the simplest forms, thirty-two in the *Guhyasamāja,* sixty-two in the *Cakrasaṃvara,* and up to one thousand and eighty in the *Kālacakra*—all are absorbed into the yogi's body. Thus, one imagines deities on one's head, on the surface of one's eyes, on the tip of one's tongue, in all of one's joints, in one's navel, on the soles of one's feet, and so forth, at thirty-two vital points as in the *Guhyasamāja*. Here, one is contemplating oneself internally, and yet populating oneself, as it were, with families of external deities, actually perceiving one's body as a temple or *mandala* palace, within which the male and female Buddhas are consorting, emanating the great bliss of the passion of their compassion. The visualizations are vividly described, but here let it suffice to say that the most extreme miniaturization of Form Bodies is involved, which in a sense trains the practitioner to confront his own reality in a vividly different manner, which prepares him effectively for the further self-re-envisionings of the perfection stage.

(5)

The perfection stage usually begins with a type of internal self-confrontation that pushes beyond the creation stage's Deity-absorption process, by departing from the normal range of self-images as a sentient being into a realm of essence, usually mentioned as the realm of "channels," "winds," and "drops" (*nādiprāṇabindu*). Thus, one envisions oneself as a network of subtle channels, arranged in three, four, five, six, or seven (depending on the system and the yogic process involved) "wheels" (*cakras*), located in the brain, throat, heart, navel, and genital regions. These wheels are not the ordinary nervous system, as has been sometimes thought, but rather are a subtle neural patterning of the nervous system, accomplished by highly advanced yogis. There are three central channels, a right known as *rasana*, a left known as *lalana*, and the all-important central one known as *avadhūti*. The opening of the central channel and the absorption therein of the winds and vital drops is a psychophysiological metaphor for the conquest of death and the attainment of enlightenment. It is believed that all living beings come close to opening this central channel at orgasm and even closer at death, but habitually their minds are distracted by passion or fear and they pass the moment without achieving any enduring state of enlightenment. Therefore, the task of the Tantric yogi on the perfection stage of the Unexcelled Yoga is to engage in the care-

ful and systematic exploration of these realms of experience
until, as it is said, death becomes for him the Body of Truth, the
between state becomes the Body of Beatitude, and re-entry into
his own previous physical aggregate or any other "mind-made-
illusory-body" (*manomaya-māyākāya*) he may choose after attaining such an advanced stage. I cannot go into this whole process in any kind of detail as it involves a complex, sophisticated
psychoneurology that is quite a study in itself, but I will quote
briefly from the Tārā meditation, just to give an idea of the type
of experience involved.

This particular sequence comes after a long and detailed self-
creation as the goddess Cintācakra, the white Tārā of long-life-
bestowing symbolism. Entering the perfection-stage practice,
still in the realm of "symbolic [with signs] yoga," the text continues:

The practitioner as Cīntācakra vividly visualizes the inside of his
body as completely empty and hollow. His body is like a tent of white
silk or a flask of white crystal, and upright in the middle thereof is the
"life channel," the *avadhūti* like a firmly planted pillar of crystal, its
upper point just not touching the top of his head, and its lower point
just not touching his "secret place." It is blocked at its upper point by
a white drop having the essence of bliss, and at its lower point by a
red drop having the essence of warmth. And the practitioner visualizes that in the middle thereof, inside the channel at the level of his
heart, is a white syllable TĀM, which is his own mind, the mind that
rides upon the steeds of the winds within his body, radiating light
and now firmly fixed in place. When this is vivid, he exhales and
holds his breath in the flask, deep in his lungs, so that his stomach
protrudes like the belly of a jar. He visualizes that the central channel
is filled with the blue-red wind of life coming from the TĀM, so that
it presses upon his "life"—the TĀM—and it cannot move either upward or downward in the central channel, for its departure in either
direction is death. And he concentrates one-pointedly thereon.[22]

From this point, the text continues into the "signless" stage of
the perfection stage:

. . . the gathering in of the body of the deity. Light radiates forth
from the seed in his heart, turning into light all the appearances of
this world which had become the mandala of noble Tārā; that light,
the entire world, dissolves into the circle of protection, which dis-

solves into the divine mansion, which melts into light and dissolves into the practitioner. He (she) himself, along with his throne, is gathered together from above downward and from below upward, and he dissolves into the wheel in his heart. The wheel dissolves into syllables, those into the syllable TĀM, the subjoined long vowel into the TA, the TA into the crescent, the crescent into the drop, and the drop into pure sound, as fine as the tip of a hair, which grows fainter and fainter until it finally disappears into nonobjectifiability. And the practitioner enters into deep contemplative union with the Clear Light, which is by its very essence Great Emptiness, the realm wherein every single aspect of the objective world and its subjective perceiver are perfect, pure as space.

This experience of innate union, beyond utter dissolution, known as a union of calm and insight, is the experience of the Body of Truth, is beyond time, ineffable, the perfect bliss of universal peace. It therefore does not last either a long time or a short time, but rather is indivisibly united with all manifestations of all the Form Bodies. And thus it is explained in the text that the yogi instantaneously and spontaneously, "like a fish leaping out of water," perfects from that clear light the full body of Cintācakra Tārā. This body radiates light out in all directions . . .

. . . cleansing the impurities of the animate and inanimate worlds, making the inanimate world into a Pure Land and raising all the animate beings it contains to the rank of holy Tārā. It makes offerings to the Victors and their sons, and it invites, in the form of white light, the knowledge of my inseparability from their body, speech, and mind. . . .

Then follows a description of the triumphal blazing forth of white, gold, red, iron-blue, emerald-green, and sapphire-blue light from the heart of the yogi/Cintācakra, which lights crystallize into a series of spherical pavilions floating in galactic space, within which the entire universe is purified and embraced and protected. And the description concludes with the reflection:

All these things are like an illusion, a moon in water, a mirage, a fancy, a reflection in a mirror, free from "true" or "false," having no essence in their appearance, inherently Transcendent Wisdom. Thus, the practitioner enters into contemplation, an Innate Union, which, like the moon in water, neither yearns after Great Bliss nor clings to the Clear Light.

V

In conclusion, we have discovered an abundant variety of spiritual experiences that can be located by degree on the scale from confrontation to realization. If I have made any point, I hope at least to have shattered any preconceptions about the monolithicity of the Buddhist traditions, and that even without going into the Theravāda tradition or into the Far Eastern traditions. If this essay has seemed long and covering a lot of territory, you should be aware that to me it seems to have barely scratched the surface, so rich and varied is the tradition. We must always remember that it spans two thousand five hundred years, a dozen different languages, half as many distinctive cultures, and many more subcultures. But I do not want to end on a note of such generalities. Let me again return to Maitreyanātha:

Although all phenomena are Buddhahood, no phenomenon whatsoever exists. Although it consists of virtuous qualities, they do not define it. It is like a jewel mine, source of the jewel of the Dharma. It is like a rain-cloud, source of the harvest of beauty.[23]

In comment, Vasubandhu explains:

all things are Buddhahood because Thusness, Reality, is free from differentiation and is manifest through purification. And yet in Buddhahood no thing exists at all with respect to its conceptually constructed reality. Buddhahood consists of virtuous qualities, since all virtues and transcendences are transformed by its presence. Yet they do not encompass or define it, for none of these is established intrinsically in the perfect reality.

One confronts a diamond, hard, brilliant, unassimilable, it flashes there before us. A raindrop does not seem like much, patters on the brow, yet it moistens us and quenches our thirst.

NOTES

1. Maitreyanātha (1979), p. 103.
2. *Ibid.*, p. 104.
3. Thurman (1979), p. 13. dKon mChog 'Jigs-med dbAng-po elucidates as follows: "The import to understand is called 'voidness arising as relativity

[appearance]' and 'relativity arising as voidness.' The cognition that realizes that internal and external relativities are free of intrinsic reality ascertains, without need of a further cognition, the viability of all systems such as causality and communication in a world consisting of mere verbal designations. [This is] the meaning of 'voidness arising as relativity.' The cognition that ascertains relativity as dependent designation in all internal and external things, not needing a further cognition, is able to generate the intense conviction about voidness of intrinsic reality. This is the meaning of 'arisal of relativity as voidness.' "

4. Maitreyanātha (1979), p. 75.

5. I still use the expression "Hīnayāna" to indicate early Indian Buddhism of the eighteen sects of Ābhidharmikas after the rise of the Mahāyāna. However, I take "hīna" and "mahā" as "individual" and "universal," in order to get away from the derogatory connotation, to indicate that each is appropriate for its specific target, the liberation of the individual and the liberation of all individuals, and hence to indicate even in the names the fact that the Hīnayāna is indispensably at the core of the Mahāyāna as well, since liberating all beings must mean liberating each one by one.

6. Govinda (1961), p. 173.

7. T. W. Rhys-David (1968), p. 188.

8. The full Sanskrit name of the work is *Prajñā nāma Mūlamadhyamakakārikā*. For a preliminary English version, see Inada (1970). The translations here are my own.

9. These arguments are unpacked in chapter 18 of the *Wisdom*. The first verse is a summary: "If the self were the aggregates, it would be subject to birth and destruction (i.e., no longer absolute). If it were other than them, it would lack any aggregative capacity (i.e., beyond the range of conditionality)."

10. Maitreyanātha (1979), p. 83.

11. Thurman (1976), p. 18.

12. *Ibid.*, pp. 91–92.

13. *Ibid.*, p. 59.

14. Cowell (1894), II, 170 ff.

15. Thurman (1976), pp. 50 ff.

16. Chang (1977), II, 442 ff., (terminology slightly altered).

17. *Ibid.*, pp. 477 ff.

18. Lhalungpa (1977), pp. 181 ff.

19. Tsong-ka-pa (1977), p. 117.

20. Beyer (1973), pp. 332–34.

21. Tsuda (1978), pp. 283–84.

22. Beyer (1973), pp. 442–58. This whole description of a Tārā practice is one of the most remarkable in the literature, vividly conveying the visualizations involved. I have picked from the translation here and there for all the quotes in the rest of this section.

23. Maitreyanātha (1979), p. 103.

WORKS CONSULTED

Beyer, S., *The Cult of Tārā* (Berkeley: University of California, 1973).

Chang, G. C. C., *The Hundred Thousand Songs of Milarepa* (Boulder, Colo.: Shambhala, 1977).

Cowell, E. B., *Buddhist Mahāyāna Texts*, SBE, XLIX, 1894 (New York: Dover, 1969).

Govinda, L. A., *Psychological Attitude of Early Buddhist Philosophy* (New York: Weiser, 1961).

Inada, K., *Nāgārjuna: Mūlamadhyamakakārikā* (Tokyo: Hokuseido, 1970).

Lhalungpa, L. P., *The Life of Milarepa* (New York: Dutton, 1977).

Maitreyanātha, "Ornament of the Scriptures of the Universal Vehicle," unpublished MS translation, Thurman, ed. (1979).

Rhys-David, T. W. R., *Buddhist Suttas* (New York: Dover, 1971).

Thurman, R. A. F., *The Holy Teaching of Vimalakīrti* (College Park: Pennsylvania State, 1976).

——— (trans.), "Song of Mother Emptiness," unpublished MS. (1979).

Tsong-ka-pa, *Tantra in Tibet* (trans. J. Hopkins) (London: Allen & Unwin, 1977).

Tsuda, S., *The Samvarodaya Tantra* (Tokyo: Suzuki, 1978).

TAITETSU UNNO

The Nature of
Religious Experience
in Shin Buddhism

Introduction

Pure Land Buddhism originated in India in the first century B.C. as an integral part of the emerging Mahāyāna movement and as a unique expression of its fundamental truth. As it passed through the Central Asian cultural centers, remaining today only as memories of a rich historical past, it underwent transformation and was introduced into China in the late second century A.D.[1] By the tenth century it had become a dominant force in the Buddhist salvific scheme embraced by the peoples of East Asia, and since then it has endured as a viable alternative to the monastic path to supreme enlightenment. The study of Pure Land Buddhism has been neglected by western scholars, but this tradition, frequently interacting with folk beliefs and magicoreligious practices,[2] as well as developing a sophisticated doctrinal system, warrants our fullest investigation as students of religious phenomena.[3]

One of the peaks in the evolution of Pure Land thought is attained in Kamakura Japan (thirteenth century), when Buddhism experienced a rejuvenation, deeply rooted in the native soil and flowering in the variegated forms of Jōdō, Jōdō-shin, Nichiren, and Zen, as well as the new growths within the traditional schools of Kegon, Hossō, Ritsu, Tendai, and Shingon. A representative figure in this creative surge is Shinran (1173–1262),[4] regarded as the founder of Jōdō-shin school (also referred to as Shin Buddhism), which today constitutes the largest body of adherents among Japanese Buddhist schools. This paper focuses upon the nature of religious experience as clarified by Shinran and maintained in Shin Buddhism, which is different from that of traditional Pure Land, as we shall see later, and from that of other forms of Mahāyāna, such as Zen Buddhism.

If we may tentatively apply the confrontation-interiority typology to these three, traditional Pure Land may be regarded as confrontational, being based exclusively upon man's dichotomous relationship to the all-pervasive compassion of Amida Buddha and his Pure Land; and Zen Buddhism may be seen as fitting into the interiority mold, stressing the nondichotomous realization of Pure Land as within one's heart and Buddha as the enlightenment potential within the self.[5] This, of course, is an oversimplification, not entirely accurate, but Shinran clearly transcends both confrontation and interiority, while at the same time affirming elements of each, such that they coexist in "double exposure," so to speak, making it impossible to reduce religious experience simply to one or the other. He inherits the essential framework of this world versus Amida's Pure Land (dichotomous), negating the possibility of enlightenment in this life; nevertheless, their dynamic interaction is to be realized and settled here and now in the transformative experience called *shinjin* (nondichotomous), normally translated as "faith," which invites misunderstanding and should be avoided. *Shinjin* has a noetic core, but, unlike satori in Zen, it is to be realized by the unenlightened person, fully cognizant of his karmic limitations and his foolish nature. The awakening of *shinjin* is crucial, for without it man is destined to continue his aimless, samsaric wandering in countless future lives, but with *shinjin* he attains "birth in the Pure Land" here and now, in spite of karmic bondage, and at the moment of death when he manifests total freedom.

Shinran's formulation, though couched in Pure Land vocabulary and informed with his original insights, advances the basic intentions of *prajñā-pāramitā* which, according to Yogācāra thinkers, consists of three modes of wisdom.[6] They are, progressively, "wisdom that strives for non-dichotomous knowing" (*prayogika-nirvikalpa-jñāna*) which originates in the world of dualities but seeks to go beyond it guided by the Buddhist path; "fundamental wisdom" (*mūla-jñāna*) which breaks through all dichotomies—thinker and thought, subject and object, this and that—into an experiential realm beyond words and concepts; and "wisdom acquired after that (fundamental wisdom)" (*tat-prṣṭha-labdha-jñāna*) which operates in the world of distinctions and differences, but now purified of ego-syntonic thought and behavior. A constant dialectic occurs between the second and third modes of wisdom, gradually eradicating the deep-rooted self-centeredness enmeshed in false constructs. This interaction parallels the creative tension found in *shinjin* as both a unitive and a disjunctive experience between man and Amida Buddha.

This paper proposes to explore the nature of religious experience in Shinran, showing that it cannot be subsumed under either confrontation or interiority but that it contains both aspects. It also suggests that Shin Buddhism may remind us of certain western forms of religious apprehension, albeit with radical differences, such as that of Paul Tillich's analysis of authentic faith. In his *Courage to Be,* for example, he states:

If participation is dominant, the relation of being-itself has a mystical character, if individualization prevails the relation of being-itself has a personal character, if both poles are accepted and transcended the relation to being-itself has the character of faith.[7]

While the actual content of being-itself remains unclear, Tillich contends that absolute faith, the state of being grasped by the power of being-itself, embraces both mystical participation and personal confidence, while avoiding both the loss of self and loss of the world. The issues involved are complex and deny any easy identification, but his view definitely parallels Shinran's concept of *shinjin*.

The Historical Background

The Pure Land, derived from the Sanskrit *sukhāvatī*, is the ideal realm of enlightened beings who are purified of blind desire (*kleśa*). This purification is not merely affective or psychological, for it includes the transformation of the world itself; hence, the Mahāyāna sūtras speak of the "purifying of the Buddha land" (*buddhakṣetrapariśuddhi*), occurring within the context of enlightenment experience and creating a realm wherein beings are born to effectuate their own enlightenment. The Pure Land ideal, thus, fulfills the goal of Buddhist practice: the supreme enlightenment of not only oneself but of all beings, ultimately and completely.

Such is the *raison d'être* of Pure Land, common to the various Mahāyāna scriptures, but it was the sūtras known as the *Larger* and *Smaller Sukhāvatīvyūha*[8] that magnified the mythic powers of great compassion to their utter limits, articulated in the forty-eight vows of Dharmākara Bodhisattva to save all beings, which successfully culminates in his becoming Amida Buddha and securing the Pure Land. Depicted in concrete worldly imagery, resplendent with gold, silver, all kinds of precious stones and rare jewels, and infused with transcendental bliss, the vision of Pure Land made supreme enlightenment tangible and accessible to the ordinary person.

The traditional belief was that the devotee would be born into such an ideal realm after death and under salutary conditions strive for Buddhahood, guided by Amida and supported by heavenly beings. Thus, one could pursue the bodhisattva path with vigor and confidence, knowing that attaining the all-important stage of nonretrogression (*avaivartika*) and being included among the "truly settled ones," destined for Buddhahood, would be only a matter of time. What was crucial and decisive for attaining birth in the Pure Land was the welcoming by Amida of the faithful at the end of his life, a belief based upon the Nineteenth Vow which promises the appearance of Amida to welcome a dying person.[9] This caught the imagination of people in all classes of Heian society (ninth to twelfth centuries), for it would fulfill the hope of both meeting the Buddha in this life and attaining birth in the next.

Such an auspicious end could be secured by the cultivation of the "mindfulness of Buddha" (*buddhānusmṛti*), a form of meditative practice which in due time came to connote the invocation of the Buddha's Name (*nien-fo* in Chinese, *nembutsu* in Japanese).[10] Since the time of Shan-tao (613–681), a towering figure in Pure Land history, recitative *nembutsu* had become a central practice to achieve the proper psychological state, "right-mindedness" (*shōnen*), to ensure Amida's welcoming at the end of life.

The Pure Land movement in the Heian period which had originated in Tendai was soon embraced by almost all of the other schools, although primarily as an adjunct to the monastic disciplines. It had a mass appeal, for it responded to the spiritual hunger especially of the disillusioned and disaffected—members of the declining aristocracy, lowly court officials, monks and nuns who had violated the precepts, and those who had been heretofore excluded from entering the gates of Buddhism: women, peasants, traders, merchants, warriors, hunters, and fishermen guilty of violence to living things. Especially in this age, pervaded with a sense of historical doom, known as *mappō*, the glorious event of Amida's welcoming was an occasion of celebration. The success of this miraculous happening was assured by the appearance of clouds tinged with purple hue, the wafting of sweet-smelling incense, the sounds of heavenly music, lightening and illumination, and a body that never decayed.[11]

Such signs of Amida's appearance at the deathbed were eagerly sought, but anxiety filled the hearts of the people, for certainty was completely lacking. As more and more people turned to Pure Land faith for refuge from the social and natural calamities of a chaotic age, greater became the fear that the auspicious occurrence would never take place and that Amida would never appear. The bankruptcy of such a faith was inevitable; however, from within this widespread disenchantment there emerged a new, existential appreciation for the Pure Land teaching which increased as the darkness of *mappō*, the end time, descended upon society. In fact, as the degeneration of the age became slowly internalized as the basic and universal human predicament, the powerful, compassionate working of Amida became increasingly clear and self-evident. Moreover, the prophecy of the historical Buddha that the Pure Land teaching would reign supreme in the end time of decadence and decline had now become a fact.[12]

The Salvation Here and Now

Such was the historical situation in which Shinran entered the Tendai novitiate in A.D. 1182, when he was nine years old, but he was also forced to abandon the monastic center (known as his "second renunciation") at the age of twenty-nine, when he encountered Hōnen (1132–1212), a charismatic teacher who had founded an independent Jōdō school to secure the *nembutsu* practice as the way to enlightenment for all, lay people and renunciants alike. The fervor of this new movement, according to the authorities, caused excesses and incited disorder in society, eventually leading to the exile in 1207 of Hōnen and his principal followers, including Shinran, to provinces remote from the capital of Kyoto. Although Shinran himself was pardoned four years later, he remained in the outlying districts for another twenty-five years, studying, reflecting, writing, and teaching the *nembutsu*. Returning to Kyoto at around the age of sixty, Shinran enters a period of renewed religious activity, his most prolific years being in his eighties and ending with his death at ninety.

Shinran's attitude to traditional Pure Land is expressed in a letter dated 1251, addressed to a follower who had questions concerning his understanding and Amida's welcoming of the faithful. To quote a passage from that letter, Shinran writes:

The idea of Amida's coming at the moment of death is for those who seek to gain birth in the Pure Land by performing religious practices, for they are practicers of self-power. The moment of death is of central concern for such people, for they have not yet attained shinjin. . . .

The person of true shinjin, however, abides in the stage of the truly settled, for he has already been grasped, never to be abandoned. There is no need to wait in anticipation for the moment of death, no need to rely on Amida's coming. At the time shinjin becomes settled, birth too becomes settled; there is no need for deathbed rites that prepare one for Amida's coming.

"Right-mindedness," then, is the settling of shinjin of the Other

Power. Because of the realization of this shinjin, a person necessarily attains supreme nirvana. Shinjin is single-heartedness, single-heartedness is the diamond-like heart, the diamond-like heart is the great mind of enlightenment, and this is Other Power that is true Other Power.[13]

Here Shinran rejects not only the goal of traditional Pure Land—anticipation of Amida's welcome in the last moments—but also all monastic disciplines, for they too frequently rely on calculative ego design, self-power. His critique is based on the powerful working of Other Power as manifested in *shinjin*, not upon his limited, fallible judgment. "Right-mindedness," too, is achieved in the settling of *shinjin*, made possible by the Primal Vow, not through human effort or determination. The awakening of *shinjin* is an experience centered on Other Power and not on the unenlightened self. It should be added that "Other Power" does not stand against "self-power"; rather, as boundless compassion it takes in self-power, making it see its own powerlessness. This is "true Other Power."

Shinran's insight into Other Power is revealed in his rereading of the famous passage known as the Fulfillment of the Eighteenth Vow in the *Larger Sukhāvatīvyūha*, which states in the original:

When sentient beings hear the Name of Amida, rejoice in trust even but once, sincerely turn over their merits toward the attainment of birth, and desire to be born in that land, then they will attain birth and will dwell in the stage of non-retrogression.[14]

The stage of nonretrogression for the Mahāyāna bodhisattva is crucial, for it determines the point from which there is only the forward momentum to enlightenment and no backsliding on the path. Since such an attainment was almost impossible for most people, according to traditional Pure Land, it was necessary to seek birth in an ideal realm in the next life and then attain that stage. But Shinran reread this passage in the light of his penetrating experience of reality and affirmed the realization of nonretrogression here and now:

When sentient beings hear the Name of Amida, rejoice and realize shinjin but once which is Amida's sincere mind giving itself to them, and desire to be born in that land, then they attain birth immediately, dwelling in the stage of non-retrogression.[15]

The key passage in the original reading which states that devotees "sincerely turn over their merits towards the attainment of birth" is now made to read by Shinran as "Amida's sincere mind giving itself to them." The religious practicer who turned over his accumulated merits and sought birth in the Pure Land now becomes the primary concern, the object, of Amida's giving. He is, furthermore, the recipient of Amida's boundless compassion not only at the end but, more significantly, at every moment of his life. In fact, the two cannot be separated, for "birth in the Pure Land" is a decisive, transformative experience here and now, determining the future of his religious life, including Buddhahood which is attained simultaneously with "birth in the Pure Land" at the end of his karmic existence.

Shinran's emphasis on the decisive importance of awakening in the present moment is stated unequivocally in his commentary on the above passage:

Then they attain birth means that when a person realizes shinjin, he is born immediately. To be born immediately means to dwell in the stage of non-retrogression. To dwell in the stage of non-retrogression is to become established in the stage of the truly settled. This is also called attainment of the stage equal to perfect enlightenment. Such is the meaning of *then they attain birth. Then* means immediately; immediately means without any passage of time, without any passage of days.[16]

The realization of Amida's compassion in the awakening of *shinjin* is simultaneously the attainment of the nonretrogressive stage, inclusion among those truly settled, and a realization equal to perfect enlightenment, all occurring in this very present and not in some unreliable future time. This new orientation of Pure Land teaching required Shinran to rethink many traditional ideas and infuse them with new significance.

A typical case is Shinran's understanding of Shan-tao's famous credo: "Life ending in the preceding moment; birth attained in the subsequent moment." This meant that the instant life ends for a person of faith, in the next instant he will be born in the Pure Land, the demarcation line for Shan-tao being physical

death. For Shinran, however, what separates the two is not physical but spiritual death; thus, "life ending in the preceding moment" is the complete acceptance of the Primal Vow of Amida,
and "birth attained in the subsequent moment" is the realization
of *shinjin* here and now by virtue of Other Power.[17]

Shinran's revolutionary insights came from his depth experience of true compassion, touched by the heart of Amida, whose
essence is the nameless and formless *dharmakāya*. This is what
provided the certainty that salvation is here and now, although
its final and ultimate consummation must await perfect Buddhahood. We must now turn our attention to that which is fundamental, *dharmakāya*, in Shinran's religious experience.

Fundamental Dharmakāya

The fundamental reality in Buddhism is called *dharmakāya*,
although it has many synonyms. It is not a cold, abstract, philosophical proposition, but, according to D. T. Suzuki, "it is very
much alive with sense and intelligence, and above all, with love
purged of human infirmities."[18] The term implies a notion of personality, because it embodies wisdom and compassion, but it is
basically a spiritual field, the vital life of *śūnyātā* (dynamic emptiness and openness). Shinran lists many equivalents of *dharmakāya*, some with philosophical connotations—the unoriginated,
thatness, suchness, thing-as-it-is, absolute equality—and others
with religious implications—extinction of blind passion, nirvana,
tranquillity, eternal bliss, Buddha-nature, Tathāgata. It is said to
fill "the countless worlds, that is, permeates the hearts and minds
of the ocean of sentient beings. Thus, it is taught that grass,
trees, and land all attain Buddhahood."[19] Since "it is impossible
for our mind to apprehend it and our words to describe it," it is
nameless and formless. This is *dharmakāya*-as-suchness (*hosshō-
hosshin*).

From this nameless and formless *dharmakāya* emerged a form,
Dharmākara Bodhisattva, who attained supreme enlightenment
to become Buddha Amida. This manifestation in form and name
is *dharmakāya*-as-compassion (*hōben-hosshin*), enabling man to
encounter that which is fundamental within the bounds of
human comprehension. Man is able to entrust himself to *dharmakāya*-as-compassion, because *dharmakāya*-as-suchness, permeat-

ing his heart and mind, comes to the fore in him, although, as a karmic being, he can neither know nor comprehend this fact.[20] But this was the source of Shinran's certainty of having attained the nonretrogressive stage in the awakening to *shinjin;* it was not something determined subjectively or logically. Just as the bodhisattva realizes suchness and touches *dharmakāya* in the stage of nonretrogression, so also does a person of *shinjin,* having been touched by *dharmakāya* as the Primal Vow of Amida, attain the nonretrogressive stage.

Here, however, it must be reiterated that the person of *shinjin* remains inexorably bound to samsaric existence, and he must live out his given life in order to exhaust his karmic responsibilities and to ultimately attain total freedom. The dichotomy between man and Buddha, this world and Pure Land, is an unbridgeable chasm which can be closed only from the side of Amida's boundless compassion. Thus, his Primal Vow works relentlessly and ceaselessly to save those who cannot be saved, many times in unexpected, extraordinary ways. The structure of Pure Land experience differs fundamentally from that of Zen in which one directly realizes *dharmakāya,* transcending time and space, to manifest it in this world. Because the Zen practicer aims for the nondichotomous experience of reality, there is no need for *dharmakāya*-as-compassion. But for the person who has been made aware of his foolish nature, cherishing samsaric bondage over nirvanic freedom, only through *dharmakāya*-as-compassion can he realize *dharmakāya*-as-suchness. The two are essentially one and no separation is possible, but without *dharmakāya* appearing as the Primal Vow, there is no way for a foolish, karmic being to reach that which is fundamental.

Primal Vow of Amida

All bodhisattvas establish vows (*praṇidhāna*), expressing their invincible wish for enlightenment which includes the selfsame enlightenment of all beings. Among the forty-eight vows fulfilled by Amida, the central one is the Eighteenth Vow, known also as the Primal Vow, which states:

If, when I attain Buddhahood, the sentient beings throughout the ten quarters, realizing sincere mind, joyful faith, and aspiration to be born in my land and saying my Name up to ten times, do not attain birth, may I not attain supreme enlightenment, excluded are those who commit the five transgressions and slander the dharma.[21]

While traditional Pure Land stressed the three attitudes—sincere mind, joyful faith, and aspiration for birth—to be essential for the religious person, Shinran considered them to be manifestations of Amida's working.[22] That is, "sincere mind" refers to the mind of Amida Buddha and not that of foolish man, who lacks it completely. The sincere mind, appearing in his mind as the Primal Vow, enables him to have "joyful faith," an impossibility for man if left to himself. From this joyful faith, made a reality by Amida, arises the "aspiration to be born in the Pure Land," an aspiration which is unthinkable for one entangled in samsaric existence. In short, what were considered to be basic requirements for the faithful are, in reality, nothing but the results of the Primal Vow working in a person devoid of any religiosity.

Now, the Primal Vow is said to be for all "sentient beings throughout the ten quarters," but it is especially directed to "those who commit the five transgressions and slander the dharma." This phrase, known as the exclusion clause (okushi-mon) challenged the exegetes down through the centuries, for it contained a contradiction: How could all-embracing compassion exclude anyone, even those guilty of the five transgressions and slandering the dharma? The latter includes the criticism of Buddha's teaching, neglect of religious life, and doubt regarding its value; and the former normally refers to the violence against mother, father, arhat, and Buddha, and disrupting the harmony of the order. Slandering the dharma is believed to be a far greater evil than the five transgressions, for it destroys the basis for repentance.

For Shinran the exclusion clause was ethically necessary, so that people would refrain from committing such evils, but religiously it focused on the person who is the primary concern of the Primal Vow. Shinran himself was the first to admit being guilty of the evils listed, not only on the conscious but on the subconscious level and not only in this life but in countless past lives. He realized that he, more than anyone else, is the object of Amida's compassion, a fact expressed by him in wonder and gratitude:

When I ponder on the compassionate vow of Amida, established through five kalpas of profound thought, it was for myself, Shinran, alone. Because I am a being bound by so much karmic evil, I feel even more deeply grateful to the Primal Vow which is designed to save me.[23]

Finite man is incapable of fulfilling any religious act which leads to supreme enlightenment, an inevitable conclusion for anyone who has truly struggled to live the highest human life possible. To such a person Amida selects and gives the one practice that is possible by anyone, at anytime and anyplace, under any circumstances: saying the *nembutsu*, "namu-amida-butsu." Hōnen called it the simplest yet highest religious practice, simplest because no conditions are attached and highest because it is not an act of finite man but of infinite compassion working through man.

Nembutsu as the act of infinite compassion is experienced as a call from Amida to return home to Life (*amitāyus*) and Light (*amitābha*), but it is also finite man's response to that call, affirming his return and arrival home in every moment, including the last, of his life. Such an affirmation, total and unconditional, of one's life leaves no room to feel the need to strive in meditative discipline, mental training, or monastic observances.

Shinjin as Awakening

While *nembutsu* practice is central both to traditional Pure Land and to Shinran himself, he considered the inner dynamic behind the recitative act, *shinjin*, indispensable. In fact, he goes so far as to say that "when the thought of wanting to say the *nembutsu* emerges from deep within, having entrusted ourselves to the inconceivable power of Amida's vow which saves us, enabling us to be born in the Pure Land, in that very moment we are grasped never to be abandoned, thus receiving the ultimate benefit."[24] This "thought of wanting to say the *nembutsu*" is, of course, neither deliberate nor calculated; it is the Other Power manifesting itself, the *dharmakāya* coming to the fore, the timeless appearing in time.

Shinjin, according to Shinran, has a dual meaning: as a noun it refers to the true and real mind of Amida Buddha, in contrast to the false and evil mind of man; and as a verb it means to entrust oneself. Thus, together, when the true and real mind of Amida covers the horizon of one's life, man entrusts himself completely to Amida. This is *shinjin,* the internal structure of which was given its classic formulation by Shan-tao:

Shinjin is the mind of profound awakening. There are two aspects. First is to decisively awaken to this self at this very moment as a being of samsara, drowning and repeating samsaric life from the deep past to this present, never having any hope of liberation. Second is to decisively awaken to the forty-eight vows of Amida which embrace sentient beings and without fail make them attain birth by transporting them without any hesitation by the power of the vow.[25]

The dialectical interaction occurring between true compassion and karmic evil intensifies *shinjin:* the greater the appreciation for Amida's boundless compassion, the deeper the realization of one's karmic evil; and the greater the awareness of karmic self, the profounder the gratitude to true compassion.

At the core of this dialectical movement, moreover, occurs a unique "transformation" (*ten*) in which karmic evil, affirmed as it is, becomes transformed into the contents of enlightenment by the power of the Primal Vow, its essential characteristic being that "evil karma, without being nullified or eradicated, is made into the highest good."[26] In the words of Shinran,

> Having gained shinjin majestic and profound
> By virtue of Amida's Unhindered Light,
> The ice of blind desire melts without fail
> To become the water of enlightenment.
>
> Evil hindrance becomes the substance of virtue
> As in the case of ice and water;
> The more the ice, the more the water;
> The more the hindrance, the more the virtue.[27]

As long as we live this human life, each person is bound by his karmic limitations. Whether those karmic hindrances are taken negatively as one's fate or affirmed positively as the gift of life is the concern of Amida's compassion, whose working transforms every possible evil into the highest good. And this not by making demands upon the being of karmic evil but by the power of enlightened suasion:

Amida remakes human beings. To remake means that he leaves our mind just as it is and places his mind upon it, taking us in. This does not mean that our mind is taken away and displaced by the mind of Amida.[28]

As long as one lives this karmic life, the dialectical tension between the awareness of karmic evil and the working of true compassion continues, deepening ever more the appreciation for both. Writing at the age of eighty-three, Shinran laments but affirms his true nature with unparalleled openness:

> Even though I return to the truth of Pure Land,
>   The mind true and real is impossible.
> This self is full of vanity, falsehood, and untruth
>   Without any trace of purity of mind.
>
> Difficult is it to be free of evil nature—
>   The heart is like snake and scorpion:
> Good acts also are mixed with poison—
>   They are but deeds vain and false.
>
> Although within this shameless, unrepenting self
>   No genuine, sincere heart exists,
> By the power of the Name granted by Amida
>   Virtue permeates the universe in all directions.[29]

This confession grew out of Shinran's life, buffeted by inner and outer turmoils beyond his control, because he took full responsibility for them and never sought to excuse himself. Such an awesome sense of responsibility, as well as penetrating insight into himself, was made possible by an experience even more fundamental, the deeply felt peace and fulfillment, having been grasped by the Primal Vow of Other Power. Singing of his joy, Shinran writes:

Now, as I ride on the ship of great compassionate vow and sail on the expansive ocean of wondrous light, the breeze of highest virtue blows peacefully and calms the waves of pain and sorrow. Quickly shall I reach the land of immeasurable light and attain unexcelled supreme nirvana.[30]

The person of *shinjin,* while living out his karmic life which made possible his encounter with true compassion, has already arrived and need not go seeking anymore; the only thing remaining is the attainment of supreme enlightenment realized at the moment of the final birth in the Pure Land. It is attained "quickly" because the process is spontaneous and effortless, all made possible by the relentless working of the Primal Vow.

But supreme enlightenment in the land of immeasurable light is not the end of the life of *shinjin*, for now as a fully enlightened being, a Buddha, he plunges back into the samsaric world to help others find their way home to Life and Light as a participant in the salvific activities of true compassion. The Pure Land is not an abode of rest; it is a waystation from which one returns to this world, for as long as there are suffering beings, the work of compassion never stops. The universe of *shinjin*, while experienced by each individual, is immense and boundless, related to what happens to our world. In summary, then, the life of *shinjin* was Shinran's actualization of the bodhisattva ideal, an actualization made possible not by ego design or self-power but by the working of Other Power within a karmically determined being. He is now an essential part of the universal Primal Vow:

> Those who attain the Pure Land of peace
> Return to this world of five defilements,
> And like Śākyamuni Buddha
> Bring endless benefits to all beings.[31]

The Process of Awakening

Shinran describes the awakening of *shinjin* as a progressive "evolution through the three vows," referring to the three stages of the Nineteenth, Twentieth, and Eighteenth Vows of Amida Buddha.[32] Simply put, the stage of the Nineteenth Vow may be called ethical, that of the Twentieth Vow semireligious, and that of the Eighteenth Vow religious. They constitute a critical analysis of Shinran's own spiritual biography, as well as a critique of contemporary beliefs and practices which fell short, according to his view, of the truly Buddhist life.

The Nineteenth Vow prescribes three essential practices: awakening a powerful aspiration for enlightenment (*bodhicitta*), a basic requirement for the bodhisattva; the pursuit of good works, including strict observance of moral precepts and meditative disciplines; and a sincere, deep wish to be born in the Pure Land. The successful fulfillment of these practices would assure the welcome by Amida at the end of one's life. Shinran devoted many years of his life to these ethical endeavors, but he could not dissolve the sense of unease that overcame him. Rather than realizing inner peace, he was consumed by deep anxiety caused by the inability to solve his existential doubts, including the threat of death. He finally realized that there was no adequate solution, for it came from the karmic evil at the core of his being.

The only possible resolution was to advance to a higher stage of practice as advocated in the Twentieth Vow: recitative *nembutsu* selected precisely for those who could not remain satisfied with the practices of the Nineteenth Vow. This was an exclusive practice centered not on man but on Amida Buddha, and nothing was required of the practicer, except the invocation of the Name, called "planting the roots of merit," and the transference of accumulated merit to all other beings. The commitment to recitative *nembutsu* was absolute; all self-power practices were to be negated. Thus, some people constantly recited the *nembutsu*, all day and night, in the belief that the greater the number of invocations, the greater the benefits derived. Shinran also had dedicated himself to "planting the roots of merit," but he continued to experience profound anxiety. Intuitively he sensed the wrongness of his practice, still rooted in self-conceit and spiritual arrogance. But now he faced a dilemma, for there were no prescribed paths to follow.

The practices encouraged in the Nineteenth and Twentieth Vows were explicit, but no clear path was indicated in the Eighteenth Vow. No human or religious act could bridge the chasm separating man from Amida, this world from the Pure Land. What is necessary is a "crosswise leap"[33] (*ōchō*) made possible by the working of Other Power. This crucial realization comes not by meditative reflection, nor by concentrated study, but by an awakening which dawns on us through constant "hearing," traditionally referred to as *chōmon*, consisting of *chō*, which is to hear the soundless sound, the voiceless voice, of Life and Light, and *mon*, which is to truly know the origin, purpose, and end of the Primal Vow of Amida. Such an awareness, obviously, is not a comprehension in the conventional sense on the subject-object level but a much deeper realization touching the very ground of our being, a realization that "we do not know the depths of karmic evil and we do not know the immensity of Tathāgata's compassion."[34] This hearing-awakening, then, goes beyond mere religious exercise or practice; it is a commitment to true and real life itself. Nothing, therefore, should stop a person from pursuing the life of *chōmon,* and thus Shinran could say:

> He who passes through all the fires
> Of three thousand great thousand worlds
> To hear the sacred Name of Amida
> Will abide forever in non-retrogression.[35]

The evolution through the three vows, culminating in the Eighteenth Vow, does not exclude the Nineteenth and Twentieth Vows, for they are all parts of Amida's salvific design to save all beings. In fact, the three vows work together constantly to release man, on both the conscious and the subconscious levels, from his deeply rooted, massive self-indulgence.

Conclusion

Shin religious experience is neither simply a mystical union nor a dualistic confrontation between a finite, karmic being and an infinite power of love or compassion. Fundamental reality, *dharmakāya,* which is none other than *śūnyātā,* breaks through all dichotomies; but at the same time it affirms man's given life, grounded in the multiple realities (*dharma*) of our dichotomous, phenomenal world, a world for which he himself must take full responsibility. What remains to be explored, then, is the nature of the confrontational relationship in Shin Buddhism, different clearly from that found in Judeo-Christian-Islamic encounter, and its basis in reality seen not as Absolute Being but as Being which is empty of all fixity.

NOTES

Whenever possible, the English translation of Shinran's work is given; if none exists, the citation is of the original source found in the standard collection of his works, vol. II of *Shinshū-shōgyō-zenshō* (hereafter SSZ II) (Kyoto: Kōkyō Shoin, 1957).

1. Very little research has been done on the origins of Pure Land Buddhism in India; an English summary of an excellent study in Japanese on this subject by Kōtatsu Fujita will appear in a forthcoming volume, *Pure Land Buddhism,* edited by Michael Solomon and James Foard.

2. A brief treatment is contained in Ichiro Hori, *Folk Religion in Japan* (Chicago: The University of Chicago Press, 1968), pp. 83–139.

3. The first significant mention of Japanese Pure Land Buddhism as "the most adequate and comprehensive and illuminating" contrast to Christianity is found in Karl Barth, *Church Dogmatics,* vol. I, 2 (Edinburgh: T. & T. Clark, 1956), 340.

4. For an introduction to his life, see Alfred Bloom, "The Life of Shinran Shonin: The Journey to Self-Acceptance," *Numen,* vol. 15, Fasc. 1 (1968), 1–62; and for an outline of his religious thought, see Taitetsu Unno, "Shinran: The New Path to Buddhahood," in the forthcoming *Pure Land Buddhism* mentioned above.

5. See, for example, *The Holy Teaching of Vimalakīrti,* translated by Robert A. F. Thurman (University Park and London: The Pennsylvania State University Press, 1976), chapter I, pp. 10–19; and *The Platform Sutra of the Sixth Patriarch,* translated by Philip B. Yampolsky (New York: Columbia University Press, 1967), pp. 156–59.

6. For an interpretative discussion, see Yoshifumi Ueda, "Thinking in Buddhist Philosophy," *The Philosophical Studies in Japan,* vol. V (1964), 73–79.

7. *Courage to Be* (New Haven: Yale University Press, 1952), pp. 156–57.

8. For an English translation from the Sanskrit text, see *Sacred Books of the East,* vol. XLIX, part 2, 1–72 and 89–102, respectively, for the *Larger* and *Smaller Sukhāvatīvyūha,* as well as the third major Pure Land scripture translated from the Chinese, under the title *Amitāyur-dhyāna-sūtra,* pp. 161–201. The Chinese translations of the *Larger* and *Smaller Sukhāvatīvyūha,* circulated in East Asia, differs slightly from the Sanskrit version. An uncritical English rendition of the standard Chinese texts are contained in *The Shinshū Seiten,* translated by Kōsho Yamamoto (compiled and edited by the Honpa Hongwanji Mission of Hawaii, Tokyo: Kenkyūsha, 1955), pp. 7–106.

9. The Nineteenth Vow states: "If, when I attain Buddhahood, I do not take a large company and appear at the moment of death before beings in the ten quarters who awaken the mind of enlightenment and practice deeds of merit, sincerely cherishing the desire to be born in my land, may I not attain the supreme enlightenment." Translated from the Chinese text of the *Larger Sukhāvatīvyūha;* see *The Shinshū Seiten,* 20. Passing references to Amida's welcoming are found in all three Pure Land sūtras.

10. The *nem* of *nembutsu* could be either "meditation" on the Buddha or "invocation" of the Buddha's Name, but the latter became the central practice in China, Korea, and Japan. A close western parallel would be the hesychast practice, known commonly as the Jesus prayer, of the Eastern Orthodox Church, which shows striking similarities to Pure Land *nembutsu* but also many radical differences, due to the structural dissimilarities of Christianity and Buddhism. For a brief but comprehensive treatment of hesychast invocation, see *On the Invocation of the Name of Jesus* by a monk of the Eastern Church (London: The Fellowship of St. Alban and St. Sergius, no date). For a comparison between the *nembutsu* and Jesus prayer, see

the bibliography in Joseph J. Spae, *Buddhist-Christian Empathy* (Chicago: The Chicago Institute of Theology and Culture, 1980), p. 117, footnote 21.

11. Belief in such signs were widespread and frequently appear in the literature of the Heian period, as well as in the lives of famous monks; for example, see Harper Havelock Coates and Ryugaku Ishizuka, *Hōnen the Buddhist Saint* (Kyoto: The Society for Publication of the Sacred Books of the World, 1949), p. 719.

12. An important prophecy for East Asian Buddhists found in the Chinese text of the *Larger Sukhāvatīvyūha, The Shinshū Seiten,* p. 72, and found as general statements in other Pure Land sutras, such as the *Smaller Sukhāvatīvyūha, ibid.,* p. 106, and *The Sacred Books of the East,* vol. XLIX, part 2, 102.

13. *Letters of Shinran: A Translation of Mattoshō,* edited by Yoshifumi Ueda (Kyoto: Hongwanji International Center, 1979), pp. 34–35.

14. *The Shinshū Seiten,* p. 39, incorporates Shinran's reading and therefore misrepresents the original text. The equivalent from the Sanskrit text is found in the English translation in *The Sacred Books of the East,* vol. XLIX, part 2, 45.

15. *The Kyōgyōshinshō,* translation of the first four chapters by D. T. Suzuki (Kyoto: Shinshū Ōtaniha, 1973), p. 89; *The Kyōgyōshinshō,* translation of all six chapters by Kōsho Yamamoto (Tokyo: Karinbunko, 1958), p. 89.

16. *Notes on "Essentials of Faith Alone": A Translation of Shinran's Yuishinshō-mon'i,* edited by Yoshifumi Ueda (Kyoto: Hongwanji International Center, 1979), pp. 34–35.

17. For Shinran's interpretation, see *Gutokushō,* SSZ II, p. 460. Shan-tao's statement is found in his *Wang-sheng li-tsan chieh,* SSZ I, p. 652.

18. *The Essence of Buddhism* (London: The Buddhist Society, 1957), p. 46.

19. *Notes on "Essentials of Faith Alone,"* p. 42.

20. The awareness of a "foolish being" and the awareness of Amida's compassion are one and the same; one is indispensable for the other. *Ibid.,* Introduction, pp. 6–8. In fact, "The Primal Vow was established out of deep compassion for us who cannot become freed from the bondage of birth-and-death through any religious practice, due to the abundance of blind passion. Since its basic intention is to effect the enlightenment of such an evil one, the evil person who entrusts himself to Other Power is truly the one who attains birth in the Pure Land. Therefore, even the good person attains birth, how much more so the evil person!"—*Tannishō: Lamenting the Deviations,* translated by Taitetsu Unno (Honolulu: Buddhist Study Center, 1977), pp. 6–7.

21. For a review of the forty-eight vows, see D. T. Suzuki, "The Shin Teaching of Buddhism" in his *Collected Writings on Shin Buddhism* (Kyoto: Shinshū Ōtaniha, 1973), pp. 42–50.

22. This is carefully developed by Shinran in *The Kyōgyōshinshō,* Suzuki translation, pp. 103–18; Yamamoto translation, pp. 103–19.

23. *Tannishō,* p. 34.

24. *Ibid.*, p. 4.

25. Quoted in *The Kyōgyōshinshō*, Suzuki translation, pp. 93–94; Yamamoto translation, p. 94.

26. *Notes on "Essentials of Faith Alone,"* p. 32.

27. *The Kōsō-wasan: Hymns on the Patriarchs by Shinran*, Ryukoku Translation Series, vol. VI (Kyoto, 1974), 62–63. The relationship suggested between ice and water reminds us of that between sin and grace in Christianity, such as found in Romans 5:20, "Law came in, to increase the trespass; but where sin increased, grace abounded all the more," but the notion of "transformation" may be unique to Shin Buddhism.

28. *The Words of St. Rennyo*, translated by Kōsho Yamamoto (Ube City: The Karinbunko, 1968), p. 28.

29. *Hitan-jukkai-san*, SSZ II, p. 527.

30. *The Kyōgyōshinshō*, Suzuki translation, p. 62; Yamamoto translation, p. 59.

31. *The Jōdō Wasan: Hymns on the Pure Land*. Ryukoku Translation Series, vol. IV (Kyoto, 1968), 48.

32. *The Kyōgyōshinshō*, Yamamoto translation, pp. 237–75, discusses the Nineteenth Vow (Temporary Gate, Birth under the Twin Shal Trees) and Twentieth Vow (True Gate of Expediency, Inconceivable Birth) as processes to the Eighteenth Vow (Sea of the Best-Selected Vow, All Wonderful Birth).

33. *The Kyōgyōshinshō*, Suzuki translation, p. 119; Yamamoto translation, p. 120.

34. *Tannishō.*

35. *The Jōdō Wasan: Hymns on the Pure Land*, p. 59.

Part III

Commentary

JOHN J. HUCKLE

Conversational Chronicle

The previous papers in this volume speak for themselves. It is the slightly immodest aim of this paper to speak for the speakers —that is, to narrate the discussions of the seminar. For more than a year participants in the seminar met, spending at each separate meeting many hours in conversation. The work of chronicling the sum of these conversations is a work necessarily more impressionistic than stenographic. It can only attempt to expose somewhat the range of issues and interests that grew out of the papers presented to the seminar and, not least important, the questions that led (and lead) to further questions.

This then is a chronicle of conversational highlights. It follows closely the original sequence of meetings, wherein the papers were presented in an order differing from the order of this volume. That sequence was: Professors Cousins, Thurman, Pagels, Kee, Green, Fishbane, Eck, Böwering, Carman, and Unno.

Many of the central questions dealt with throughout the period of the seminar recurred—whether in new or only slightly altered guises. However, it seems fair—and it is convenient as well —to distinguish two phases of the seminar. This distinction is fundamentally a matter of emphases. The first phase, ending with Howard Kee's paper on Pauline mysticism, was especially a time of methodological clarification, as well as increasing methodological complexification. Specifically, the usefulness of the original typology of "confrontation" and "interiority" was reassessed. (The results of that discussion are treated thoroughly in Peter Berger's introduction to this volume.) In the second phase, while not abandoning its original scholarly impulse, discussion tended to focus on the wider religious implications of the phenomena under study. This last, perhaps as prelude to formal and systematic theological and philosophical considerations.

How does one "get at" both the dynamics and nature of religious experience? What is the determinative effect of language upon such experience? Certainly it must be more than window dressing—an essentially superfluous "outside" that can be stripped away to lay bare the unchanging essence "inside." In that case, at what level of inquiry can we investigate religious traditions which present such experience, especially highly sophisticated and abstract systematic presentations (e.g., Thurman on several Mahayana sources). Are the questions that can be asked of such systems from any other point of view than their own relevant, or are we engaged in an exercise of comparative epistemologies?

If one maintains that distinct experiences are irreducible, one to the other, must one also maintain that they are antagonistic? In the case of Gnosticism and orthodox Christianity chosen by Elaine Pagels, there seems a clear example of a successful use of the types of "confrontation" and "interiority" in order to examine the interaction of distinct religious experiences, which are, in this case, mutually antagonistic. Here we also see what seems to be a clear case of the resolution of a conflict of disparate religious experiences predominantly in favor of one type. In the second century, orthodox Christianity defined its experience of Jesus in predominantly confrontational terms while rejecting definitions in terms of pure interiority as heretical. In this instance, sharp boundaries are drawn between the two types of experience. Yet, as such, they are not mutually exclusive types (even in the New Testament itself); there are clear cases in the history of religions of reconciliation and compromise, of the ascendancy of one or the other type, of uneasy truces. How do they coexist in the same tradition or material and why do they coexist in the way that they do? What are the motives of interaction?

How far can the relationship between experiences of confrontation and interiority be understood sociologically—especially in regard to the function of one kind of experience or the other in the assertion and maintenance of institutional and/or personal identity? For example, in her chosen case, Pagels suggests that the confrontational mode provided a precarious second-century Christianity with a more useful instrument for its survival through institutionalization.

Beyond sociological explanations (but not apart from them), is it valid to maintain an "autonomous religious dynamic" which exists alongside of other nonreligious motives, but is not reducible to them? What does this consideration say to the way the polarities interrelate?

Can the question be put simply but, at the same time, with many layers of complexity: What gives religious experience its accent of reality?

In certain cases, such questions may be best approached through the original typology; however, in other instances, the polarities of "confrontation" and "interiority" are obviously inadequate. If we assume that the "confrontation" and "interiority" typology is attempting to get at something, what can be done with it? The nature of religious experience may be entirely too complex for this typology to work successfully and comprehensively. Its unsuitability for the case of Franciscan mysticism has already been maintained (Cousins on Franciscan mysticism); the invalidity of any attempt to bifurcate East-West along the line of this typology has also been amply demonstrated (Thurman on Mahayana Buddhism). Finally, if Kee's interpretation of Paul is accepted, the typology seems completely undermined. If Paul's confrontation is completely interior, apart from any occurrence in the objective, external sensory world, the "confrontation" and "interiority" conceptuality is inapplicable.

There is the further and related question of the language matrix of religious experience. What, if anything, is our analysis imposing upon the material under study and what distortion of that material may be involved? Given certain life-worlds, may it not be methodologically misleading even to isolate some experiences as specifically "religious"? At the same time, even with experiences we identify as religious, we are not in a line of interpretation reaching back to pure experience, but in a circle of interpretations.

It may be possible that the "confrontation" and "interiority" typology, as well as other polar conceptualizations, might function as a kind of code to address the question central to the seminar: Is there some great divide running through religions? If so, what is it? To get at this question, it is possible to propose a paradigmatic case: Elijah and the prophets of Ba'al. The early traditions of Israel irreconcilably oppose Israel's experience of God to that of nature mysticism and sacred sexuality. As well, this antagonism has dominated the history of Judaism and Christianity. Are both experiences, in fact, irreconcilable along the divide of religious motivations? Is it possible now, given changed sociocultural reasons, to re-evaluate sacred sexuality in a broader spectrum? With this case as an example, the problem then is whether certain religious experiences are essentially incompatible or whether they only appear to be incompatible under very specific circumstances. Furthermore, how "very specific circumstances" determine the shape of religious experience does not yet seem clear. The "embeddedness" of experience in its language matrix needs to be further clarified before it is possible to decide whether consideration of an experience "in a broader spectrum" re-evaluates that experience or creates a new one.

If we pause to assess the past and future direction of the seminar what can we agree upon? In that each discussion has pushed further the conversation of the seminar, the seminar has been successful. However, during the course of conversations certain options have become evident. One option is to continue our predominantly descriptive scholarly approach to questions. Another is to approach questions in a more overtly philosophical or theological way. This option taken would move us into a direct relation with broader issues that have surfaced during the course of the seminar. This last option itself includes a number of directions.

In relation to our starting typology, the papers have shown that the categories "interiority" and "confrontation" are more intertwined than originally proposed. Should we now try to find a methodology or synthesis that will give a clearer philosophical expression to these categories as they develop out of the papers?

At the same time, the material we have been studying is especially open to theological interests. Most philosophers and theologians do not deal with the issues raised here. One must be wary, however, of entering the "swamp" of epistemology. Even so, it does not seem possible to avoid theological and philosophical questions. It is necessary to move beyond the field of scholarly expertise to raise broad conceptual issues which must be looked at if one is not to function naïvely. Though there have been hints, this group has not really addressed the underlying reality of the symbols it has been dealing with.

How to do this is not completely clear. It may be necessary to wade the swamp, to examine epistemology and epistemological presuppositions, not only of method but also of material. This would raise questions that surfaced earlier. In any case, the material is particularly rich for philosophy and theology and for a critique of both.

Deep personal concerns have also emerged through our discussions. For example, some of us here, speaking from within Judaism, see the opportunity to address issues raised here as contemporary Jews. What do these issues mean in relation to Jewish tensions and how do other religious modalities challenge us as Jews? How can these issues be discussed across religious traditions?

In fact, any consideration of a contemporary theological agenda will necessarily both broaden and sharpen the questions we are raising here: questions of the negotiability of nonreducible religious experiences, of challenges to the authority of religious traditions, of the relativizing thrust of certain religious experiences—perhaps, ultimately, of the truthfulness of an experience.

Hasidism is a case in point where many of these questions are illuminated. Was the Hasidic retreat motivated by the perception that the kind of Jewish mysticism to which Hasidism gave rise could lead to the radical relativization of Judaism? Whatever the "all [is God]" is, Hasidism must have realized it is very different from the traditional notion of God passed down in Judaism. In fact, is not mysticism itself a relativizing force within religions—a force which undermines the claims of all historical traditions? If God is all what does it matter what route one takes?

Hasidism pulled back from a course that, it perceived, would have radically delegitimated Judaism. Its universalism called into question the necessity of revelation as a mediating principle and so threatened to negate Jewish existence. However, its universal pantheism was "negative universalism": over and against this universal pantheism the commandments were relativized but not over and against other religions. The Hasidim did not raise the problem of other religions even if, as an experiential and cognitive structure, universal pantheism potentially includes the problem of other religions.

Could Hasidism have maintained in one complex its mysticism and the unique claim of its tradition? If we can say that the tension between inner Torah and outer Torah is a projection upon Jewish history by Gershom Scholem, then perhaps they can both coexist. There would be times when one kind of experience would be needed and times when another would be needed. One would then move in and out of the different experiences. Would the effect of this alternation be destructive of the tradition? How, in fact, do syncretistic impulses alter the integrity of a tradition?

It might be useful to distinguish historical and typological syncretisms, the former shaped by influences from without, the latter, like the Jewish Kabbalah, representing a syncretism from within. The ancient Israelite situation represents a case of historical syncretism whose actual intentions, due to the nature of the biblical material, are not always clear. Was Yahweh always outside the plenum? In any case, the "pure Yahwism" of official theology seems to have remained the property of an intellectual elite. For this official Yahwism, all syncretistic impulses were destructive adulterations. Need we admit that? How far can syncretism go before a religion loses its original character and becomes something else? Who decides? Is this established at a very subjective level by people deciding at a certain point what can or cannot be tolerated? If so, could not others, with more comparative materials at hand, pass judgment on the correctness of such decisions?

The plenum of the divine expresses a yearning for contact with the concrete life of the god and not just submission to the god's will. Yahwism shares with Calvinism this denial of the plenum, this lust for differentiation. Both represent extreme cases of "mythological deprivation" (a mistake?). Conceived positively, syncretism represents a type of mediating position (between differentiation and nondifferentiation) which may, in turn, become a type itself (a combination of unity and differentiation). However, rather than a syncretistic mixture, might not this new type (following Ewert Cousins's conceptualization) represent equally primordial experience even if it manifests itself in later historical periods? Hypothetically, if such a type had existed in the biblical setting, it might have been some kind of emanationism. God is really other, yet known through the very concrete perceptions that are emanations of his/her/its presence.

Can one speak, in any meaningful way, of a common human pattern of religious experience? And if one can, is it possible to identify it as the experience of the plenum, essentially an experience of nondifferentiation that is rooted in the rhythms of nature? If this can be conceived as the case, the development of various religious traditions would bring about ruptures in the plenum. Despite these ruptures, might there not always be a recurrence of the plenum, movements within religious traditions themselves which reject the sharp polarization between deity and humanity, experiences rooted in the "near shore"? As always, it is necessary to address the question of "official" religion and the large "underground" of belief and practice, which, to a large extent, determines the life of any religious tradition.

Both of these experiences would have to be specified phenomenologically, that of the plenum and that of the rupture. Both of these poles seem to function in all the traditions we have seen rather than to distinguish traditions, but they can be formulated in contrast even if they can be and have been mediated.

Or again, rather than mediation, should one speak of a primordial gestalt which joins both plenum and rupture, both immanence and transcendence, and is not reducible to either?

Considering the thrust of most mysticism—broadly understood —toward unity and nondifferentiation in an individual context, what can be said about individuation? Should it be regarded as episodic, a deviation from what human destiny really is, or is it an important epistemological gain? Can distinct salvation experiences such as those which stress the disappearance of the personality and those which polarize God and man be reconciled? Can one any longer afford to negate the truth of either experience?

Increasingly the issues raised in our discussions have been placed in more personal and contemporary settings. If certain options are rejected (e.g., forms of fundamentalism or reductionism), how is one to define oneself in relation to a specific religious tradition? Or, further, what is the authority of any specific religious experience? For some, it may be that the contemporary scene is characterized both by a loss of the sense of the God of history and by a longing to rejoin the plenum, to experience the concrete presence of God. Are we moving to a new re-encounter with the plenum and, concomitantly, a refusal to renegotiate with the God of will? Specifically, need one any longer involve oneself in an exegetical stance vis-à-vis one's own tradition? Generally, the enterprise of exegetical renegotiation seems a waste of time. Such a recognition of one's syncretism may be particularly difficult and painful for some. For example, Jewish identity has always defined itself negatively; it has striven to establish its difference; but this may no longer be possible. Given the possibility of affirming a variety of religious perceptions, need this affirmation be an agent that invalidates one religious tradition or another?

Knowledge of one's past is essential for movement into the future. One is challenged even more to know one's tradition in order to know where one stands in the present. Religious traditions may serve as "sources of wisdom" rather than "cores of truth" from which one may draw when confronted by the vast experience of mankind. The task of theology may have irrevocably changed, its horizon expanded through sheer accumulation of knowledge.

One's religious tradition is no longer a self-contained, taken-for-granted world within which one can rest secure. In fact, such a world is neither there nor possible. For the Jewish and Christian backgrounds of these traditions the major challenge is confrontation with the plenum as embodied in Asian religions. However, this does not require the liquidation of the tradition. The authentic experience of each is self-validating. One can speak of the truth of Judaism as well as of Christianity, i.e., the sense of reality embodied by the tradition.

The last few paragraphs are the finest expression of the accomplishments of the seminar which was the basis of this book. Dying, Gertrude Stein—sibylline, if anyone can be so described—asked, "What is the answer?" Replying to herself, this knowing lady answered, "What is the question?" Knowing its business, the seminar had a comparable clear vision of the priorities of discourse—along with the imagination to interrogate both gods and men.

HARVEY COX

The Battle of the Gods?
A Concluding
Unsystematic Postscript

The conversation that emerged around the papers assembled in this book was, as chiefs of state announce after the meetings they hold, "a valuable, frank, and informative exchange." More than that, it was often spirited, sometimes baffling, never acrimonious. Still, most of us agreed by the end of these discussions that what had happened had been mainly prolegomena. Absorbing prolegomena perhaps, maybe even indispensable, but prolegomena nonetheless.

We had begun with a sharp challenge. Since answering the challenge of the "new" religious movements (or the newly perceived challenge of very old ones) with deprogrammers, stepped-up proselytizing, or steely indifference seemed unattractive, how should we then respond? The exact nature of the issue posed by these traditions, mostly originating in the Orient, was phrased in somewhat different ways. Some saw it as a confrontation between monotheism and "nonmonotheism." Others preferred to define it as the difference between confrontational and interiority models of the divine-human interaction. The papers themselves, however, soon revealed the severe limitations of both these typologies. Still, the underlying question of how a person can cope seriously with the challenge of global religious pluralism at the level of what appear to be impossibly, even bewilderingly, contradictory truth claims was never far from our consciousness. As the only practicing "professional" theologian in the group (I grant that all human beings possess the inborn right to be amateur generals, football coaches, and theologians), it fell to me at the end of the series to reflect on what the conversation had meant and to make a few suggestions about how it might continue. Having now read through the papers again, and recalled the discussions, I have only two observations to make. Both touch on the question of our method, and both are sketchy.

Before I suggest these two items, however, it seems important to say that a possible theological agenda arising from the challenge presented by religious pluralism would not have to be invented out of whole cloth. After all, Emerson and Thoreau were reading the *Bhagavad Gita* in the early nineteenth century. Swami Vivekananda made his whirlwind tour of America, winning hearts for the Vedanta, nearly a century ago. Religious pluralism is not a new arrival on our shores. Also, theological concern about the questions raised in our discussions—the significance of different varieties of religious experience—has a venerable intellectual history. We would ignore that history, as the truism truly puts it, only at the peril of repeating its mistakes.

It is fashionable nowadays in some theological circles to lament the whole period of Protestant theological history that stretches from Karl Barth to Jürgen Moltmann, from dialectical to political theology, from the early twenties to the late seventies, as a kind of regrettable interruption, a tedious detour. Partisans of this view of theological history often suggest that if only we had continued along the road so admirably marked out by Ernst Troeltsch (on religious pluralism) or William James (on religious experience) we would not find ourselves so directionless in coping with these issues today.

As will become clearer in the pages that follow, I do not myself subscribe to this reading of the history of our discipline. I

believe we are where we are in theology today for perfectly un-
derstandable reasons, and that although we may need to retrace
a few steps before we take the next ones, there is no call for nos-
talgia or recrimination. Still, it seems obvious to me that any informed discussion of how the claims of the Christian message
can be reconciled with the modern mind's gnawing awareness of
the historical relativity of all such claims must eventually deal
with Ernst Troeltsch. I say this as a Protestant Christian theologian in part, but not wholly, because Troeltsch worked within
my tradition. I also say this because historic Christianity seems
to have asserted its *universal* claim more strongly and more con-
sistently than any of the other traditions we have discussed—with
the possible exception of Islam (and even there there are questions as Gerhard Böwering's paper on the Sufi Theory of Sahl at-
Tustari suggests). Also, Protestant theologians have dealt with
the dilemma of the historical relativity of Christianity more con-
sistently then Catholics have, some might even say obsessively.
Some scholars even argue today that the problem of unbelief
and doubt, the products of the onslaught of science, critical
scholarship, and pluralism, are peculiarly Protestant—perhaps
even "bourgeois"—problems, stemming from the impact of the
Enlightenment, and have relevance for others only as they too
have been infected by the modern, critical, Protestant outlook.
There may be something to this argument. It implies that the issues faced in this book are especially those of modern western,
educated people. They are not the "religious" problems faced by
those whose lives are defined by poverty, enforced idleness, or
some form of external domination. My point is that the problem
we faced in our group is a peculiar problem for Christians, at
least historically, in a way that it has not been for Hindus or
Buddhists. It is not even a problem in the same way for Jews, although when it is phrased in the "monotheism versus nonmonotheism" idiom, it becomes one.

What about Roman Catholic work on the challenge of religious pluralism? There has been a lot of it. When I visited India
in the fall of 1978 I met members of Catholic contemplative or-
ders who were deeply absorbed in the study and practice of Indian spiritual disciplines. The Vatican established its Secretar-
iat for Non-Christian Religions before the World Council of

Churches began its program on Dialogue with Persons of Other Living Faiths and Ideologies. Also, at the theological level both Karl Rahner and Bernard Lonergan have done valuable work on these issues, as has the American Catholic John Donne. Thomas Merton was devoting himself almost completely to the significance of oriental spirituality for Christians at the time of his tragically early death. But since both Rahner and Lonergan employ a philosophical approach that is not familiar to many Protestants, and also because more than a few Protestant theologians suspect that neither has truly taken the plunge into the icy currents of historical relativity, but that both keep one toe on the ontological bottom, the "problem" remains. Donne and Merton are helpful in their own ways. But neither addresses the challenge the way it presented itself in our discussions. Hence, the route "back to Troeltsch and from Troeltsch forward" seems unavoidable.

Ernst Troeltsch is still best known for his monumental *Social Teachings of the Christian Churches*. But he also pursued a related, lifelong interest in the question of how Christian faith and the perplexing variety of seemingly rival religious truth claims could be sorted out. His courageous trek through this intimidating jungle of historical, philosophical, and theological thickets never brought him to any satisfying clearing. Nevertheless his pioneering exploration marked some paths and alerted those who would follow to the inevitable dangers such a venture entails. We may not be able to follow Troeltsch all the way today. But we can still learn much from him, even from his mistakes.

Like many people who try to grapple with the issue of truth, pluralism, and relativism today, Troeltsch thought of himself, at least at the outset of his career, more as a philosopher than as a theologian. Schooled, as are all German philosophers, on both Kant and Hegel, Troeltsch began by assuming that hidden under the multivarious surface of the several religious traditions, and obscured by their nonrational and culturally particular idiom, the careful observer could discern an inner core which was both rational and common to all of them. His position, though an enormously sophisticated one, inevitably calls to mind the countless armchair comparativists I meet on trains and planes who when I tell them I am a theologian always assure me good-naturedly—usually without having smelled the Ganges or wrestled with a *koan*—that "underneath it all, every religion really teaches the same thing." When I ask them what that "same thing" is, it almost always turns out to be belief in some power "beyond ourselves" and making some effort to do good to our neighbors.

Though it is tempting to be derisive about this commonly held conviction, or to drown it as I have sometimes tried to do in a maelstrom of examples of child sacrifice, holy war, *suttee*, evil-eye spells, and the astonishing fact that many Buddhists claim *not* to believe in God, I have come to believe that such a cold-water shock treatment is a little unfair. It should be remembered that the all-the-same-underneath theory does express—albeit confusedly—a profound truth. It testifies to the pervasive human conviction that despite appearances to the contrary, all human life, however diverse, does rest on some universal ground. It reminds us that most people devoutly hope that reality is ultimately coherent, not as fragmentary and absurd as it often seems. So we can understand and affirm this theory as a *symbol*. But we cannot go very far with it as a theory. Troeltsch himself soon learned this and discarded the theory to move on to another phase.

In his next stage, Troeltsch sought to hold on to the *Absolutheit* of the reality to which he believed Christian faith points and to hold with equal vigor to the irreducibly variegated sociocultural (we might now add psychological, gender-specific, and maybe even somatic) modes by which this single truth is perceived and appropriated. God who is *beyond* the relativities of history is known only *through* the relativities of history. Although the formula at first sounds quite similar to the all-the-same-underneath theory, it is not. It does not claim that the various religious traditions ultimately teach the same thing but only that the transcendental source (or Transcendental Source?) of all religious experience, however varied, is one (One), while all concrete religious expressions, rituals, and beliefs are radically conditioned by their respective cultures. This is something quite different.

This second position, though rarely defended by fellow airline passengers, still creates formidable problems for the Christian theologian, and perhaps for those of other traditions as well. It might even create serious problems for the airline passenger-cum-theologian if thought about enough. Why, one might ask, does some Transcendental Source reveal Him- or Her- or Itself in such a confusing anarchy of ways? Why do religious people burn down each other's temples and refute each other's teachings if one benevolent deity is inspiring them all? In addition, this theory produces that inevitable vertigo which sets in when one recognizes that if the other person's faith system is culturally determined, then so is mine. The sociology of knowledge is a sharp blade, but it can also cut the hand of its wielder.

To Troeltsch's credit, he did not recoil from the full import of these unsettling implications of his theory. He conceded that if Hinduism and Buddism were the historically conditioned responses of other civilizations to the Absolute, so then must Christianity be no more than the highest synthesis of our own civilization's values and beliefs. One can imagine the chagrin that many western Christians, not only missionaries and evangelists but also those who complacently believed that European Christendom had something to bring to the lesser breeds without the law, felt when they heard Troeltsch's message. He himself did not dwell very much on the relativity of Christianity with reference to the other world religions. He chose rather to emphasize that since Christianity was a *historical* movement, it was not a finished product or a closed system. It was open to future change and development. Still, many heard his words as cutting the aorta of what seemed the utterly basic universalism of God's creation of the whole world and Christ's redemption of all humankind.

Karl Barth responded not so much to the philosophical theology of Troeltsch as to the cultural crisis of the First World War, the revolutions it loosed in Europe, and the theological crisis all this precipitated. Barth's work is often interpreted as a condemnation of everything Troeltsch stood for, even as an arrogant denial of Troeltsch's painful sensitivity to the multiplexity and human religiousness. I believe this is a false picture. Contemporaries often exaggerate the differences between thinkers addressing the same issue, but those who look at both in retrospect see more in common. Clearly this is the case with Barth and Troeltsch. Both were preoccupied with the same challenges:

the decline of European Christendom, and the emergence into view (it had always been there) of worldwide religious and ideological pluralism. Both wondered how the Message of Christ could make itself heard in such a changed and changing world.

Although his disciples and advocates rarely mention it, Barth had no trouble accepting Troeltsch's belief that "Christianity" was a product of western civilization. What interested him, however, was the question of what, if anything, could be said about what Troeltsch had called the "Absolute," whose reality neither man denied and which both identified as the source of all religious expressions. In Barth's early writings the answer to the question of how much we can know about this Absolute is clear: "Not much." Human beings cannot know God since, in Barth's famous metaphor, God touches the world only as a tangent touches the edge of a circle, giving it its boundary, but not intersecting it. Later, however, Barth argued that this utter hiddenness and remoteness of God had to do only with the blindness of *natural* human knowledge. By grace God had become human, whether all human beings were aware of it or not. Consequently, even in the natural state, every human being already lived within God's grace, defined by that grace in every aspect of his or her being.

It is critical to point out here that Barth did not present this fleshed-out vision of Troeltsch's somewhat neuter Absolute in some frantic effort to preserve a tiny patch of dry sod from Troeltsch's all-inclusive historical-relative flood. He did so, interestingly, because he thought Troeltsch was not accepting historicity and particularity seriously enough. Specifically he felt Troeltsch was not accepting his own (and Barth's and everyone's) particularity as a human being whose very quest for God is already fulfilled, in principle, by God's unconditional acceptance of all people and by God's unreserved identification with all things human. Although Barth's position is difficult to grasp and impossible to summarize, it has two important things to say to the discussion about religious pluralism. One is that we all enter into it as persons whose concrete histories and personal life trajectories have already been touched and shaped, in their own gritty singularity, by God's grace. This grace does not intrude only in ecstatic moments but provides the very substance of our beings as personal and social creatures. It is also what has brought us, presumably, to an inquiry about the relative validity of different religious "truth claims." Barth's deepened and expanded doctrine of grace also suggests that since God has not united Himself with humankind at the "religious" level but rather at all levels, and especially at whatever dimension of the human is most characteristically human (Barth thought it was our capacity for love and "cohumanity"), "religion" may not be the most useful category to use in asking the question we want to ask.

Barth does not flinch in the least at the assertion that Christianity is indeed the creation of western culture. For him, the coming of God into the world in Jesus Christ is not a "religious" event at all, but calls all religion and all religions into radical question. For this reason, Christianity as such has absolutely nothing to teach Hindus or Muslims. They are to be seen *not* in the first instance as adherents of "another religion," but rather as fellow humans, as *Mitmenschen,* whose cultural and personal specificity is just as much a gift of God's grace as ours is. Speaking to them and listening to them should thus proceed always with the recognition that God's disclosure of the paradigm of divine-human and human-human community already includes them, and us. For Barth, the task of the Christian is to seek to realize this human community in love and to confess our faith with joy but without—as another generation would put it—"laying our trip on them."

For Barth, the fact that Christianity carries the word "Christ" within it gives Christians no advantage whatever over anyone else. God is no respecter of persons. Since what is disclosed for all to see in Jesus Christ is that God has already chosen and redeemed all people, not just Christians or believers or "spiritual people," for Barth any claim that Christianity is a superior religion is simply beside the point, largely because the mode of God's reality in the world is not fundamentally a matter of religion. It was the brilliant, young, and somewhat flamboyant theologian Dietrich Bonhoeffer who was especially intrigued by this last point in Barth's thinking and decided to work out a "nonreligious interpretation of the Gospel." But he died dangling from a Gestapo noose in 1945 before he could even begin his work.

I have always regretted the fact that no one has yet been able to take even the next step in the revolutionary direction Bonhoeffer suggested. Such a program might have critical significance for the questions asked by these essays. It may well be that Bonhoeffer saw better than Barth himself did the real implications of his program, and Barth failed because he did not take his own premises seriously enough. The fear voiced by many of his admirers that Barth's "transcendental realism" (their term, not his) would eventually degenerate into a mere reassertion of orthodoxy seemed to come true. The irascible old curmudgeon of Basel churned out volume after volume of a *Church Dogmatics* that seemed distressingly oblivious to the fact that the universal message it elucidated was the product of a white European male—and a Swiss at that. What had begun as a promise to subvert and revolutionize all theology ended as one more theological system. Troeltsch's question—and ours—got lost in the footnotes.

It is not quite the case that the Barthian movement left us with no resources to deal with religious pluralism. What it did was to promise a refreshingly new approach to an old question— and then not deliver on its promise. It implied a fundamental critique of the culture-boundedness of the previous discussion—but it never followed through. It hinted at subverting our age-old habit of thinking of Christianity as one religion among others (a habit which has also been criticized, in quite a different way, by W. C. Smith). It suggested that the subject "doing" the theology is not the faceless observer of pure science, as though any such creature ever existed in any field, but a unique human person whose very intellectual inquiry is already part of a search impelled by God's encompassing providence. But it never developed the implications of its initial shattering critique of the bland epistemology of the Enlightenment. Today it is the liberation theologians who have begun to insist so emphatically on the historical specificity of the knower, the human subject of all thought (including theology), and to suggest that whether that subject is black or white, rich or poor, male or female, makes a difference that cannot be excluded from theology's critical understanding of its own task.

Today hardly anyone reads Barth. But Troeltsch's problem has returned with a vengeance. The journals teem with scholarly articles on the phenomenology of religion and on various comparative themes. The main job openings for young religion scholars in an increasingly tight market are those in nonwestern religions. On every hand it is declared that religious pluralism is the single most important issue facing Christian theology. The group that prepared these essays represents neither a rump nor a remnant but the lead edge of a bull market in theological activity.

We have not finished with the Germans. In addition to those who descry the shade of Troeltsch in what we must do, there are also those who advise that Schleiermacher is also an essential ancestor to consult. Friedrich Schleiermacher was probably the progenitor of all truly modern theology. Living a century before Troeltsch, he stated more persuasively than anyone before him ever had that valid theology must begin with the experience of the religious person. Though Schleiermacher's ideas fell upon stony soil during the period of dialectical, Barthian, and hermeneutical theologies, still they keep reappearing—in part, I suspect, because there is something fundamentally sound about them. Any theology which is divorced from human experience will die and deserves to. It is now sometimes suggested consequently that we can once again take up his program using more refined methods that have been developed since his time. This would mean that the ideologies that bolster the various religious systems could be "bracketed," at least temporarily, and one could examine the root experience, the primal *ding an sich*, which is only later symbolized, institutionalized, and systematized by devotees, clerics, and theologians. This process, it is theorized, may at least clarify what "truth claims" are really being made, and this in turn will eliminate spurious conflicts and make the choices clearer if not easier.

Such a process appears intriguing, at least at first blush. When we think about it more carefully, however, in the light of what we have learned from the history I have just rehearsed, it seems less promising. To make the judicious examination of religious experience the key to coping with the plethora of claims and refutations made by different religious traditions quickly collides with two obstacles. The first is, *who* is doing the inquiring and *why?* Here the whole vexed issue of the concrete historicity of the subject (the inquirer) and his or her purpose and motivation comes into view. The second difficulty is the precarious quality of the category "religious experience" itself. It should be recalled that since the halcyon days of Schleiermacher we have not only witnessed the development of phenomenology but also weathered Maslow's peak experiences, LSD, cassette music-to-meditate-by, and a raging contagion of altered states and induced moods littering the premises with what are alleged to be religious experiences. Let me say a bit more about these two obstacles in the order I have mentioned them.

The first problem, that of the status of the observer, requires little discussion here since it has become a familiar criticism of the alleged neutrality of the scientific method. What has never been made clear to me, however, is why those who employ the phenomenological method (recognizing that there are many such methods) feel they are somehow exempt from this difficulty. The question is an especially serious one when it comes to the analysis of experiences and phenomena with such weighty, if not "ultimate," significance as those usually classified as religious. Whatever else it is or is not, religion is usually agreed to have something to do with the most basic and inclusive frame of reference within which a person or a people lives. It has to do with "ultimate concern." If all people, including scholars of religion, have a "religion" in this sense (a point Paul Tillich never tired of reiterating), then where does one put one's feet in order to conduct such an observation, except (either consciously or unconsciously) somewhere within one's own "religion"? There is, it seems clear, no place to stand that will not color what is selected to be examined, what is seen, what is deemed important, what is overlooked. And there is nowhere to stand that will not be profoundly influenced by the outcome of the inquiry.

I am not simply raising the familiar general problem of the relationship of the investigator to the object, an issue which is heatedly discussed in the philosophy of science. Though some would deny it, there are others that claim a carefully refined scientific method can minimize subjective distortion. Be that as it may, what must be examined in this case, if the phenomenological analysis of religious experience is to have any value at all, is not just an event but what that event *means* to a human person.

Since religious experience, we are told, must strike its experiencer as being in some sense significant not just for him/her but for me as well, the observer now becomes the observed, the one addressed. Like Rilke's bust of Apollo, the phenomenon returns the observer's gaze and says, "You must change your life."

I repeat that I am not speaking of the general problem of science (although that would be a question worth pursuing on another occasion). Nor am I concerned at the moment with the allegedly incommunicable quality of mystical ecstasy (which in any case John Carman shows in his essay on bhakti is not always claimed). What I am recalling is that no religious tradition I know of would concede that the inner meaning of its core experiences is available to tourists, voyeurs, or comparativists. Such folk, it is usually claimed, will not only *not* grasp the meaning of what is happening but will inevitably misunderstand. Wilfred Smith has demonstrated in his exegesis of the Koran, for example, that Islam simply has no term for a person who truly understands the revelation but does not follow it. Such a person would literally be a contradiction in terms.

I need to say immediately that I do *not* hold to the popular—and extreme—version of this objection which claims, "You have to *be* a parent, a chicano, a schizophrenic, or a Sikh to be able to say anything about it." I have learned much about myself, and some of it has been all too painfully true, from people who do not belong to one or another of my social categories. Eloquent and informative histories, ethnologies, and descriptions of the rites, practices, and ideas of religious movements have been written by nonadherents. The foregoing papers testify to the validity of such undertakings. Many scholars have developed an admirable degree of genuine empathy for whatever it is they are studying. What I am arguing is that as soon as one begins to ask not just what is true for *them,* but what is true for *me,* the game changes. Put more candidly, the game is over. It is over because the question of what is ultimately true for me, presumably what I would live or die for, is by definition not something about which I can play a game.

Last year a student of mine conducted an exemplary study of young Hasidic Jewish women living in Brooklyn. She began the project as an ultraliberal Jew, leaning toward a reconstructionist perspective. As a convinced feminist she also harbored some deep suspicions about how such energetic and vital young Hasids could be held within the practices of what appeared to be an almost completely male-dominated religious system. As she lived with these young women, asked them about their lives, got to know them, however, she soon came to feel they were questioning her as much as she was questioning them. The bust of Apollo spoke. When one moves, even without fully intending to do so, beyond careful and sympathetic description into asking (or being asked) what this means for me, any pose of neutrality or detachment disappears. Further, we begin to recognize that the implicit standards we bring with us when we try to decide what is true and what is not in the realm of ultimate meanings have been fed to us with our mothers' milk.

It is important to reiterate here what has been said many times before, that the modern "science" of *Religionswissenschaft* is in no way exempt from the limitations I have just described. It is philosophically informed by a modern world view which, whatever else may be said in its favor—and there is much that is positive to be said—is no more privileged than any other world view. Peter Berger has pointed this out on numerous occasions. In fact the most helpful way to understand the underlying significance of the modern "scientific" (including phenomenological) study of religion is to understand it as another example of how one religious tradition views another one—like Muslims studying Christianity or Buddhists studying Judaism. I emphasize however that I do *not* employ this analogy here to cast doubt on the validity of such study. Quite the opposite. I believe we have much to learn from the way members of one religious tradition try to understand another and do so without recourse to spurious notions of neutrality. What my argument calls into question is not the comparative study of religious traditions but the fiction of the faceless subject, the "ideal observer," the historyless, genderless, classless, faithless cipher of laboratory-induced fantasies.

What all this means is that we cannot begin the next stage of any inquiry into "truth claims" until we have purged ourselves, not of our subjectivity, but of futile and self-defeating efforts to deny it. Any true understanding of the claims of someone else's religious tradition on me requires not only that I be aware of how I stand with reference to my own tradition's claims but that I also make it part of the process. What is required is not neutrality but dialogue, not some extrahistorical touchstone by which conflicting claims can be tested, but a willingness to let my truth be tested and altered by another's. What is needed, to mix terms that are not usually mixed, is a combination of testimony and vulnerability, a recognition that the highest of personal stakes are inevitably involved, and a readiness to change, to *be* changed, in unexpected ways by the encounter.

Raymond Panikkar used to warn his students on the first day of his course in comparative mysticism that if they were not open to the possibility of being converted during the semester they should immediately drop the course. I do not know if any of his students were ever converted. I do know that in my own experience a genuine encounter with persons of another religious tradition threatens my security and subverts my familiar world in ways I had not anticipated. Others have had the same shock. This is also true, I should add, for encounters with fellow Christians who experience our common faith from a radically different perspective. Once the phantom of subjectless analysis is laid to rest and communication between genuine historical persons, replete with their respective particularities, begins, something extraordinary can happen. One enters into such a dialogue expecting to exchange ideas and feelings but quickly finds out that one's most fundamental categories for construing the world and one's place within it are jolted and upset. The center does not hold. One tries to retreat to containing what one is experiencing in one's existing conceptual models, but it soon becomes clear that this obscures and falsifies the whole thing. Yet in the midst of this disturbing experience one is aware of a security, a bond with the other person, a communion perhaps that persists despite the clash of categories. This can also happen, I repeat, with people who read different and threatening meanings into the same symbols that guide us. The discovery of the underlying tie that binds such disparate persons into something shared comes as a surprise and as a gift. That which binds is not a common core of teaching, not even, I believe, some universal but culturally particularized "religious experience." Whatever it is, it has always come to me as something mysterious and gratuitous, not as the product of my efforts. I know of no method now in existence which can begin to make sense of this. Until I find one, I will have to continue to call it grace.

Translated into even more theological terms, perhaps what I am talking about is the paradoxical transcendence of God which comes to us both as an awesome strangeness and as a friend and companion. There are stories in many religious traditions of God coming in the form of a stranger whose true identity is discovered only after the hesitant hosts grant the needed hospitality. In our all-too-predictable world it may be through the unwelcome poor and the unexpected stranger, both of whom threaten our customary ways of living, that God is disclosing Himself (or Herself) to us. In any case, what we need as we begin following the questions these essays sharpen is a method that not only allows but *requires* the historical subjectivity and the existential commitments of the participants to become an integral part of the endeavor.

The second problem, that of returning to a tradition's primal religious experience in the mode of Schleiermacher with, say, some help from Merleau-Ponty or one of the more recent phenomenologists is that "religious experience," as we have already mentioned, has become an inexact, mercurial, and I believe ultimately inadequate concept. I realize that at Harvard we are taught to breathe the name of William James with reverence. But it is one of the more thankless responsibilities of theologians to raise questions about the categories people use in discussing religion. Such a category is "religious experience." Recognizing the boldness and even brilliance of *The Varieties of Religious Experience,* I would like, nonetheless, to appeal not to a Cantabridgian forefather but to one from Yale. I venture this with some assurance that it will fall within the venerable oriental religious tradition of honoring the transmission, since the figure I wish to invoke was the teacher of my teacher, Douglas Clyde Macintosh, who was the mentor of H. Richard Niebuhr.

Macintosh was a near-contemporary of James, but I find what he had to say about religious experience even more valuable. In 1919 Macintosh published a book entitled *Theology as an Empirical Science.* As the title indicates, Macintosh shared in his own way our current concern with the real experience of actual people in any vital theology. He did not want to be a merely deductive or exegetical theologian. But, even sixty years ago, Macintosh saw some of the pitfalls of empiricism that William James seemed to overlook.

Part of Macintosh's strength lay, I believe, in the fact that his classical training as a theologian alerted him to issues in the study of religion that even the most thoughtful psychologist might miss. Also, no one named Macintosh can have wholly escaped a healthy Scottish Calvinist awareness of sin and of how sin traps even very pious individuals into using God and religion to bless and bolster their own projects. Macintosh saw how, in the liberal theological tradition of which he was proud to be a part, God all too easily became identified with what I or my people want anyway. Where, he wondered, was the awesome holiness of God, the thunder of Sinai, the righteous One who stands in judgment over His *own* people? He was therefore uncomfortable about the central role "religious experience" had begun to play in liberal theology, coming to believe as his career went on that *God*, and not religious experience, had to become the critical focus of theology again—albeit a God whose judgment and mercy are encountered in and through those human experiences in which truth, beauty, and rationality were affirmed in both personal and corporate life.

What is important to underline here is that the human experiences Macintosh was interested in were not those of mystical transport, blinding ecstasy, or beatific vision. They were experiences of political justice, social transformation, and personal renewal. It was here that my own teacher, H. Richard Niebuhr, picked up and enlarged on Macintosh's work. Drawing also on Troeltsch and Barth (to both of whom he dedicated *The Meaning of Revelation*), as well as on the ideas of George Herbert Mead and Josiah Royce, Niebuhr taught us to think of the biblical events not as the exclusive but rather as the normative locus of God's revelation. He then went on to encourage us to look for the ordering, judging, and liberating action of God not just in Christianity and not just in religious history but wherever such response-requiring events take place, in however "secular" a city.

I clung to Niebuhr's teaching with a special fervor, I suppose, because he spoke so directly to my condition at the time. I had come to divinity school puzzled about how to put my piety (I had been reared in an evangelical Baptist setting) and my politics (I had been a part of the student left at the university) together. He showed me how to do it then. But does his perspective, drawing together as it does a half century of the best in Protestant theology, say anything to the issues raised in this collection?

I believe so. Niebuhr's emphasis on the reality of the historical subject, the "responsible self," revelation as the meaning events have for the "inner history" of peoples, excludes any comparative-religion analysis which does not make the comparer integral to the comparison. Also his "radical monotheism," influenced in large measure by Barth but also by his teacher Macintosh, rules out any exclusive focus on religious experience as a starting point. His work points toward a careful combination of historical, exegetical, and empirical methods—each securing the other from its characteristic excesses and misuses. Following such a method would suggest that any people's "religious" qualities must be discerned in the symbols, values, stories, heroes, and struggles which give shape to their *whole* historical and cultural experience. Otherwise we allow the prejudices of the day to define what we mean by "religious experience," and in today's climate this would make it hard to avoid dealing mainly with the spectacular, the once-in-a-lifetime, the mind-blowing, the exotic, rather than with the customary, the pedestrian, the enduring, the commonplace. We might be drawn too quickly into analyzing trances and visions while forgetting the cup of cold water and the blow struck for freedom. We need a method that will help us understand not so much "religious experience" but the religious dimension of *all* experience—some of which may not appear at first to be religious at all.

These then are the two modest methodological items I would propose for the next step in our enterprise. We need a method that will draw us from description to dialogue, one that will make clear that the truth we seek reveals itself only to those who reveal themselves. We need a method that will enable us to set aside our own preferences about what a religious experience is or ought to be, that makes the whole world our parish and directs us not to an isolated sector of human life but to a stratum that underlies it all.

Finally, let us remember that there is much at stake. As I compose these pages I have just finished reading a collection of essays by Latin American theologians entitled *La Lucha de los Dioses* (*The Struggle of the Gods*) subtitled "The Idols of Oppression and the Search for a Liberating God." In the long opening essay of this volume, Pablo Richard argues expertly that the real issue between Moses and the Golden Calf (Exodus 32) was *not* one of a spiritual versus a material deity, and not even of monotheism versus something else. The battle was over what *kind* of God Moses had revealed to the Israelites, namely a God who would not permit them to languish in bondage but called them to dangerous and sacrificial effort in the crucible of history. Other writers in *La Lucha de los Dioses* return time and again to the fact that for millions of people today, theological arguments have an immediate political meaning. Islam is only the clearest example. To try to understand its history or its meaning today apart from its political history would be futile. Some gods console and comfort. Others summon people to anger and subversion. In any case, these "political" meanings of religious experience, often viewed as extrinsic or derivative by purists, must be seen as part of a whole.

The writers of *La Lucha de los Dioses* also reminded me once again of something I have already mentioned briefly but is worth repeating, especially in the context of a discussion of *different* religious traditions. These Latin Americans emphasized that often the most acrimonious battles of the gods take place not *between* different traditions but *within* the same one. We all know this in our own experience. Encountering adherents of another tradition can, as I have said, jolt and unnerve us. But when we see *our* saints and stories used in ways we find repellent it enrages and sickens us. When I read that the Ku Klux Klan members who murdered demonstrators in Greensboro, North Carolina, last year followed up the massacre by singing "What a Friend We Have in Jesus," a hymn on which I was raised, I felt my teeth clench and my palms dampen. No doubt there has been entirely too much blood let in struggles *between* religious groupings, but the mayhem that goes on *within* our own tradition should remind us that simply sharing a common symbol does not solve everything. Religious groups are almost always harder on the heretic than on the pagan. Further proof, if we needed it, that what we must understand is not the symbols themselves but what they mean to real people.

The material we are handling is highly inflammable stuff. It is well to remember that when Isaiah ventured into the Temple in the incident recorded in Isaiah 6, he was not yet a prophet and probably had little intention of becoming one. We do know that it was a tumultuous time in the history of Israel. We do not know what Isaiah was looking for when he entered the Temple or what was on his mind. It may have been a routine cultic act. Whatever he was looking for, we can be relatively sure, I think, that it was not what William James was looking for when he sniffed the nitrous oxide in Cambridge 2500 years later. What happened to the unsuspecting Isaiah was that he was touched on the lips by a burning coal borne by an awesome and terrifying winged creature. After that he was never the same.

Perhaps this fearsome scene, rather than a decorous seminar room equipped with ashtrays and folding chairs, provides a better metaphor for the kind of task we are about. We may not be touched by seraphim. But we will surely not be the same when it is over.

About the Editor

PETER L. BERGER is University Professor at Boston University. He is the author of *A Rumor of Angels, Sacred Canopy, Invitation to Sociology, Pyramids of Sacrifice, The Heretical Imperative,* and *Sociology Reinterpreted,* among other books.

About the Contributors

GERHARD BÖWERING is Associate Professor of Islamic Studies in the Department of Religious Studies at the University of Pennsylvania. He is a member of the American Oriental Society, the Association of Asian Studies and the Medieval Academy of America, and a contributor to the Encyclopaedia of Islam and the Encyclopaedia Iranica. His publications have focused on two major areas of Islamic research, Qur'anic commentary and Islamic mysticism (Sufism). They include *The Mystical Vision of Existence in Classical Islam, The Dreams and Labors of a Central Asian Sufi,* and a number of articles on Islamic topics.

JOHN B. CARMAN is Professor of Comparative Religion at Harvard Divinity School and the director of the Center for the Study of World Religions. He is the author of *The Theology of Rāmānuja,* the co-author of *Village Christians and Hindu Culture,* and the translator of W. Brede Kristensen's lectures in phenomenology of religion, published under the title *The Meaning of Religion.*

EWERT H. COUSINS is Professor of Theology at Fordham University, where he was the director of the Graduate Program in Spirituality, 1975–80, and a visiting professor at Columbia University. He is the chief editorial consultant for the sixty-volume series The Classics of Western Spirituality, and he is the translator and editor of the Bonaventure volume in the series. He is the author of *Bonaventure and the Coincidence of Opposites* and the editor of *Process Theology* and *Hope and the Future of Man.*

HARVEY COX is Victor Thomas Professor of Divinity at Har-

vard. He is the author of, among other books, *Feast of Fools,
Secular City,* and *Turning East.*

DIANA ECK is Associate Professor of Hindu Religious Studies
in the Department of Sanskrit and Indian Studies at Harvard
University. She has done extensive fieldwork in India, and her
book *Banāras, City of Light* will be published next year.

MICHAEL FISHBANE is Associate Professor of Biblical Studies at
Brandeis University where he holds the Lane Chair in Jewish
History and Social Ethics. He is the author of many studies in
scholarly journals and encyclopedias, in both Hebrew and Eng-
lish, and is the author, most recently, of *Text and Texture: Close
Readings of Selected Biblical Texts.*

ARTHUR GREEN is Associate Professor of Religious Studies at
the University of Pennsylvania. He is the author of *Tormented
Master: A Life of Rabbi Nahman of Bratslav,* and has also
translated two volumes of Hasidic sources into English.

JOHN J. HUCKLE is currently doing graduate studies in sociology.

HOWARD CLARK KEE is Professor of New Testament at Boston
University, where he is Chairman of Graduate Studies in the
Biblical-Historical Field. He is the author of, among other books,
*Understanding the New Testament, Jesus in History: An
Approach to the Study of the Gospels,* and *Christian Origins in
Sociological Perspective.*

ELAINE PAGELS is Professor of Religion at Barnard College,
Columbia University. She is the author of *The Johannine Gospel
in Gnostic Exegesis, The Gnostic Paul: Gnostic Exegesis of the
Pauline Letters, The Gnostic Gospels* and numerous scholarly
articles. She has participated in the editing and translating of
Nag Hamadi texts.

ROBERT A. F. THURMAN is Associate Professor of Religion at
Amherst College.

TAITETSU UNNO is Professor of World Religions and chairman
of the Department of Religion at Smith College. A specialist in
East Asian Buddhism, he has published articles on Hua-yen and
Pure Land thought. Currently he is engaged in a ten-year proj-
ect, under the auspices of the Hongwanji International Center in
Kyoto, to translate all of the works of Shinran into English.